CPython

A Complete Guide to CPython's Architecture and Performance

Chien-Lung Kao

Apress®

CPython: A Complete Guide to CPython's Architecture and Performance

Chien-Lung Kao
Taipei, T´ai-pei, Taiwan

ISBN-13 (pbk): 979-8-8688-1768-7 ISBN-13 (electronic): 979-8-8688-1769-4
https://doi.org/10.1007/979-8-8688-1769-4

Copyright © 2025 by Chien-Lung Kao

This work is subject to copyright. All rights are reserved by the Publisher, whether the whole or part of the material is concerned, specifically the rights of translation, reprinting, reuse of illustrations, recitation, broadcasting, reproduction on microfilms or in any other physical way, and transmission or information storage and retrieval, electronic adaptation, computer software, or by similar or dissimilar methodology now known or hereafter developed.

Trademarked names, logos, and images may appear in this book. Rather than use a trademark symbol with every occurrence of a trademarked name, logo, or image we use the names, logos, and images only in an editorial fashion and to the benefit of the trademark owner, with no intention of infringement of the trademark.

The use in this publication of trade names, trademarks, service marks, and similar terms, even if they are not identified as such, is not to be taken as an expression of opinion as to whether or not they are subject to proprietary rights.

While the advice and information in this book are believed to be true and accurate at the date of publication, neither the authors nor the editors nor the publisher can accept any legal responsibility for any errors or omissions that may be made. The publisher makes no warranty, express or implied, with respect to the material contained herein.

Managing Director, Apress Media LLC: Welmoed Spahr
Acquisitions Editor: Celestin Suresh John
Development Editor: James Markham
Editorial Assistant: Gryffin Winkler

Cover designed by eStudioCalamar

Cover image designed by kuritafsheen77 on freepik

Distributed to the book trade worldwide by Springer Science+Business Media New York, 1 New York Plaza, New York, NY 10004. Phone 1-800-SPRINGER, fax (201) 348-4505, e-mail orders-ny@springer-sbm.com, or visit www.springeronline.com. Apress Media, LLC is a Delaware LLC and the sole member (owner) is Springer Science + Business Media Finance Inc (SSBM Finance Inc). SSBM Finance Inc is a **Delaware** corporation.

For information on translations, please e-mail booktranslations@springernature.com; for reprint, paperback, or audio rights, please e-mail bookpermissions@springernature.com.

Apress titles may be purchased in bulk for academic, corporate, or promotional use. eBook versions and licenses are also available for most titles. For more information, reference our Print and eBook Bulk Sales web page at http://www.apress.com/bulk-sales.

Any source code or other supplementary material referenced by the author in this book is available to readers on GitHub. For more detailed information, please visit https://www.apress.com/gp/services/source-code.

If disposing of this product, please recycle the paper

Table of Contents

About the Author xi

Chapter 1: Reading the CPython Source Code 1

What Is CPython? 1

Why Read the Source Code? 1

Where to Begin? 2

    Obtaining the Source Code 2

    Development Tools 3

Can I Understand This Without Knowing C? 4

Chapter 2: Overview of the CPython Project Structure 5

Project Structure 5

Building the Project 7

    Greet CPython! 8

    A (Very) Basic Module 11

    Saying Goodbye on Exit 13

Chapter 3: Everything Is an Object: Part 1 15

What Is an "Object"? 15

    The Previous and Next Object 17

    Garbage Collection Mechanism 18

    PyTypeObject 22

Summary 24

TABLE OF CONTENTS

Chapter 4: How Objects Are Created in CPython 25
Running the Program! 25
Step 0: Code Analysis 25
Step 1: Transformation to AST 26
Step 2: Compilation to Bytecode 27
Step 3: Instantiating an Object 29
Summary 31

Chapter 5: Everything Is an Object: Part 2 33
PyTypeObject 33
Basic Members 34
Methods and Operators 34
Access Methods 35
Other 35
The List Type 36
Printing a List 37
Using the Bracket Operator 39
List Methods 41
List Addition 42
Number of Elements 44
List Comparison 45
Summary 47

Chapter 6: Defining a Custom Built-in Type 49
Creating a New Type 49
Defining Methods 50
Implementing the Type 51
Making It a Built-in Type 53
Building and Running 54
Parameterized Initialization 55

TABLE OF CONTENTS

Chapter 7: What Happens During Module Import 61
Different Ways of Importing 61
The import Instruction 62
The from .. import .. Instruction 66
Crazy Side-Effects! 67
The Behind-the-Scenes Hero: meta_path 69
Summary 71

Chapter 8: The Internal Representation of Integers 73
How Are Numbers Created? 73
Integer Objects 75
Astronomical Numbers! 77
Small Integers 78

Chapter 9: Floating Point Numbers in CPython 81
What Is a "Floating Point Number"? 81
The Structure of Floating Point Numbers 82
About Floating Point Numbers 83
Floating Point Arithmetic 84
Infinity! 86
Not a Number! 87
Comparing Floating Point Numbers 88
Floating Point Performance 89

Chapter 10: Inside the String Object: Part 1 91
Creating a String 91
String Objects 92
The Fundamental String Structure 95
String Operations 96
Encoding Conversion 96
Strings Are Immutable 98

v

Chapter 11: Inside the String Object: Part 2 101

String Operations 101
Copying Strings 101
String Slicing 104

Performance 107
String Interning 107

Chapter 12: What Happens When Python Starts 111

Using a Debugger 111
Program Entry Point 112
Reading the Program File 115
Building the Abstract Syntax Tree 117
Creating the Code Object 118
Ready for Liftoff! 119

Chapter 13: From Source to Bytecode: How .py Becomes .pyc 121

Having a .pyc Is All You Need 121
"Maybe" a .pyc File? 123
Magic Number, Magic! 125
Unpacking a .pyc File 129

Chapter 14: The List Object and Its Internal Management 133

Internal Structure of Lists 133
Creating and Initializing a List 134

Memory Management 137
When Is More Memory Needed? 138
The Over-allocation Formula 140

Common List Operations 141
Appending Elements 141
Inserting Elements 142
Removing Elements 143

Chapter 15: The Dictionary Object: Part 1 145
The Internal Structure of Dictionaries 145
Creating a Dictionary 147
Adding Elements 149
Handling Hash Collisions 154
Looking Up Elements 157

Chapter 16: The Dictionary Object: Part 2 159
Dictionary Memory Management Techniques 159
Adding More Elements 159
Should We Request More Capacity? 162
How Much Space to Allocate? 166
Returning Memory: Does It Happen? 167

Chapter 17: The Tuple Object and Its Immutability 169
Tuple Design 169
Creating a Tuple 170
Empty Tuples 172
Non-empty Tuples 173
Deallocation Mechanism 174
Common Tuple Operations 177
Modifying Tuples 177
Tuple Unpacking 178

Chapter 18: Inside the Python VM: Code Objects 181
Functions Are Also Objects 181
Preparing to Create a Function 184
Code Object 185

TABLE OF CONTENTS

Chapter 19: Inside the Python VM: Function Objects 191
Creating Function Objects 191
What Do the Parameters Look Like? 193
Accessing Function Attributes 194
Calling a Function 195
What Is "Vectorcall"? 196

Chapter 20: Inside the Python VM: Frame Objects 199
Frame Object 199
The Life Cycle of a Frame Object 201

Chapter 21: Inside the Python VM: Namespaces and Scopes 205
Variable Scope 205
Local Variables (L) 206
Global and Built-in Variables (G, B) 207
Enclosing Variables (E) 211

Chapter 22: Inside the Python VM: Cells and Closures 215
Creating a Cell Object 215
Closures 217
Free Variables 219
From the Python Perspective 220

Chapter 23: Classes and Where They Come From 223
Creating a Class 223
The Mastermind Behind the Scenes 226
Selecting the Metaclass 227
Preparing the Namespace 228
The Birth of a Class! 229
Chicken or the Egg? 231

TABLE OF CONTENTS

Chapter 24: Class Inheritance in CPython 233
Classes and Inheritance 233
    Creating a Class 233
    How Does Inheritance Work? 235
    Method Lookup 236

Chapter 25: Method Resolution Order and C3 Linearization 243
The C3 Linearization Algorithm 243
    Whose Method Gets Called? 244
MRO Calculation 245
    Single Inheritance 245
    Multiple Inheritance 249
    A More Complex Inheritance Example 250
    What If It Can't Be Calculated? 253

Chapter 26: The Role of super() in Multiple Inheritance 257
Algorithm Implementation 257
    Preparation Before Merging 257
    Merging 260
Family Feuds 262
    Super! 263
    Whose Child Is It? 265
    Solving Family Feuds 269
    Specifying the Superclass 270
    Quick Quiz: Who Am I? 271

Chapter 27: The Generator Object and the Yield Statement 273
The Generator Class 274
    yield, Please! 278
    Next, Please! 279

TABLE OF CONTENTS

Chapter 28: How Iterators Work Internally 283
The Iterator Protocol 283
Halt! Password, Please! 285
Different Types of Iterators? 291

Chapter 29: Understanding Descriptors in Python 295
When Calling Methods 295
Attribute Lookup Process 296
Process Summary 300
Method Descriptors 301

Chapter 30: Exception Handling Internals in CPython 305
Exception Handling 305
Stacking Up 306
Exception Table 307
Entry Portals 308
Exception Type Matching 308
Handling the Exception 310
Finally! 311

Index 313

About the Author

Chien-Lung Kao is a seasoned programmer with over 30 years of hands-on experience and 15 years as an educator, specializing in JavaScript, Ruby, and Python. He is a respected author of several books on Ruby on Rails and Git published in Taiwan, sharing his in-depth knowledge and insights with a global audience. Kao has also been a featured speaker at conferences and tech events across Asia, including Taiwan and Japan, where he connects with developers and tech enthusiasts on advanced programming techniques and industry trends.

CHAPTER 1

Reading the CPython Source Code

What Is CPython?

If this is your first time hearing the name "CPython," you might think it's a new implementation of Python. But no, CPython isn't a new toy or a new programming language—it's the very same Python interpreter that most people use every day. What some may not know is that Python was originally developed in the C programming language, so when people mention "Python" without any further clarification, they are typically referring to CPython.

Why Read the Source Code?

Why? For no particular reason—just for fun. And having fun is important!

If your goal in reading this book is to dramatically improve your Python programming skills by exploring the CPython source code, you might be a little disappointed. While reading the CPython source can enhance your understanding of Python to some degree, the primary benefit is the opportunity to improve your C programming skills, since most of the CPython code base is written in C.

Therefore, if you simply want to learn Python syntax, an introductory Python book would be a better choice. The main purpose of delving into the CPython source code is to uncover some of the "black magic" behind the language. For example, what exactly are "objects" in Python? How are modules loaded? How does Python manage memory? These are the kinds of topics this book will focus on.

CHAPTER 1   READING THE CPYTHON SOURCE CODE

Where to Begin?
Obtaining the Source Code

Although the entire CPython project is available to browse directly on GitHub, it's more efficient to download the CPython source code onto your local computer for in-depth exploration. The next chapter will guide you through where and how to download it.

While the latest version of Python is currently 3.13, this book references the CPython source code for version 3.12.6. Source code can vary between different versions, especially for changes beyond minor releases. If you want to follow along exactly, it's recommended to use the same version as I do to ensure that we're viewing the same content.

Additionally, because the CPython source code can be quite complex at times, I may occasionally omit sections for clarity. For example, the original code might look like this:

```c
// file: Include/object.h

struct _object {
    _PyObject_HEAD_EXTRA

#if (defined(__GNUC__) || defined(__clang__)) \
        && !(defined __STDC_VERSION__ && __STDC_VERSION__ >= 201112L)
    // On C99 and older, anonymous union is a GCC and clang extension
    __extension__
#endif
#ifdef _MSC_VER
    // Ignore MSC warning C4201: "nonstandard extension used:
    // nameless struct/union"
    __pragma(warning(push))
    __pragma(warning(disable: 4201))
#endif
    union {
        Py_ssize_t ob_refcnt;
#if SIZEOF_VOID_P > 4
        PY_UINT32_T ob_refcnt_split[2];
#endif
    };
```

```
#ifdef _MSC_VER
    __pragma(warning(pop))
#endif

    PyTypeObject *ob_type;
};
```

There are several `#ifdef` conditional compilation directives, some related to the operating system, others to debugging information. Most of the time, these may not be directly relevant to the core topic at hand, so for the sake of focus, I might simplify the code like this:

```
// file: Include/object.h
struct _object {
    _PyObject_HEAD_EXTRA

    union {
        Py_ssize_t ob_refcnt;
    };

    PyTypeObject *ob_type;
};
```

To be clear, it's not that the omitted portions are unimportant, but removing them helps us concentrate on the essentials.

Development Tools

There are many tools you can use to read source code, such as Vim, Visual Studio Code (hereafter referred to as VS Code), or even full-featured IDEs like Visual Studio. These editors provide helpful features for source code navigation, such as jumping quickly to definitions of functions, macros, constants, or searching for keywords—all of which make source code exploration more efficient.

In this book, I will use VS Code for source code exploration. If you haven't installed it yet, you can download it from the official VS Code website.

Besides VS Code, I have also started using a new editor called Zed, which is developed in Rust. While it doesn't have as many plugins as VS Code, its performance is significantly better, especially for larger files or projects with numerous lines of code—this difference is noticeable. I highly recommend trying it out.

- **VS Code**: https://code.visualstudio.com/
- **Zed**: https://zed.dev/

Can I Understand This Without Knowing C?

Here's the bottom line: Even if you don't grasp everything 100%, it's perfectly fine. Skimming through the code can still be a valuable learning experience.

Learning is not always linear; you don't need to understand every single line to gain insights. Sometimes, just examining code structure, function calls, or variable names can be informative. It's like piecing together a puzzle—you don't have to complete every piece to get a sense of the overall picture.

To be honest, I'm not a C expert either. Fortunately, we live in an age of advanced AI tools such as ChatGPT that can help explain what's going on when things get confusing. As I go through the source code, I'm learning C along the way too. Even if it feels like "the blind leading the blind," you'll eventually get a sense of the bigger picture.

Also, not every part of the CPython project is written in C—some modules are written in Python. If you're already comfortable with Python, you might want to start by looking at those modules, which tend to be more approachable. However, if you're a complete beginner and have never written any kind of code before, you might find it challenging to keep up. For this reason, I assume readers have some basic programming knowledge—it doesn't have to be Python; any language will do—as long as you're familiar with concepts like variables, functions, loops, and control flow.

Ready to get started? In the next chapter, we'll take a look at the CPython project structure and walk through compiling the source code on your own machine, so you can build your very own version of Python!

CHAPTER 2

Overview of the CPython Project Structure

In this chapter, we'll take a look at the overall structure of the CPython project and try building the project ourselves. We'll even make some small modifications to the CPython source code to get a taste of what it's like to be a Python Core Developer (just for fun, of course)!

Project Structure

First, let's grab a copy of the project from GitHub:

```
$ git clone git@github.com:python/cpython.git -b v3.12.6 --depth=1
```

In this book, I am using version `3.12.6` of CPython. If you're using a different version, some source code details might vary. Excluding some less important files, the directory structure of the freshly cloned CPython project from GitHub looks like this:

```
CPython
├── Doc
├── Grammar
├── Include
├── Lib
├── Mac
├── Misc
├── Modules
├── Objects
├── PC
├── PCbuild
```

CHAPTER 2   OVERVIEW OF THE CPYTHON PROJECT STRUCTURE

```
├── Parser
├── Programs
├── Python
└── Tools
```

Here's a brief introduction to what each directory contains:

- `Doc`: As the name suggests, this directory contains all the documentation, written in reStructuredText (`.rst`) format. It's actually pretty good bedtime reading if you're struggling to fall asleep!

- `Grammar`: Files for defining how Python's grammar and parser rules work.

- `Include`: C language header files used throughout the project. If you plan to write extensions for CPython, you'll probably need files from here.

- `Lib`: The standard library—this directory contains modules written in Python. If you're familiar with Python, you'll find this folder relatively approachable.

- `Modules`: Similar to the `Lib` directory, but the modules here are written in C.

- `Mac`: Tools and files specific to macOS.

- `Misc`: A collection of miscellaneous files. I personally use such folders to store files that I can't categorize elsewhere.

- `Objects`: The source code for all Python built-in object types, such as `str` or `list`. You'll see files from this directory quite often in this book.

- `PCbuild`: Files for building Python on Windows, especially with Visual Studio. There are project files you can open directly.

- `PC`: Similar to `PCbuild`, but targeted at older Windows versions. Most files are obsolete, but some are retained for compatibility.

- `Parser`: Code for converting `.py` files into tokens that Python can understand. This part is a bit more advanced.

- **Programs**: Contains source code related to CPython executables.
- **Python**: Contains the interpreter source code itself. This is a more advanced area, but if you're interested in how the interpreter works, it's worth checking out.
- **Tools**: Utilities for Python development and maintenance.

For the purposes of this book, you'll most often see the Include, Lib, Modules, Objects, and Python directories. These are the core source files of the CPython interpreter, and if you want to understand the inner workings of Python, you'll spend most of your time here.

Building the Project

After downloading the project, switch into the project directory and run the ./configure command:

```
$ cd cpython
$ ./configure
```

The ./configure command will print out a lot of information that might look intimidating at first. What it's really doing is checking your system environment and dependencies to make sure nothing important is missing. Once everything checks out, a Makefile will be generated. This file describes how the make command should go about compiling the whole project.

If you add the --prefix parameter to ./configure, like so:

```
$ ./configure --prefix=/tmp/my-python
```

With the --prefix option, when you run make install later, the compiled Python (and related files) will be installed under /tmp/my-python. However, I'm not planning to run make install just yet, so you can leave off the --prefix for now. We'll revisit it if we need to run other tools (like pip) later.

Next, run the make command. This command will compile the whole project according to the rules defined in the generated Makefile:

```
$ make
```

The compilation process may take a while. If it finishes without any errors, you should find a new executable named python.exe in the root directory—even on macOS, the filename is python.exe. I know it might seem odd to see .exe on macOS, but it's intentional: since there's already a Python/ directory in the CPython project, using python.exe helps avoid a naming conflict.

If you want to "install" the Python version you just built, you can run:

```
$ make install
```

If you passed a --prefix argument to ./configure earlier, the make install command will install Python to that location. But even if you skip installation, you can still directly run the newly built python.exe. Try running it to launch the familiar REPL environment:

```
$ ./python.exe
Python 3.12.6+ (heads/3.12:b2a7d718e3b, Sep 15 2024, 23:31:57) [Clang 15.0.0 (clang-1500.3.9.4)] on darwin
Type "help", "copyright", "credits" or "license" for more information.
>>> import sys
>>> sys.version
'3.12.6+ (heads/3.12:b2a7d718e3b, Sep 15 2024, 23:31:57) [Clang 15.0.0 (clang-1500.3.9.4)]'
```

A + after the version number indicates that this is not an official release, but rather a "development" or custom-compiled version.

Greet CPython!

Now, let's make a small change to the CPython source code to create a custom effect. For example, I'd like to print a "Hello" message upon entering the REPL and a "Bye" message when exiting, just to make things a bit friendlier! To achieve this, I need to locate the code responsible for entering the REPL. This is in Python/pythonrun.c, and by looking up the _PyRun_InteractiveLoopObject() function, you'll find a do...while... loop—the very loop that implements the "Read-Eval-Print Loop" (REPL):

```c
// file: Python/pythonrun.c

int
_PyRun_InteractiveLoopObject(FILE *fp, PyObject *filename,
PyCompilerFlags *flags)
{
    PyCompilerFlags local_flags = _PyCompilerFlags_INIT;
    // ... omitted ...

    do {
        ret = PyRun_InteractiveOneObjectEx(fp, filename, flags);
        // ... omitted ...
    } while (ret != E_EOF);
    return err;
}
```

This segment is fairly straightforward—the main logic lives within the do… while… loop. If I want to greet the user before the REPL loop starts, I can simply call printf() right before do. To look a bit more "programmatic," I'll define a say_something() function in this file, which simply prints the passed-in string:

```c
// file: Python/pythonrun.c

void
say_something(const char *message)
{
    printf("==============\n");
    printf("%s\n", message);
    printf("==============\n");
}
```

Because we'll call say_something() inside _PyRun_InteractiveLoopObject(), the function definition must appear before its first use. Now, let's call it:

```c
// file: Python/pythonrun.c

int
_PyRun_InteractiveLoopObject(FILE *fp, PyObject *filename,
PyCompilerFlags *flags)
```

```
{
    PyCompilerFlags local_flags = _PyCompilerFlags_INIT;
    // ... omitted ...

    say_something("Hello CPython");  // added this line
    do {
        ret = PyRun_InteractiveOneObjectEx(fp, filename, flags);
        // ... omitted ...
    } while (ret != E_EOF);

    say_something("Bye"); // added this line
    return err;
}
```

This way, "Hello CPython" will print when you enter the REPL, and "Bye" will print upon exit. Unlike Python or JavaScript, where changes take effect immediately, with C, you need to recompile the code first. So re-run make to rebuild CPython. This time, only the changed files are rebuilt, so it should finish faster than before.

Run the following to see the effect:

```
$ ./python.exe
Python 3.12.6+ (heads/3.12-dirty:b2a7d718e3b, Sep 16 2024, 14:46:05) [Clang 15.0.0 (clang-1500.3.9.4)] on darwin
Type "help", "copyright", "credits" or "license" for more information.
=============
Hello CPython
=============
>>> 1 + 2
3
>>> print("Hey you!")
Hey you!
>>> ^D
=============
Bye
=============
```

As soon as you enter the REPL, you'll see "Hello CPython". When you exit (by pressing Ctrl+D), "Bye" is printed as well. Success!

However, there is a minor issue. In Python 3.12, you can exit the REPL not only with Ctrl+D but also by typing `exit()`. Currently, `exit()` does not print "Bye", since the original `do...while...` loop condition only checks for `ret != E_EOF`. We'll tackle this shortly, but first, let's improve the `say_something()` function a bit. I want to make it reusable in other parts of the code base, so I'll reorganize it into a separate module. This will also demonstrate how to structure modules in C!

A (Very) Basic Module

To define a module in C, you typically declare function prototypes in a `.h` header file, then implement the functionality in a corresponding `.c` source file. This is common practice in C. Following the conventions in the CPython project, such header files are usually placed in the `Include` directory and source files in `Modules`, `Python`, or `Objects`. Extension modules (C Extensions) are typically in `Modules`, while core features are found in `Python` or `Objects`. Since our `say_something()` function modifies interpreter behavior, placing it in the `Python` directory makes sense.

Let's start by creating a `greeting.h` file in the `Include` directory. The filename can be something else if you prefer. The contents are as follows:

```
// file: Include/greeting.h
```

```
#ifndef _PY_GREETING_H
#define _PY_GREETING_H

extern void say_something(const char *message);

#endif
```

The `#ifndef` and `#define` lines implement a header guard, which prevents this file from being included more than once and causing compilation errors. `_PY_GREETING_H` is just an arbitrary name; the key is that it doesn't clash with any others. Next, in the `Python` directory, create a `greeting.c` file:

```
// file: Python/greeting.c
```

```
#include <stdio.h>
#include "greeting.h"
```

CHAPTER 2   OVERVIEW OF THE CPYTHON PROJECT STRUCTURE

```c
void say_something(const char *message)
{
  printf("=============\n");
  printf("%s\n", message); // Print the incoming message
  printf("=============\n");
}
```

This is functionally identical to before, but now we include "greeting.h" so the compiler knows about `say_something()`.

Now we need to tell CPython to compile these files so that `say_something()` is available. In the CPython project, all files to be compiled are listed in `Makefile.pre.in`, which serves as a template for generating the `Makefile`. Let's add `greeting.c` to the build by finding the PYTHON_OBJS list and inserting our greeting object file:

```
# file: Makefile.pre.in

PYTHON_OBJS=    \
        Python/_warnings.o \
    ... omitted ...
        Python/suggestions.o \
        Python/perf_trampoline.o \
        Python/greeting.o \
        Python/$(DYNLOADFILE) \
        $(LIBOBJS) \
        $(MACHDEP_OBJS) \
        $(DTRACE_OBJS) \
        @PLATFORM_OBJS@
```

After saving the file, you need to re-run `./configure` to regenerate the `Makefile`. Once that's complete, run `make` again to rebuild CPython. This will compile `greeting.c` into `greeting.o`. Now, anywhere you'd like to use this function, just include `greeting.h`, for example:

```c
// file: Python/pythonrun.c

#include "pycore_pylifecycle.h"   // _Py_UnhandledKeyboardInterrupt
#include "pycore_pystate.h"       // _PyInterpreterState_GET()
#include "pycore_sysmodule.h"     // _PySys_Audit()
```

```
#include "pycore_traceback.h"      // _PyTraceBack_Print_Indented()
#include "greeting.h"

// ... omitted ...
```

As long as you include greeting.h, you can call your custom say_something() function wherever you like.

Saying Goodbye on Exit

Back to the REPL: earlier, we mentioned that quitting with exit() doesn't print "Bye", because calling exit() does not trigger the ret != E_EOF condition in the loop. In Python/pythonrun.c, search for the handle_system_exit() function. This is the function that's called when exit() is used to leave the REPL. Let's add a call to say_something("Bye"); here:

```
// file: Python/pythonrun.c

static void
handle_system_exit(void)
{
    int exitcode;
    if (_Py_HandleSystemExit(&exitcode)) {
        say_something("Bye");  // <-- add this line
        Py_Exit(exitcode);
    }
}
```

Rebuild with make, and it should work as expected:

```
$ ./python.exe
Python 3.12.6+ (heads/3.12-dirty:b2a7d718e3b, Sep 16 2024, 15:41:49) [Clang 15.0.0 (clang-1500.3.9.4)] on darwin
Type "help", "copyright", "credits" or "license" for more information.
============
Hello CPython
============
>>> print("Hey")
```

CHAPTER 2   OVERVIEW OF THE CPYTHON PROJECT STRUCTURE

```
Hey
>>> exit()
=============
Bye
=============
```

　　Done! How does it feel to make your own modifications to the CPython source code?

　　When learning Python, you may have heard the saying "everything in Python is an object." In the next chapter, let's start from this idea and take a look at what these "objects" actually look like under the hood!

CHAPTER 3

Everything Is an Object: Part 1

In most Python courses, articles, or tutorial videos, you often hear the statement "everything in Python is an object." Integers, floats, and strings are all objects; lists and dictionaries obviously look like objects; and even functions and classes are also objects. Since everything is an object, let's take a look at what an object actually looks like in CPython.

What Is an "Object"?

In CPython, objects are represented using the `PyObject` struct. Let's see how `PyObject` is defined. In the `Include/pytypedefs.h` file, you'll find:

```
// file: Include/pytypedefs.h

// ... omitted ...
typedef struct PyGetSetDef PyGetSetDef;
typedef struct PyMemberDef PyMemberDef;

typedef struct _object PyObject;
typedef struct _longobject PyLongObject;
typedef struct _typeobject PyTypeObject;
typedef struct PyCodeObject PyCodeObject;
// ... omitted ...
```

As expected, PyObject is indeed a struct. If you look up _object, you'll find its definition in Include/object.h:

```
// file: Include/object.h

struct _object {
    _PyObject_HEAD_EXTRA

#if (defined(__GNUC__) || defined(__clang__)) \
        && !(defined __STDC_VERSION__ && __STDC_VERSION__ >= 201112L)
    // On C99 and older, anonymous union is a GCC and clang extension
    __extension__
#endif
#ifdef _MSC_VER
    // Ignore MSC warning C4201: "nonstandard extension used:
    // nameless struct/union"
    __pragma(warning(push))
    __pragma(warning(disable: 4201))
#endif
    union {
        Py_ssize_t ob_refcnt;
#if SIZEOF_VOID_P > 4
        PY_UINT32_T ob_refcnt_split[2];
#endif
    };
#ifdef _MSC_VER
    __pragma(warning(pop))
#endif

    PyTypeObject *ob_type;
};
```

This looks a bit complicated, so let's remove the conditional compilation directives like #ifdef to focus on the core structure. What remains is:

```
// file: Include/object.h

struct _object {
    _PyObject_HEAD_EXTRA
```

```
    union {
        Py_ssize_t ob_refcnt;
    };
    PyTypeObject *ob_type;
};
```

The _object struct is quite straightforward—it contains a macro _PyObject_HEAD_EXTRA and two member variables, ob_refcnt and ob_type. Let's examine each of them one by one.

The Previous and Next Object

Starting with the macro _PyObject_HEAD_EXTRA, if you trace its definition, you'll find it in the same file:

```
// file: Include/object.h

#ifdef Py_TRACE_REFS
/* Define pointers to support a doubly-linked list of all live heap
objects. */
#define _PyObject_HEAD_EXTRA            \
    PyObject *_ob_next;           \
    PyObject *_ob_prev;

#define _PyObject_EXTRA_INIT _Py_NULL, _Py_NULL,

#else
#  define _PyObject_HEAD_EXTRA
#  define _PyObject_EXTRA_INIT
#endif
```

In C, #define is used to create macros. Macros are neither variables nor functions—they are code snippets that are replaced during compilation, making the code more readable and reusable. Notice the comment just above the macro:

> Define pointers to support a doubly linked list of all live heap objects.

This means that the _PyObject_HEAD_EXTRA macro actually defines _ob_next and _ob_prev pointers, which are used to link all Python objects together into a doubly linked list. Python objects are stored on the heap, which, unlike the stack, does not necessarily occupy contiguous memory locations. After allocation, objects may be scattered throughout the heap. So how does Python know what the previous or next object is? Python uses a "doubly linked list" data structure to connect all objects. This makes it easy to find the previous or next object and allows objects to be added or removed efficiently (O(1)), though searching through the list is slower (O(n)).

From the source code, you can see that the _PyObject_HEAD_EXTRA macro is typically empty during normal compilation and only includes the _ob_next and _ob_prev pointers when Py_TRACE_REFS is defined. This feature is usually enabled for debugging or tracking object reference counts; in the Python versions most of us use, objects do not form a doubly linked list.

Garbage Collection Mechanism

ob_refcnt is a variable of type Py_ssize_t, which is essentially a long integer. refcnt stands for Reference Count (RC), which is how Python handles garbage collection. When an object is referenced, such as being assigned to a variable or stored in a list or dictionary, its ob_refcnt increases. Conversely, when the reference is removed, ob_refcnt decreases. When the value of ob_refcnt drops to 0, it means no one needs this object anymore, and it can be reclaimed by the Garbage Collector (GC), releasing its resources back to the system.

Here, ob_refcnt is encapsulated in a union; this is usually done to allow for extension or modification of struct fields under different compilation conditions. Let's trace how ob_refcnt is initialized:

```
// file: Objects/object.c

PyObject *
_PyObject_New(PyTypeObject *tp)
{
    PyObject *op = (PyObject *) PyObject_Malloc(_PyObject_SIZE(tp));
    if (op == NULL) {
        return PyErr_NoMemory();
    }
```

```
    _PyObject_Init(op, tp);
    return op;
}
```

The purpose of the _PyObject_New() function is pretty clear—it requests a block of memory suitable for the given type and then initializes the object. In other words, it's a function for creating PyObject objects. Now, let's follow _PyObject_Init():

```
// file: Include/internal/pycore_object.h

static inline void
_PyObject_Init(PyObject *op, PyTypeObject *typeobj)
{
    assert(op != NULL);
    Py_SET_TYPE(op, typeobj);
    if (_PyType_HasFeature(typeobj, Py_TPFLAGS_HEAPTYPE)) {
        Py_INCREF(typeobj);
    }
    _Py_NewReference(op);
}
```

In the last line of the function, you can see a call to _Py_NewReference(), which is the function responsible for setting ob_refcnt. Let's continue to follow it:

```
// file: Include/internal/pycore_object.h

void
_Py_NewReference(PyObject *op)
{
    new_reference(op);
}
```

Almost there—let's take a look at the new_reference() function:

```
// file: Objects/object.c

static inline void
new_reference(PyObject *op)
{
    if (_PyRuntime.tracemalloc.config.tracing) {
```

CHAPTER 3   EVERYTHING IS AN OBJECT: PART 1

```
        _PyTraceMalloc_NewReference(op);
    }
    // Skip the immortal object check in Py_SET_REFCNT; always set
       refcnt to 1
    op->ob_refcnt = 1;
}
```

Aha! Here you can see that the `ob_refcnt` of the passed-in object is set to 1. This means every newly created object's `ob_refcnt` has a default value of 1. Why is this necessary? Well, without setting it to 1, the object would be considered unused and scheduled for deletion immediately upon creation.

Since we're here, let's also quickly look at how `ob_refcnt` is incremented and decremented:

```
// file: Include/object.h

static inline Py_ALWAYS_INLINE void Py_INCREF(PyObject *op)
{
    // Explicitly check immortality against the immortal value
    if (_Py_IsImmortal(op)) {
        return;
    }
    op->ob_refcnt++;
}
```

It's simply incremented using ++. What about decrementing?

```
// file: Include/object.h

static inline Py_ALWAYS_INLINE void Py_DECREF(PyObject *op)
{
    // Non-limited C API and limited C API for Python 3.9 and older access
    // directly PyObject.ob_refcnt.
    if (_Py_IsImmortal(op)) {
        return;
    }
    _Py_DECREF_STAT_INC();
    if (--op->ob_refcnt == 0) {
```

```
        _Py_Dealloc(op);
    }
}
```

Decrementing just uses -- on the op parameter to decrease the count. Here, if ob_refcnt drops to 0, it triggers a call to _Py_Dealloc(). If you continue to trace into _Py_Dealloc(), you will observe the object's life cycle, such as invoking its tp_dealloc method. Further details about this will be covered when we discuss Type objects.

Did you notice the "immortal" object design in the above code?

Immortal Objects

If you paid attention to the code earlier, you'll notice that when incrementing or decrementing ob_refcnt, if the object is "immortal," the operation does nothing—the ob_refcnt value remains unchanged. Let's look at how the _Py_IsImmortal() function is implemented:

```
// file: Include/object.h

static inline Py_ALWAYS_INLINE int _Py_IsImmortal(PyObject *op)
{
#if SIZEOF_VOID_P > 4
    return _Py_CAST(PY_INT32_T, op->ob_refcnt) < 0;
#else
    return op->ob_refcnt == _Py_IMMORTAL_REFCNT;
#endif
}
```

As you can probably deduce, simply assigning a special value to ob_refcnt marks the object as immortal. What is this special value? On 64-bit systems, it's a negative value. On 32-bit systems, since the ob_refcnt range is smaller, Python uses a specific fixed value _Py_IMMORTAL_REFCNT instead of a negative number to indicate immortality.

Why have "immortal" objects? In Python, certain objects—such as None, True, and False—are frequently used and don't change. They should not and do not need to be collected. This design prevents repeated creation and destruction of these commonly used objects.

CHAPTER 3   EVERYTHING IS AN OBJECT: PART 1

PyTypeObject

The last member of PyObject, ob_type, is a pointer to a PyTypeObject. So, what is PyTypeObject?

`// file: Include/pytypedefs.h`

```
typedef struct _object PyObject;
typedef struct _longobject PyLongObject;
typedef struct _typeobject PyTypeObject;
typedef struct PyCodeObject PyCodeObject;
typedef struct _frame PyFrameObject;
```

It turns out that PyTypeObject is just an alias for the _typeobject struct. Let's check its definition:

`// file: Include/object.h`

```
struct _typeobject {
    PyObject_VAR_HEAD
    const char *tp_name; /* For printing, in format "<module>.<name>" */
    Py_ssize_t tp_basicsize, tp_itemsize; /* For allocation */

    /* Methods to implement standard operations */

    destructor tp_dealloc;

    // ... omitted ...

    /* Type attribute cache version tag. Added in version 2.6 */
    unsigned int tp_version_tag;

    destructor tp_finalize;
    vectorcallfunc tp_vectorcall;

    /* bitset of which type-watchers care about this type */
    unsigned char tp_watched;
};
```

This struct has many member variables. For example, tp_name is the name of the type, and tp_dealloc is the destructor, which can be customized for different types. The tp_doc is what you see when you print the .__doc__ attribute of an object. For illustration, let's change the value of tp_name in the List type (PyList_Type) and recompile CPython to see what happens:

```c
// file: Objects/listobject.c

PyTypeObject PyList_Type = {
    PyVarObject_HEAD_INIT(&PyType_Type, 0)
    "list-Hello-World",  // <-- changed here
    sizeof(PyListObject),
    0,
    (destructor)list_dealloc,                    /* tp_dealloc */
    // ... omitted ...
    PyObject_GC_Del,                             /* tp_free */
    .tp_vectorcall = list_vectorcall,
};
```

I changed the tp_name of PyList_Type from "list" to "list-Hello-World". After recompiling with make, when I use the built-in type() function in the Python REPL to print the type, the type name appears as list-Hello-World:

```
$ ./python.exe
Python 3.12.6+ (heads/code-review-dirty:914b9826fe6, Sep 17 2024, 17:11:15)
[Clang 15.0.0 (clang-1500.3.9.4)] on darwin
Type "help", "copyright", "credits" or "license" for more information.
=============
Hello CPython
=============
>>> a = [1, 2, 3]
>>> type(a)
<class 'list-Hello-World'>
>>>
```

There's not much use for this, and you shouldn't do it in practice—it's just a fun demonstration.

We'll cover more members of _typeobject in later sections as they become relevant. For now, let's look at the very beginning: PyObject_VAR_HEAD:

```
// file: Include/object.h
```

```
#define PyObject_VAR_HEAD      PyVarObject ob_base;
```

Looking up the definition of PyVarObject, you'll find it right next to the previously mentioned _object:

```
// file: Include/object.h
```

```
typedef struct {
    PyObject ob_base;
    Py_ssize_t ob_size; /* Number of items in variable part */
} PyVarObject;
```

PyVarObject has two members: ob_base, which is a PyObject, and ob_size, which indicates the "size" or "count" of items in the variable part. What does this mean? For example, in a list, ob_size is the number of elements in the list; for a string, it indicates the string's length. For mutable objects (like lists), ob_size changes when elements are added or removed. For immutable objects (like strings or tuples), ob_size remains constant—no methods are provided to change it.

Summary

PyObject is the core struct representing objects in CPython. It plays a crucial role in Python's internals. ob_refcnt is used to track how many times an object is referenced; when this count drops to 0, the object is reclaimed. The ob_type member points to a PyTypeObject, which describes the object's type and encapsulates its behavior and characteristics—much of Python's object-oriented functionality revolves around this. Thanks to ob_type, each PyObject can have a different type, enabling features like polymorphism and inheritance.

We'll pause our introduction to PyTypeObject here for now. In the next section, we'll take a look at how an object is created in the world of Python.

CHAPTER 4

How Objects Are Created in CPython

Let's start with a very simple, albeit not very useful, piece of Python code:

```
class Cat:
    pass
kitty = Cat()
```

This Python code looks quite straightforward. Defining a class and then creating an instance (object) from it is a common operation in Python. But do you know what's happening behind the scenes when the `kitty` instance is created from the `Cat` class? If you've written Python classes before, you are probably familiar with the `__init__()` function and know its purpose. However, you may not be as familiar with another similar function called `__new__()`. In the following, we'll take a look at what happens under the hood when an object is created by examining the CPython source code and also explore the difference between these two functions.

Running the Program!
Step 0: Code Analysis

Although Python does not require compilation like C, the interpreter still has to understand the code we write. The first step is tokenization. Tokenization is the process where the source code is split into individual tokens. To illustrate, here's a simple example:

```
a = 1 + 2
```

This line of code would be broken down into the following tokens:

- NAME (a)
- EQUAL (=)
- NUMBER (1)
- PLUS (+)
- NUMBER (2)

The purpose of this process is to convert raw source code into syntactically meaningful fragments that can be understood by the interpreter. In CPython, this process is handled in `Parser/tokenizer.c`, with the key function being `_PyTokenizer_Get()`:

```
// file: Parser/tokenizer.c

int _PyTokenizer_Get(struct tok_state *tok, struct token *token) {
  int result = tok_get(tok, token);
  if (tok->decoding_erred) {
    result = ERRORTOKEN;
    tok->done = E_DECODE;
  }
  return result;
}
```

The `tok_get()` function inside is responsible for transforming the source code into tokens. This function deals with various details, including processing regular strings and the handy F-Strings. The list of tokens is stored in `Grammar/Tokens`, so if you ever want to add new keywords or syntax to Python, those are the files to look at.

Step 1: Transformation to AST

Once your code has been split into tokens, the next step is turning these tokens into an Abstract Syntax Tree (AST). The goal here is to allow the interpreter to understand the structure and meaning of your code.

As mentioned in earlier chapters, within the CPython project structure, there are directories named `Grammar` and `Parser` dedicated to these tasks. The actual process of parsing into an AST is somewhat complex and goes beyond the scope of this book, so for now, it's enough to know that this step takes place.

Step 2: Compilation to Bytecode

Next, the parsed AST is compiled into bytecode. Wait—compiled? Isn't Python an interpreted language? That's correct. While Python is interpreted, the interpreter first compiles your code into an intermediate form known as bytecode, which is then executed.

This might not feel so obvious if you're working with a single `.py` file. As an example: if you have `a.py` and `b.py` and `a.py` contains `import b`, the contents of `b.py` will be compiled to bytecode and stored in a file named `b.cpython-312.pyc` within the `__pycache__` directory. The naming convention is easy to figure out: `cpython-312` refers to the version of the Python interpreter (Python 3.12 in this case).

So, if you have ever seen a `__pycache__` directory in your Python project, those are the compiled bytecode files. The next time the same piece of Python code is run, the interpreter first checks whether a matching `.pyc` file exists and if recompilation is necessary. If the `.pyc` file is present and doesn't need to be recompiled, it is loaded and executed directly by the Python Virtual Machine (VM).

The code responsible for compiling an AST to bytecode can be found in the CPython project at `Python/compile.c`. The function `_PyAST_Compile()` takes the AST and produces an executable code object. You can explore how your own code is translated into bytecode using Python's built-in `dis` module:

```
$ python -m dis demo.py
```

The output might look like this:

```
0             0 RESUME                   0

1             2 PUSH_NULL
              4 LOAD_BUILD_CLASS
              6 LOAD_CONST               0 (<code object Cat>)
              8 MAKE_FUNCTION            0
             10 LOAD_CONST               1 ('Cat')
```

CHAPTER 4   HOW OBJECTS ARE CREATED IN CPYTHON

```
                    12 CALL                        2
                    20 STORE_NAME                  0 (Cat)
     4              22 PUSH_NULL
                    24 LOAD_NAME                   0 (Cat)
                    26 CALL                        0
                    34 STORE_NAME                  1 (kitty)
                    36 RETURN_CONST                2 (None)

Disassembly of <code object Cat>:
     1               0 RESUME                      0
                     2 LOAD_NAME                   0 (__name__)
                     4 STORE_NAME                  1 (__module__)
                     6 LOAD_CONST                  0 ('Cat')
                     8 STORE_NAME                  2 (__qualname__)

     2              10 RETURN_CONST                1 (None)
```

The numbers at the start (such as 0, 1, and 4) are line numbers in your original source code. Two key points to note here: the LOAD_BUILD_CLASS instruction is used to create the class, and the resulting class is stored in the Cat variable via STORE_NAME. In CPython, the code corresponding to the LOAD_BUILD_CLASS operation is the following:

```
// file: Python/bltinmodule.c

static PyObject *
builtin___build_class__(PyObject *self, PyObject *const *args,
Py_ssize_t nargs, PyObject *kwnames)
{
    PyObject *func, *name, *winner, *prep;

    // ... code omitted ...

    return cls;
}
```

Let's examine a relevant excerpt:

```
// file: Python/bltinmodule.c
```

```
if (meta == NULL) {
    /* if there are no bases, use type: */
    if (PyTuple_GET_SIZE(bases) == 0) {
        meta = (PyObject *) (&PyType_Type);
    }
    /* else get the type of the first base */
    else {
        PyObject *base0 = PyTuple_GET_ITEM(bases, 0);
        meta = (PyObject *)Py_TYPE(base0);
    }
    Py_INCREF(meta);
    isclass = 1;  /* meta is really a class */
}
```

From this, you see that if no metaclass and no parent class are specified (as in our Cat example), the metaclass defaults to type, i.e., PyType_Type. We'll dedicate a full chapter later to the relationship between classes and metaclasses.

There is much more to the builtin___build_class__() function worth discussing, but we'll address it in more detail in later chapters on object-oriented programming. For now, suffice it to say that this function returns a class, but in reality, that class is itself a PyObject. This means that in Python, classes are also just objects.

Once the class is created, the next step is to instantiate an object.

Step 3: Instantiating an Object

If you look at the latter part of the previously shown bytecode, you'll see this:

```
              // ... code omitted ...
              10 LOAD_CONST              1 ('Cat')
              12 CALL                    2
              20 STORE_NAME              0 (Cat)

    4         22 PUSH_NULL
              24 LOAD_NAME               0 (Cat)
              26 CALL                    0
              34 STORE_NAME              1 (kitty)
              36 RETURN_CONST            2 (None)
              // ... code omitted ...
```

CHAPTER 4   HOW OBJECTS ARE CREATED IN CPYTHON

When you execute `kitty = Cat()`, you are essentially "calling" the class object. Python has many special (magic) methods with double underscores at both ends—__call__ is one of them. Any object with a __call__ method can be "called" like a function.

Even though our custom Cat class does not implement __call__, its metaclass is type, which does have this method. Thus, "calling" or "executing" the Cat class triggers the tp_call member of the type class:

```
// file: Objects/typeobject.c

PyTypeObject PyType_Type = {
    PyVarObject_HEAD_INIT(&PyType_Type, 0)
    "type",                                  /* tp_name */
    sizeof(PyHeapTypeObject),                /* tp_basicsize */
    sizeof(PyMemberDef),                     /* tp_itemsize */
    (destructor)type_dealloc,                /* tp_dealloc */
    // ... code omitted ...
    0,                                       /* tp_hash */
    (ternaryfunc)type_call,                  /* tp_call */
    0,                                       /* tp_str */
    (getattrofunc)_Py_type_getattro,         /* tp_getattro */
    .tp_vectorcall = type_vectorcall,
};
```

You'll see that the tp_call member points to a function called type_call. Here is a relevant excerpt of the implementation:

```
// file: Objects/typeobject.c

static PyObject *
type_call(PyTypeObject *type, PyObject *args, PyObject *kwds)
{
    PyObject *obj;

    // ... code omitted ...

    obj = type->tp_new(type, args, kwds);
    obj = _Py_CheckFunctionResult(tstate, (PyObject*)type, obj, NULL);
```

```c
    if (obj == NULL)
        return NULL;

    // ... code omitted ...
    type = Py_TYPE(obj);
    if (type->tp_init != NULL) {
        int res = type->tp_init(obj, args, kwds);
        if (res < 0) {
            assert(_PyErr_Occurred(tstate));
            Py_SETREF(obj, NULL);
        }
        else {
            assert(!_PyErr_Occurred(tstate));
        }
    }
    return obj;
}
```

Within the type_call() function, the type->tp_new() function is called first to create the object. If successful, type->tp_init() is then called to initialize the object. These tp_new() and tp_init() functions in C correspond to the __new__ and __init__ methods in Python, respectively.

Summary

If you write a class and instantiate it, the process goes through these steps:

Compilation stage:

1. Convert source code into tokens.
2. Parse tokens into an AST.
3. Compile the AST into bytecode.

Execution stage:

1. Call the class with parentheses (), which actually invokes the tp_call() member method.

CHAPTER 4 HOW OBJECTS ARE CREATED IN CPYTHON

2. The default `tp_call()` of the type class calls the `tp_new()` function to create the object.

3. It then calls the object's `tp_init()` function to initialize the object.

As a side note, type itself is quite interesting. You might be used to calling `type("hello kitty")` to get the class name of a string. Many think of `type()` as just a function, but it's actually both an object and a class. In the implementation of `type_call()`, you'll find this section:

```
// file: Objects/typeobject.c
```

```
    /* Special case: type(x) should return Py_TYPE(x) */
    /* We only want type itself to accept the one-argument form (#27157) */
    if (type == &PyType_Type) {
        assert(args != NULL && PyTuple_Check(args));
        assert(kwds == NULL || PyDict_Check(kwds));
        Py_ssize_t nargs = PyTuple_GET_SIZE(args);

        if (nargs == 1 && (kwds == NULL || !PyDict_GET_SIZE(kwds))) {
            obj = (PyObject *) Py_TYPE(PyTuple_GET_ITEM(args, 0));
            return Py_NewRef(obj);
        }

        /* SF bug 475327 -- if that didn't trigger, we need 3
           arguments. But PyArg_ParseTuple in type_new may give
           a msg saying type() needs exactly 3. */
        if (nargs != 3) {
            PyErr_SetString(PyExc_TypeError,
                            "type() takes 1 or 3 arguments");
            return NULL;
        }
    }
```

From the comments and code, you can see that if three arguments are provided, you can use `type()` to create a new class. If a single argument is passed, `type()` returns the type of that argument. This is why `type(123)` returns `<class 'int'>` and `type('hello kitty')` returns `<class 'str'>`.

CHAPTER 5

Everything Is an Object: Part 2

In the core implementation of CPython, `PyTypeObject` plays a significant role.

You may have heard the saying "Everything is an object" in Python. Every object has its type, and `PyTypeObject` is the fundamental structure that describes these types. It is one of Python's core structures, defining the behavior, attributes, and methods of all Python types. In this chapter, let's continue exploring some interesting design aspects hidden within.

PyTypeObject

In CPython, `PyTypeObject` is the foundation of all Python objects. It defines their behavior, attributes, and methods. Here is the definition of `PyTypeObject`:

```
// file: Include/object.h
```

```c
struct _typeobject {
    PyObject_VAR_HEAD
    const char *tp_name; /* For printing, in format "<module>.<name>" */
    Py_ssize_t tp_basicsize, tp_itemsize; /* For allocation */

    // ... omitted ...
};
```

To avoid taking up too much space, only a portion of the structure is shown here. You can find the complete definition of `PyTypeObject` in the original `Include/object.h` file. This structure contains all the information needed for a type, such as the type's name, size, methods, attributes, and how it handles memory allocation, attribute access, object creation, and destruction.

Let's briefly organize and categorize its parts:

Basic Members

- `tp_name`: The name of the type, for example, the result of calling `type()` on `int` or `list`.

- `tp_basicsize`, `tp_itemsize`: The source code comments state `/* For allocation */`, indicating that these fields describe the memory size occupied by the object.

- `tp_dict`: The attribute dictionary, which stores the type's attributes. This corresponds to the `__dict__` attribute discussed previously, but here, since we are talking about types, it's slightly different from the `.__dict__` of instances or objects. That said, types themselves are also objects—this is where things can get confusing.

- `tp_base`: The base type; this field is used to describe inheritance relationships.

Methods and Operators

- `tp_new`: The function called when an object is being created.

- `tp_init`: The function called after the object has been created.

- `tp_alloc`: The function responsible for allocating memory for the object.

- `tp_dealloc`: The function called when the object is about to be collected by the GC.

- `tp_call`: The function invoked when the object is called as a function (i.e., when parentheses () are used).
- `tp_str` and `tp_repr`: As the names suggest, these are related to the magic methods `__str__` and `__repr__` we previously introduced in advanced object-oriented programming.

Access Methods

- `tp_as_number`: Defines how the object behaves as a numeric type, such as handling arithmetic and bitwise operations
- `tp_as_sequence`: Defines how the object behaves as a sequence type, enabling operations like indexing, slicing, and concatenation
- `tp_as_mapping`: Defines how the object behaves as a mapping type, such as key/value access and length calculation

This part is especially interesting and will be discussed in more detail later.

Other

- `tp_flags`: Flags indicating type features.
- `tp_doc`: As you might guess, this is the type's documentation string.
- `tp_methods`: Used to define various methods provided by the type. These can be called like built-in methods in Python, and they point to a `PyMethodDef` structure.
- `tp_members`: Structure for defining member variables for the type.
- `tp_getset`: Related to property access in Python.
- `tp_descr_get` and `tp_descr_set`: Related to Python's descriptor protocol.
- `tp_richcompare`: Used for determining how the type handles comparisons.

Looking at the definition of PyTypeObject alone may still feel a bit abstract, so let's use the built-in list type as a concrete example to see how this structure is applied in practice.

The List Type

The list type is defined in the CPython source code as follows:

```
// file: Objects/listobject.c

PyTypeObject PyList_Type = {
    PyVarObject_HEAD_INIT(&PyType_Type, 0)
    "list",
    sizeof(PyListObject),
    0,
    (destructor)list_dealloc,                   /* tp_dealloc */
    0,                                          /* tp_vectorcall_offset */
    0,                                          /* tp_getattr */
    0,                                          /* tp_setattr */
    0,                                          /* tp_as_async */
    (reprfunc)list_repr,                        /* tp_repr */
    0,                                          /* tp_as_number */
    &list_as_sequence,                          /* tp_as_sequence */
    &list_as_mapping,                           /* tp_as_mapping */
    PyObject_HashNotImplemented,                /* tp_hash */
    0,                                          /* tp_call */
    0,                                          /* tp_str */
    PyObject_GenericGetAttr,                    /* tp_getattro */
    0,                                          /* tp_setattro */
    0,                                          /* tp_as_buffer */
    Py_TPFLAGS_DEFAULT | Py_TPFLAGS_HAVE_GC |
        Py_TPFLAGS_BASETYPE | Py_TPFLAGS_LIST_SUBCLASS |
        _Py_TPFLAGS_MATCH_SELF | Py_TPFLAGS_SEQUENCE,  /* tp_flags */
    list___init___doc__,                        /* tp_doc */
    (traverseproc)list_traverse,                /* tp_traverse */
    (inquiry)_list_clear,                       /* tp_clear */
```

```
    list_richcompare,                /* tp_richcompare */
    0,                               /* tp_weaklistoffset */
    list_iter,                       /* tp_iter */
    0,                               /* tp_iternext */
    list_methods,                    /* tp_methods */
    0,                               /* tp_members */
    0,                               /* tp_getset */
    0,                               /* tp_base */
    0,                               /* tp_dict */
    0,                               /* tp_descr_get */
    0,                               /* tp_descr_set */
    0,                               /* tp_dictoffset */
    (initproc)list__init__,          /* tp_init */
    PyType_GenericAlloc,             /* tp_alloc */
    PyType_GenericNew,               /* tp_new */
    PyObject_GC_Del,                 /* tp_free */
    .tp_vectorcall = list_vectorcall,
};
```

Fields that are set to 0 indicate that the corresponding structure members are not implemented.

Printing a List

Let's first examine what `tp_repr` of `PyList_Type` does:

```
// file: Objects/listobject.c

static PyObject *
list_repr(PyListObject *v)
{
    // ... omitted ...
    if (Py_SIZE(v) == 0) {
        return PyUnicode_FromString("[]");
    }
    // ... omitted ...
```

```
    _PyUnicodeWriter_Init(&writer);
    writer.overallocate = 1;
    /* "[" + "1" + ", 2" * (len - 1) + "]" */
    writer.min_length = 1 + 1 + (2 + 1) * (Py_SIZE(v) - 1) + 1;

    if (_PyUnicodeWriter_WriteChar(&writer, '[') < 0)
        goto error;

    for (i = 0; i < Py_SIZE(v); ++i) {
        if (i > 0) {
            if (_PyUnicodeWriter_WriteASCIIString(&writer, ", ", 2) < 0)
                goto error;
        }

        // ... omitted ...
    }

    writer.overallocate = 0;
    if (_PyUnicodeWriter_WriteChar(&writer, ']') < 0)
        goto error;

    Py_ReprLeave((PyObject *)v);
    return _PyUnicodeWriter_Finish(&writer);
    // ... omitted ...
}
```

You can see that if the list is empty, it prints [ ]; if it has elements, it prints each element separated by commas and enclosed in square brackets. There's an interesting calculation for string length:

```
writer.min_length = 1 + 1 + (2 + 1) * (Py_SIZE(v) - 1) + 1;
```

For instance, for [1, 2, 3], the total space required is:

- "[": Opening bracket
- "1": First element
- ", 2": Separator and subsequent elements for each after the first
- "]": Closing bracket

At first glance, this formula may look odd, but by computing the required minimum string length up front, the `PyUnicodeWriter()` can allocate enough memory in one go, avoiding repeated reallocations during string concatenation and increasing efficiency.

Using the Bracket Operator

Earlier, we mentioned `tp_as_sequence` and `tp_as_mapping`. One deals with sequence types like lists or tuples, and the other deals with mapping types like dictionaries. Take a look at the following code example:

```
a = (0, 1, 2)          # This is a tuple
b = [0, 1, 2]          # This is a list
c = { 0: 0, 1: 1, 2: 2 }  # This is a dictionary
print(a[0])
print(b[0])
print(c[0])
```

In Python, using brackets to access values seems perfectly natural. But from the interpreter's perspective, how does it determine whether the bracket operation is for a tuple, a list, or a dictionary? In other words, how does it know to look for `tp_as_sequence` or `tp_as_mapping`?

Let's use Python's built-in `dis` module to examine the bytecode generated by the code above. You'll find that for all three objects, the operation uses the `BINARY_SUBSCR` instruction. Let's see what this instruction does:

```c
// file: Python/bytecodes.c

inst(BINARY_SUBSCR, (unused/1, container, sub -- res)) {
    #if ENABLE_SPECIALIZATION
    _PyBinarySubscrCache *cache = (_PyBinarySubscrCache *)next_instr;
    if (ADAPTIVE_COUNTER_IS_ZERO(cache->counter)) {
        next_instr--;
        _Py_Specialize_BinarySubscr(container, sub, next_instr);
        DISPATCH_SAME_OPARG();
    }
    STAT_INC(BINARY_SUBSCR, deferred);
    DECREMENT_ADAPTIVE_COUNTER(cache->counter);
```

CHAPTER 5   EVERYTHING IS AN OBJECT: PART 2

```
    #endif  /* ENABLE_SPECIALIZATION */
    res = PyObject_GetItem(container, sub);
    DECREF_INPUTS();
    ERROR_IF(res == NULL, error);
}
```

You can see that the real action happens in the `PyObject_GetItem()` function. Digging into that:

```
// file: Objects/abstract.c

PyObject *
PyObject_GetItem(PyObject *o, PyObject *key)
{
    // ... omitted ...
    PyMappingMethods *m = Py_TYPE(o)->tp_as_mapping;
    if (m && m->mp_subscript) {
        PyObject *item = m->mp_subscript(o, key);
        return item;
    }

    PySequenceMethods *ms = Py_TYPE(o)->tp_as_sequence;
    if (ms && ms->sq_item) {
        // ... omitted ...
    }
    // ... omitted ...
}
```

This code shows that when the bracket operator is used, it first looks at the `tp_as_mapping` member and checks if `mp_subscript` is implemented. If not, it then checks the `tp_as_sequence` member for `sq_item`.

In other words, even if both `mp_subscript` and `sq_item` are present, when using the brackets operator, the lookup order is `mp_subscript` first, then `sq_item`. If neither is implemented, you'll get an error message like `'object is not subscriptable'`, for example:

```
>>> user = 9527
>>> user[123]
```

```
Traceback (most recent call last):
  File "<stdin>", line 1, in <module>
TypeError: 'int' object is not subscriptable
```

List Methods

Next, let's look at the tp_methods member, which defines the set of methods provided by the type. For lists, it's implemented like this:

// file: Objects/listobject.c

```
static PyMethodDef list_methods[] = {
    {"__getitem__", (PyCFunction)list_subscript, METH_O|METH_COEXIST,
     PyDoc_STR("__getitem__($self, index, /)\n--\n\nReturn self[index].")},
    LIST___REVERSED___METHODDEF
    LIST___SIZEOF___METHODDEF
    LIST_CLEAR_METHODDEF
    LIST_COPY_METHODDEF
    LIST_APPEND_METHODDEF
    LIST_INSERT_METHODDEF
    LIST_EXTEND_METHODDEF
    LIST_POP_METHODDEF
    LIST_REMOVE_METHODDEF
    LIST_INDEX_METHODDEF
    LIST_COUNT_METHODDEF
    LIST_REVERSE_METHODDEF
    LIST_SORT_METHODDEF
    {"__class_getitem__", Py_GenericAlias, METH_O|METH_CLASS, PyDoc_
    STR("See PEP 585")},
    {NULL,            NULL}          /* sentinel */
};
```

These names are mostly self-explanatory. For example, if we follow the macro LIST_APPEND_METHODDEF:

```
// file: Objects/clinic/listobject.c.h
```

```
#define LIST_APPEND_METHODDEF    \
    {"append", (PyCFunction)list_append, METH_O, list_append__doc__},
```

We find that it refers to the `list_append` function, which is used to add an element to a list. Other methods work similarly.

List Addition

When two lists are added together using the + operator:

```
[1, 2, 3] + [4, 5, 6]
```

Earlier, we mentioned the `tp_as_sequence` member, which defines how an object behaves as a sequence type (indexing, slicing, concatenation, and so on). For lists, `tp_as_sequence` points to the `list_as_sequence` structure:

```
// file: Objects/listobject.c
```

```c
static PySequenceMethods list_as_sequence = {
    (lenfunc)list_length,                   /* sq_length */
    (binaryfunc)list_concat,                /* sq_concat */
    (ssizeargfunc)list_repeat,              /* sq_repeat */
    (ssizeargfunc)list_item,                /* sq_item */
    0,                                      /* sq_slice */
    (ssizeobjargproc)list_ass_item,         /* sq_ass_item */
    0,                                      /* sq_ass_slice */
    (objobjproc)list_contains,              /* sq_contains */
    (binaryfunc)list_inplace_concat,        /* sq_inplace_concat */
    (ssizeargfunc)list_inplace_repeat,      /* sq_inplace_repeat */
};
```

Here, sq_concat handles concatenation and points to the function list_concat(). Let's follow it:

```c
// file: Objects/listobject.c

static PyObject *
list_concat(PyListObject *a, PyObject *bb)
{
    // ... omitted ...
    size = Py_SIZE(a) + Py_SIZE(b);
    if (size == 0) {
        return PyList_New(0);
    }
    np = (PyListObject *) list_new_prealloc(size);

    // ... omitted ...
    return (PyObject *)np;
}
```

From the source code, when two lists are added together, a new list is created and returned. Even if both lists are empty, a new empty list is still created.

Just below sq_concat is a similar member called sq_inplace_concat, which is triggered when using the += assignment operator. It currently points to list_inplace_concat():

```c
// file: Objects/listobject.c

static PyObject *
list_inplace_concat(PyListObject *self, PyObject *other)
{
    PyObject *result;

    result = list_extend(self, other);
    if (result == NULL)
        return result;
    Py_DECREF(result);
    return Py_NewRef(self);
}
```

This function calls `list_extend()`, which adds the elements of other to self. Therefore, the += operation on a list will modify the original list rather than creating a new one, unlike the + operator.

Number of Elements

In Python, you can use the `len()` function to get the number of elements in a list:

```
len([1, 2, 3])  # 3
```

This is straightforward, but how does it work under the hood? Why can the `len()` function be used on many different types?

Let's trace the `len()` function, which is a built-in defined in Python/bltinmodule.c:

```
// file: Python/bltinmodule.c

static PyObject *
builtin_len(PyObject *module, PyObject *obj)
{
    Py_ssize_t res;

    res = PyObject_Size(obj);
    if (res < 0) {
        assert(PyErr_Occurred());
        return NULL;
    }
    return PyLong_FromSsize_t(res);
}
```

The implementation is simple: it just calls `PyObject_Size()`. Digging into `PyObject_Size()`:

```
// file: Objects/abstract.c

Py_ssize_t
PyObject_Size(PyObject *o)
{
    // ... omitted ...
    PySequenceMethods *m = Py_TYPE(o)->tp_as_sequence;
```

```
    if (m && m->sq_length) {
        Py_ssize_t len = m->sq_length(o);
        assert(_Py_CheckSlotResult(o, "__len__", len >= 0));
        return len;
    }
    return PyMapping_Size(o);
}
```

This function first checks the tp_as_sequence member and, if present, uses the sq_length method of PySequenceMethods, which points to list_length():

```
// file: Objects/listobject.c
static Py_ssize_t
list_length(PyListObject *a)
{
    return Py_SIZE(a);
}
```

This function returns the length of the object. If the type is not a sequence type (i.e., it lacks tp_as_sequence), it calls PyMapping_Size(), which invokes the type's tp_as_mapping member's mp_length function to return the length.

The Python documentation for the len() function says:

> Return the length (the number of items) of an object. The argument may be a sequence (such as a string, bytes, tuple, list, or range) or a collection (such as a dictionary, set, or frozen set).

This explains why len() can be used on string, list, tuple (sequence types), or dictionary and similar mapping types.

- len: https://docs.python.org/3/library/functions.html#len

List Comparison

Finally, let's close this chapter with a deceptively simple but tricky question:

```
a = float("nan") # NaN
b = float("nan") # NaN
```

CHAPTER 5 EVERYTHING IS AN OBJECT: PART 2

```
print([a] == [a]) # A. What does this print?
print([a] == [b]) # B. What does this print?
```

In many languages, floating point numbers follow the IEEE 754 standard, in which NaN is not equal to anything, including itself. But what happens if you put them in lists? The result is surprising.

When lists are compared, Python uses the `tp_richcompare` member of `PyList_Type`, which is implemented by the `list_richcompare()` function:

```
// file: Objects/listobject.c

static PyObject *
list_richcompare(PyObject *v, PyObject *w, int op)
{
    // ... omitted ...
}
```

This function is a little lengthy, so let's highlight two main points. First, if the lengths differ (for equality or inequality), the function returns immediately:

```
// file: Objects/listobject.c

vl = (PyListObject *)v;
wl = (PyListObject *)w;

if (Py_SIZE(vl) != Py_SIZE(wl) && (op == Py_EQ || op == Py_NE)) {
    /* Shortcut: if the lengths differ, the lists differ */
    if (op == Py_EQ)
        Py_RETURN_FALSE;
    else
        Py_RETURN_TRUE;
}
```

If the two lists have the same number of elements, each corresponding pair of elements is compared for object identity (i.e., their memory address):

```
// file: Objects/listobject.c

for (i = 0; i < Py_SIZE(vl) && i < Py_SIZE(wl); i++) {
    PyObject *vitem = vl->ob_item[i];
    PyObject *witem = wl->ob_item[i];
```

```
    if (vitem == witem) {
        continue;
    }
    // ... omitted ...
}
```

Back to the original question:

```
a = float("nan") # NaN
b = float("nan") # NaN

print([a] == [a]) # A. What does this print?
print([a] == [b]) # B. What does this print?
```

For `[a] == [a]`, the number of elements is the same, then the objects are compared by memory address. The variable a compared to itself means they are the same object, so the result is `True`.

In `[a] == [b]`, although the number of elements is the same and both variables hold NaN, they are two different objects in memory from Python's perspective, so the result is `False`.

Summary

Although we used the `list` type as our main example, other built-in types follow a similar implementation. In CPython, all types are defined using the `PyTypeObject` structure, which specifies the type's name, size, methods, attributes, and how it handles memory allocation, attribute access, object creation, and destruction. These methods and attribute implementations are what define the behavior and features of Python objects.

In the next chapter, we will leverage what we've learned so far to write a simple type in CPython and see how these components work together.

CHAPTER 6

Defining a Custom Built-in Type

In the previous chapter, we took a look at the `PyType_Type` structure and used the `PyList_Type` structure for lists as an example. In this chapter, I'll demonstrate a similar approach to create our own built-in type named `PyKitty_Type` and even make it perform backflips!

Before we begin, please note: Don't do this in CPython for production purposes. This is purely an experimental exercise just for fun.

Creating a New Type

First, I'll create two files: `kittyobject.c` and `kittyobject.h`. The header (`.h`) file is relatively straightforward and should be placed inside the `Includes` directory:

```
// file: Includes/kittyobject.h

#ifndef Py_KITTYOBJECT_H
#define Py_KITTYOBJECT_H

#include "Python.h"

extern PyTypeObject PyKitty_Type;

#endif
```

I plan to declare a type called `PyKitty_Type`. You can choose any name you like, as long as it does not conflict with the names of other built-in types. Next, the implementation in the `.c` file is a bit more involved. I'll place it in the `Objects` directory alongside the list implementation (`listobject.c`):

```
// file: Objects/kittyobject.c
```

```c
#include <Python.h>
#include "kittyobject.h"

typedef struct {
  PyObject_HEAD
} KittyObject;
```

Here, similar to `PyListObject`, I define a structure called `KittyObject`. You may add any additional member variables here as you see fit. I use the `PyObject_HEAD` macro instead of `PyObject_VAR_HEAD` (as used in `PyListObject`), because `PyObject_VAR_HEAD` includes an `ob_size` field for the size of the object. For `PyKittyObject`, we don't need it, so `PyObject_HEAD` is sufficient and simpler.

Defining Methods

Next, I want objects created from this type not only to be able to do backflips but also to greet politely. Let's define two simple functions:

```
// file: Objects/kittyobject.c
```

```c
static PyObject *
kitty_greeting(KittyObject *self, PyObject *Py_UNUSED(ignored))
{
  printf("Hello, Kitty\n");
  Py_RETURN_NONE;
}

static PyObject *
kitty_backflip(KittyObject *self, PyObject *Py_UNUSED(ignored))
{
  printf("I can do backflip!\n");
  Py_RETURN_NONE;
}
```

You can choose any function names you like, as long as they do not conflict with others. Here, I've followed the naming pattern in listobject.c, prefixing the function names with the type, such as kitty_greeting and kitty_backflip. Their implementations are straightforward—just printing a message with printf().

To make the Python REPL output stand out for instances of our new type, I'll define a custom function for the tp_repr member, here called kitty_repr:

```
// file: Objects/kittyobject.c

static PyObject *
kitty_repr(KittyObject *self)
{
  return PyUnicode_FromString("♥ Hello Kitty ٩(´ᴗ`*)و🍟");
}
```

By convention, __repr__ is intended to display information useful to developers, such as the memory address of the object. Here, however, I'm deliberately returning a playful string just for fun.

Finally, following the example of list_dealloc in listobject.c, I'll implement a kitty_dealloc function to handle memory deallocation:

```
// file: Objects/kittyobject.c

static void
kitty_dealloc(KittyObject *self)
{
  Py_TYPE(self)->tp_free((PyObject *)self);
}
```

Implementing the Type

Now it's time to set up the internals of PyKitty_Type:

```
// file: Objects/kittyobject.c

PyTypeObject PyKitty_Type = {
    PyVarObject_HEAD_INIT(&PyType_Type, 0)
    .tp_name = "kitty",
    .tp_basicsize = sizeof(KittyObject),
```

51

CHAPTER 6　DEFINING A CUSTOM BUILT-IN TYPE

```
    .tp_itemsize = 0,
    .tp_flags = Py_TPFLAGS_DEFAULT,
    .tp_alloc = PyType_GenericAlloc,
    .tp_new = PyType_GenericNew,
    .tp_free = PyObject_Del,
    .tp_dealloc = (destructor) kitty_dealloc,
    .tp_doc = "Hello, Kitty",
};
```

This follows the PyList_Type approach in listobject.c with a few adjustments. To achieve an effect similar to strings <class 'str'> or lists <class 'list'>, I set tp_name to "kitty".

As we learned in the previous chapter, simply defining kitty_greeting, kitty_backflip, or kitty_repr isn't enough; we need to attach them to our PyKitty_Type so that they can actually be invoked:

```
// file: Objects/kittyobject.c

PyTypeObject PyKitty_Type = {
    PyVarObject_HEAD_INIT(&PyType_Type, 0)
    "kitty",
    // ... (omitted) ...
    .tp_doc = "Hello, Kitty",
    .tp_repr = (reprfunc)kitty_repr,
};
```

Here, I've set the kitty_repr function to the tp_repr member. The other two methods should be placed in the tp_methods array, so let's prepare them:

```
// file: Objects/kittyobject.c

static PyMethodDef kitty_methods[] = {
    {"greeting", (PyCFunction)kitty_greeting, METH_NOARGS, "Hello"},
    {"backflip", (PyCFunction)kitty_backflip, METH_NOARGS, "Backflip"},
    {NULL, NULL}
};
```

This approach follows the list_methods definition in listobject.c. Next, set the pointer for the tp_methods member:

```c
// file: Objects/kittyobject.c
```

```c
PyTypeObject PyKitty_Type = {
    PyVarObject_HEAD_INIT(&PyType_Type, 0)
    "kitty",
    // ... (omitted) ...
    .tp_doc = "Hello, Kitty",
    .tp_repr = (reprfunc)kitty_repr,
    .tp_methods = kitty_methods,
};
```

This completes most of the implementation code for our new type.

Making It a Built-in Type

Next, I want this type to be available as a built-in—usable without any `import` statements, like lists or tuples. To do this, open `Python/bltinmodule.c` and locate the `_PyBuiltin_Init()` function. Inside this function, you'll find a macro called SETBUILTIN; add our PyKitty_Type there:

```c
// file: Python/bltinmodule.c
```

```c
PyObject *
_PyBuiltin_Init(PyInterpreterState *interp)
{
    // ... (omitted) ...
    SETBUILTIN("tuple",              &PyTuple_Type);
    SETBUILTIN("type",               &PyType_Type);
    SETBUILTIN("zip",                &PyZip_Type);
    SETBUILTIN("kitty",              &PyKitty_Type);
    debug = PyBool_FromLong(config->optimization_level == 0);
    if (PyDict_SetItemString(dict, "__debug__", debug) < 0) {
        Py_DECREF(debug);
        return NULL;
    }
    // ... (omitted) ...
}
```

CHAPTER 6   DEFINING A CUSTOM BUILT-IN TYPE

Don't forget to include the .h file as well:

```
// file: Python/bltinmodule.c
```

```
#include "kittyobject.h"
```

Building and Running

Finally, make a small edit to your Makefile:

```
// file: Makefile.pre.in
```

```
OBJECT_OBJS=    \
        // ... (omitted) ...
        Objects/unicodeobject.o \
        Objects/unicodetype.o \
        Objects/unionobject.o \
        Objects/weakrefobject.o \
        Objects/kittyobject.o \
        @PERF_TRAMPOLINE_OBJ@
```

Make sure to include `Objects/kittyobject.o`.

Now you're ready to compile:

```
$ ./configure
$ make
```

Assuming everything builds successfully, let's give it a try:

```
>>> kitty
<class 'kitty'>
>>> type(kitty)
<class 'type'>
```

Awesome! The kitty type exists, and it's available without an import. Let's check a bit further:

```
>>> help(kitty)
class kitty(object)
 |  Hello, Kitty
 |
 |  Methods defined here:
 |
```

Looks like the tp_doc member works as expected. Now, let's instantiate our new object:

```
>>> cc = kitty()
>>> cc
♥ Hello Kitty ٩('ʊ`*)و🍟
```

See? Our custom type really stands out! Let's try calling the methods:

```
>>> cc.greeting()
Hello, Kitty
>>> cc.backflip()
I can do backflip!
```

Everything is working. However, at the moment, the kitty type does not support initialization with arguments—so the greeting is always simply "Hello, Kitty", which isn't very interesting. Next, let's add support for initializing the object with a parameter.

Parameterized Initialization

Right now, the kitty type is a bit boring and always greets in the same way. We'd like to give it a name upon creation, like this:

```
c = kitty()
c.greeting()   # Hello

k = kitty("Nancy")
k.greeting()   # Hello, Nancy
```

CHAPTER 6   DEFINING A CUSTOM BUILT-IN TYPE

If a parameter is provided, the greeting should include the name; otherwise, it should default to just "Hello".

To achieve this, our current `KittyObject` structure needs a place to store the name. We'll add a name member variable:

```
// file: Objects/kittyobject.c
```

```c
typedef struct {
  PyObject_HEAD
  PyObject *name;
} KittyObject;
```

In Python classes, extra initialization parameters are typically handled in the __init__ method, which maps to the `tp_init` member in `PyTypeObject`. Let's implement this:

```
// file: Objects/kittyobject.c
```

```c
static int
kitty_init(KittyObject *self, PyObject *args, PyObject *kwds)
{
  static char *kwlist[] = {"name", NULL};
  PyObject *name = NULL;

  if (!PyArg_ParseTupleAndKeywords(args, kwds, "|U", kwlist, &name)) {
    return -1;
  }

  if (name != NULL) {
    Py_INCREF(name);
  }

  Py_XSETREF(self->name, name);
  return 0;
}
```

A brief explanation:

- The function PyArg_ParseTupleAndKeywords() parses the provided arguments into Python objects.
- The Py_INCREF() function increments the reference count of the object so that it is not garbage-collected at the end of the function.
- Py_XSETREF() sets the name member variable on our type.

Now, connect this function to the .tp_init member in PyKitty_Type:

```
// file: Objects/kittyobject.c

PyTypeObject PyKitty_Type = {
    PyVarObject_HEAD_INIT(&PyType_Type, 0) "kitty",
    // ... (omitted) ...
    .tp_repr = (reprfunc)kitty_repr,
    .tp_methods = kitty_methods,
    .tp_init = (initproc)kitty_init,
};
```

Lastly, update the original kitty_greeting function so it prints the name if provided:

```
// file: Objects/kittyobject.c

static PyObject *
kitty_greeting(KittyObject *self, PyObject *Py_UNUSED(ignored))
{
  if (self->name != NULL) {
    printf("Hello, %s!\n", PyUnicode_AsUTF8(self->name));
  } else {
    printf("Hello!\n");
  }

  Py_RETURN_NONE;
}
```

Recompile, and let's test:

```
>>> c = kitty()
>>> c.greeting()
```

CHAPTER 6   DEFINING A CUSTOM BUILT-IN TYPE

```
Hello!
>>> k = kitty("Nancy")
>>> k.greeting()
Hello, Nancy!
>>>
```

Success! Next time, you can show your friends your Python that can do backflips!

Full source code:

// file: Includes/kittyobject.h

```
#ifndef Py_KITTYOBJECT_H
#define Py_KITTYOBJECT_H

#include "Python.h"

extern PyTypeObject PyKitty_Type;

#endif
```

// file: Objects/kittyobject.c

```
#include <Python.h>
#include "kittyobject.h"

typedef struct {
  PyObject_HEAD
  PyObject *name;
} KittyObject;

static PyObject *
kitty_greeting(KittyObject *self, PyObject *Py_UNUSED(ignored))
{
  if (self->name != NULL) {
    printf("Hello, %s!\n", PyUnicode_AsUTF8(self->name));
  } else {
    printf("Hello!\n");
  }

  Py_RETURN_NONE;
}
```

```c
static PyObject *
kitty_backflip(KittyObject *self, PyObject *Py_UNUSED(ignored))
{
  printf("I can do backflip!\n");
  Py_RETURN_NONE;
}

static PyObject *
kitty_repr(KittyObject *self)
{
  return PyUnicode_FromString("❤ Hello Kitty ٩('O`*)و🍟");
}

static void
kitty_dealloc(KittyObject *self)
{
  Py_XDECREF(self->name);
  Py_TYPE(self)->tp_free((PyObject *)self);
}

static int
kitty_init(KittyObject *self, PyObject *args, PyObject *kwds)
{
  static char *kwlist[] = {"name", NULL};
  PyObject *name = NULL;

  if (!PyArg_ParseTupleAndKeywords(args, kwds, "|U", kwlist, &name)) {
    return -1;
  }

  if (name != NULL) {
    Py_INCREF(name);
  }

  Py_XSETREF(self->name, name);
  return 0;
}
```

```c
static PyMethodDef kitty_methods[] = {
    {"greeting", (PyCFunction)kitty_greeting, METH_NOARGS, "Hello"},
    {"backflip", (PyCFunction)kitty_backflip, METH_NOARGS, "Backflip"},
    {NULL, NULL}
};

PyTypeObject PyKitty_Type = {
    PyVarObject_HEAD_INIT(&PyType_Type, 0) "kitty",
    .tp_basicsize = sizeof(KittyObject),
    .tp_itemsize = 0,
    .tp_flags = Py_TPFLAGS_DEFAULT,
    .tp_alloc = PyType_GenericAlloc,
    .tp_new = PyType_GenericNew,
    .tp_dealloc = (destructor) kitty_dealloc,
    .tp_free = PyObject_Del,
    .tp_doc = "Hello, Kitty",
    .tp_repr = (reprfunc)kitty_repr,
    .tp_methods = kitty_methods,
    .tp_init = (initproc)kitty_init,
};
```

CHAPTER 7

What Happens During Module Import

Regardless of whether it's a built-in or a third-party package, I'm sure everyone has used the import keyword to bring in a module when writing Python programs. So, can you guess what the differences are among the following three ways of importing?

```python
# Style A
import sys
print(sys.version)

# Style B
import sys as s
print(s.version)

# Style C
from sys import version
print(version)
```

Different Ways of Importing

In terms of result, all three will successfully print version and display the current Python version. If you look at the compiled bytecode, you'll find that Style A and Style B are almost identical. The main difference is that Style A stores the module as sys using the STORE_NAME instruction, while Style B with the as keyword stores it as s.

```
1            2 LOAD_CONST               0 (0)
             4 LOAD_CONST               1 (None)
             6 IMPORT_NAME              0 (sys)
             8 STORE_NAME               0 (sys)
```

CHAPTER 7   WHAT HAPPENS DURING MODULE IMPORT

```
  4          46 LOAD_CONST              0 (0)
             48 LOAD_CONST              1 (None)
             50 IMPORT_NAME             0 (sys)
             52 STORE_NAME              3 (s)
```

Both styles use the IMPORT_NAME instruction to import the module; other differences are minimal. However, the from ... import ... syntax differs slightly in its execution:

```
  7          90 LOAD_CONST              0 (0)
             92 LOAD_CONST              2 (('version',))
             94 IMPORT_NAME             0 (sys)
             96 IMPORT_FROM             2 (version)
             98 STORE_NAME              2 (version)
            100 POP_TOP
```

Besides IMPORT_NAME, there's also an IMPORT_FROM instruction. Let's take a look at what these two instructions do.

The import Instruction

Starting with IMPORT_NAME, you can find its source code in Python/bytecodes.c:

```
// file: Python/bytecodes.c

inst(IMPORT_NAME, (level, fromlist -- res)) {
    PyObject *name = GETITEM(frame->f_code->co_names, oparg);
    res = import_name(tstate, frame, name, fromlist, level);
    DECREF_INPUTS();
    ERROR_IF(res == NULL, error);
}
```

The initial inst macro is simply for simplifying switch-case statements. The real work is done by the import_name() function:

```
// file: Python/ceval.c

static PyObject *
import_name(PyThreadState *tstate, _PyInterpreterFrame *frame,
            PyObject *name, PyObject *fromlist, PyObject *level)
```

```
{
   // ... omitted ...
}
```

Let's continue to see what happens inside:

```
// file: Python/ceval.c

// ... omitted ...
import_func = PyObject_GetItem(frame->f_builtins, &_Py_ID(__import__));
if (import_func == NULL) {
    if (_PyErr_ExceptionMatches(tstate, PyExc_KeyError)) {
        _PyErr_SetString(tstate, PyExc_ImportError, "__import__ not
          found");
    }
    return NULL;
}
// ... omitted ...
```

Here, it retrieves the __import__ function from the built-ins; if not found, you'll get an "**import** not found" error. "But how could a built-in like __import__ be missing?" you may wonder. Under normal circumstances, it should always be there, but you can purposely delete it as follows:

```
# It exists at first
>>> __import__
<built-in function __import__>

# Delete it with the del keyword
>>> import builtins
>>> del builtins.__import__

# Now try importing another module
>>> import sys
Traceback (most recent call last):
  File "<stdin>", line 1, in <module>
ImportError: __import__ not found
```

CHAPTER 7   WHAT HAPPENS DURING MODULE IMPORT

And indeed, we get the expected error message. This is just for experimentation—don't sabotage yourself or your coworkers like this without good reason! Let's return to the original import_name() function:

```
// file: Python/ceval.c

// ... omitted ...
if (_PyImport_IsDefaultImportFunc(tstate->interp, import_func)) {
    Py_DECREF(import_func);
    int ilevel = _PyLong_AsInt(level);
    if (ilevel == -1 && _PyErr_Occurred(tstate)) {
        return NULL;
    }
    res = PyImport_ImportModuleLevelObject(
                name,
                frame->f_globals,
                locals == NULL ? Py_None :locals,
                fromlist,
                ilevel);
    return res;
}
// ... omitted ...
```

The real import work happens in the PyImport_ImportModuleLevelObject() function. Let's continue tracing:

```
// file: Python/import.c

PyObject *
PyImport_ImportModuleLevelObject(PyObject *name, PyObject *globals,
                                 PyObject *locals, PyObject *fromlist,
                                 int level)
{
  // ... omitted ...
}
```

Within this function, you'll find the following:

```
// file: Python/import.c

mod = import_get_module(tstate, abs_name);
if (mod == NULL && _PyErr_Occurred(tstate)) {
    goto error;
}
```

If you trace into the import_get_module() function, you'll see that Python tries to fetch the module from the sys.modules dictionary first. If found, it uses it directly; otherwise, it proceeds to execute import_find_and_load():

```
// file: Python/import.c

static PyObject *
import_find_and_load(PyThreadState *tstate, PyObject *abs_name)
{
    // ... omitted ...

    mod = PyObject_CallMethodObjArgs(IMPORTLIB(interp), &_Py_ID(_find_
    and_load), abs_name, IMPORT_FUNC(interp), NULL);

    // ... omitted ...
}
```

Here, it calls the _find_and_load() function from the importlib module to find and load the module. This importlib is written in Python, not C. The _find_and_load() function is not a public API, so if you want to call it in REPL, you'll need to use importlib._bootstrap._find_and_load(). However, it's recommended to use importlib's import_module() function for importing modules directly.

Now that we've gotten to the importlib module, let's see what _find_and_load() does:

```
# file: Lib/importlib/_bootstrap.py

def _find_and_load(name, import_):
    module = sys.modules.get(name, _NEEDS_LOADING)
    if (module is _NEEDS_LOADING or
```

Chapter 7: What Happens During Module Import

```
            getattr(getattr(module, "__spec__", None), "_initializing",
        False)):
        with _ModuleLockManager(name):
            module = sys.modules.get(name, _NEEDS_LOADING)
            if module is _NEEDS_LOADING:
                return _find_and_load_unlocked(name, import_)

    # ... omitted ...

    return module
```

Finally, we're seeing some Python code! In this function, Python first tries to fetch the module from the `sys.modules` dictionary. If it exists, it returns it immediately; if not, it calls the `_find_and_load_unlocked()` function to load the module. Tracing into `_find_and_load_unlocked()`, you'll see the imported module is added to `sys.modules`, so subsequent imports can use it directly.

The from .. import .. Instruction

Next, let's look at the IMPORT_FROM instruction. You can find its definition in Python/bytecodes.c:

```
// file: Python/bytecodes.c

inst(IMPORT_FROM, (from -- from, res)) {
    PyObject *name = GETITEM(frame->f_code->co_names, oparg);
    res = import_from(tstate, from, name);
    ERROR_IF(res == NULL, error);
}
```

Here, it calls the `import_from()` function. Let's follow up:

```
// file: Python/ceval.c

static PyObject *
import_from(PyThreadState *tstate, PyObject *v, PyObject *name)
{
    PyObject *x;
```

```
        PyObject *fullmodname, *pkgname, *pkgpath, *pkgname_or_unknown,
        *errmsg;

        if (_PyObject_LookupAttr(v, name, &x) != 0) {
            return x;
        }
        // ... omitted ...
}
```

This tries to look up the attribute name from the module object v. If found, it returns that attribute. If not, the execution continues below. Here, v is the module that was previously imported by the IMPORT_FROM instruction. In other words, the from parameter stores the already-imported module. Looking further:

```
// file: Python/ceval.c

fullmodname = PyUnicode_FromFormat("%U.%U", pkgname, name);
if (fullmodname == NULL) {
    Py_DECREF(pkgname);
    return NULL;
}
x = PyImport_GetModule(fullmodname);
```

Here, fullmodname combines the package and attribute name to form the full module name, then tries to retrieve it from sys.modules via PyImport_GetModule(). Although programming textbooks suggest using meaningful variable names, here the variable x means the module—maybe the author didn't want to overthink the name :)

In short: the import statement calls import_name(), which utilizes the importlib module for lookup and import. The from.. import.. statement relies on import_from(), which first tries to fetch the attribute from the object and only then checks sys.modules.

Crazy Side-Effects!

While following _find_and_load_unlocked(), I stumbled upon a comment: # Crazy side-effects! that caught my attention:

 # file: Lib/importlib/_bootstrap.py

```python
def _find_and_load_unlocked(name, import_):
    # ... omitted ...
    if parent:
        if parent not in sys.modules:
            _call_with_frames_removed(import_, parent)
        # Crazy side-effects!
        if name in sys.modules:
            return sys.modules[name]
        parent_module = sys.modules[parent]
```

What kind of side-effect could be so wild that the developers had to leave this comment in the CPython source code? How crazy is "crazy"? In fact, this code is handling circular import situations. Let's illustrate this with an extreme example. Assume we have the following project structure:

```
├── hello
│   ├── __init__.py
│   ├── child.py
│   └── parent.py
└── main.py
```

File contents are as follows:

```python
# file: hello/__init__.py

from .parent import give_me_child
# file: hello/child.py

class ChildClass:
    pass
# file: hello/parent.py

from .child import ChildClass


def give_me_child():
    return ChildClass()
# file: main.py

import hello.child
```

What happens when you run `main.py`? Let's see:

1. Python prepares to import `hello.child`. Before doing so, it attempts to import the `hello` package.

2. While importing the `hello` package, Python executes `__init__.py`.

3. In `__init__.py`, Python tries to import `give_me_child` from the `parent` module—so it has to execute `parent.py`.

4. The first line in `parent.py` is `from .child import ChildClass`, so Python now tries to import the `child` module—the very module we wanted to import initially!

5. `child` is imported and added to the `sys.modules` dictionary.

6. Execution returns to `parent.py`, completing the definition of `give_me_child`.

7. Finally, execution returns to `main.py`, but now `hello.child` is already in `sys.modules`, so it's used directly.

That's the reason for the "Crazy side-effects!" comment. During the import process for `child`, higher-level modules or packages may import it again, so `child` gets imported even before the original request finishes.

The Behind-the-Scenes Hero: meta_path

When reviewing `import_find_and_load()`, I noticed something interesting:

```
// file: Python/import.c

static PyObject *
import_find_and_load(PyThreadState *tstate, PyObject *abs_name)
{
    // ... omitted ...
    PyObject *sys_path = PySys_GetObject("path");
    PyObject *sys_meta_path = PySys_GetObject("meta_path");
    PyObject *sys_path_hooks = PySys_GetObject("path_hooks");
```

```
    if (_PySys_Audit(tstate, "import", "OOOOO",
                    abs_name, Py_None, sys_path ? sys_path : Py_None,
                    sys_meta_path ? sys_meta_path : Py_None,
                    sys_path_hooks ? sys_path_hooks : Py_None) < 0) {
        return NULL;
    }
    // ... omitted ...
}
```

sys.path is straightforward—a list that determines the search order for modules. But what is sys.meta_path? Let's print it in the REPL:

```
>>> import sys
>>> sys.meta_path
[<class '_frozen_importlib.BuiltinImporter'>,
 <class '_frozen_importlib.FrozenImporter'>,
 <class '_frozen_importlib_external.PathFinder'>]
```

It's a list, consisting of three classes: BuiltinImporter, FrozenImporter, and PathFinder. The first two can be found in Lib/importlib/_bootstrap.py, while the last one is in Lib/importlib/_bootstrap_external.py.

These Importer or Finder classes are responsible for importing modules. In brief, BuiltinImporter handles built-in modules, FrozenImporter deals with "frozen modules" (which are compiled into the interpreter and don't require disk access—resulting in faster startup, better performance, and enhanced security), and PathFinder is the most complex. It manages searching for modules through the file system paths by traversing each path in sys.path to look for matching modules.

All these classes implement a find_spec() class method. As seen previously in the _find_and_load_unlocked() function, there's a segment like this:

```
# file: Lib/importlib/_bootstrap.py

def _find_and_load_unlocked(name, import_):
    # ... omitted ...

    spec = _find_spec(name, path)
    # ... omitted ...
```

Let's check the implementation of _find_spec():

```
# file: Lib/importlib/_bootstrap.py
def _find_spec(name, path, target=None):
    meta_path = sys.meta_path

    # ... omitted ...

    for finder in meta_path:
        with _ImportLockContext():
            try:
                find_spec = finder.find_spec
            except AttributeError:
                continue
            else:
                spec = find_spec(name, path, target)

    # ... omitted ...
```

In summary, when using these Finder classes, Python iterates through `sys.meta_path` in order, first using `BuiltinImporter`. If it fails, it tries `FrozenImporter`, and finally, `PathFinder`.

If you find these three built-in Finders insufficient, you can even create your own custom Finder. For detailed specifications, consult the official documentation.

- The meta path: https://docs.python.org/3.12/reference/import.html#the-meta-path

Summary

Tracing the source code revealed that Python's module import mechanism is much more complex than I imagined. The import process is completed through close cooperation between C and Python: the efficiency of C paired with the flexibility of Python. Importing involves module search, loading, initialization, and handling circular imports. The use of the `sys.modules` dictionary as a cache ensures that importing the same module multiple times doesn't consume extra resources—Python simply fetches it from `sys.modules`.

Complex though it may be, the module import mechanism is quite fascinating to explore…Well, at least I think so!

CHAPTER 8

The Internal Representation of Integers

In the world of Python, integers are among the most fundamental and frequently used data types. Have you ever wondered what happens behind the scenes when you create a number in Python, for example: n = 9527? In some programming languages, the size of numbers can be limited by the operating system—for instance, 232 or 264. Exceeding this limit can result in an "Overflow," but why is Python capable of handling integers of arbitrary size? And why do integers between -5 and 256 have certain special properties? In this chapter, we'll explore these questions in detail.

How Are Numbers Created?

Let's start with a simple Python statement:

n = 9527

Let's look at the corresponding bytecode:

```
1           2 LOAD_CONST               0 (9527)
            4 STORE_NAME               0 (n)
```

It's quite straightforward. The LOAD_CONST instruction loads the constant 9527 onto the stack, and the STORE_NAME instruction assigns it to the variable n. But how is the value 9527 actually created? If the bytecode execution only "loads" this constant, when exactly is this constant created?

The bytecode process is divided into two phases: compilation and execution. During the compilation phase, the function responsible for generating integers in Python is PyLong_FromLong():

CHAPTER 8   THE INTERNAL REPRESENTATION OF INTEGERS

// file: Objects/longobject.c

```
PyObject *
PyLong_FromLong(long ival)
{
    PyLongObject *v;
    unsigned long abs_ival, t;
    int ndigits;

    // ... omitted ...

    return (PyObject *)v;
}
```

This function converts an integer into a PyLongObject. We'll delve into the details of the function in a moment. Next, this object is inserted into the code object's constant table, co_consts:

// file: Python/compile.c

```
static Py_ssize_t
compiler_add_const(PyObject *const_cache, struct compiler_unit *u, PyObject *o)
{
    assert(PyDict_CheckExact(const_cache));
    PyObject *key = merge_consts_recursive(const_cache, o);
    if (key == NULL) {
        return ERROR;
    }

    Py_ssize_t arg = dict_add_o(u->u_metadata.u_consts, key);
    Py_DECREF(key);
    return arg;
}
```

Here, u->u_metadata.u_consts refers to co_consts, which is a tuple containing all constants needed by the code object. This covers the compilation phase of the bytecode process.

Moving on to the execution phase, the compiled bytecode is executed by the virtual machine (VM). Let's see what the LOAD_CONST instruction does during execution:

```
// file: Python/bytecodes.c

inst(LOAD_CONST, (-- value)) {
    value = GETITEM(frame->f_code->co_consts, oparg);
    Py_INCREF(value);
}
```

As you can see, during execution, Python fetches the precompiled constant object from the current Frame's code object constant table, co_consts, rather than creating a new one by calling PyLong_FromLong() again. This is much more efficient. Concepts like Frame and Code Object will be explained in detail in later chapters. For now, you can consider Frame as the current function's execution environment and Code Object as the function's actual code.

Integer Objects

As mentioned earlier, the PyLong_FromLong() function creates a PyLongObject during bytecode compilation and stores it in co_consts. So, what does a PyLongObject look like?

```
// file: Include/cpython/longintrepr.h

struct _longobject {
    PyObject_HEAD
    _PyLongValue long_value;
};
```

The structure is quite simple; it has only one member variable, long_value, which is of type _PyLongValue:

```
// file: Include/cpython/longintrepr.h

typedef struct _PyLongValue {
    uintptr_t lv_tag; /* Number of digits, sign and flags */
    digit ob_digit[1];
} _PyLongValue;
```

CHAPTER 8 THE INTERNAL REPRESENTATION OF INTEGERS

The `lv_tag` field, as indicated by the comment "Number of digits, sign and flags," holds metadata such as the number of digits, the sign, and some additional information about the integer. The `ob_digit` array stores the actual value of the integer. Although its size is 1, there can be multiple digits required to represent large numbers.

On a 64-bit system, the structure of `lv_tag` looks like this:

In this diagram, S, T, and DATA denote the meaning of each bit. S indicates the sign (0 for positive, 1 for negative), T is a flag indicating whether this is a "small integer," and DATA (the largest portion) stores the number of digits needed for the number. For example, let's consider the number 9527:

First, the S bit records the sign: 0 for positive, 1 for negative. So for 9527, the S bit is 0.

CPython has a concept called "small integers," which will be discussed in detail later. These are integers in the range from -5 to 256. If an integer falls within this range, the T bit is 0; otherwise, it is set to 1. Although 9527 is not particularly large, it falls outside the small integer range, so the T bit in its `lv_tag` is set to 1.

The DATA part is more involved. In Python, a `digit` unit (as defined by PYLONG_BITS_IN_DIGIT in the source code) can hold 30 bits on a 64-bit system. The binary representation of 9527 is 10010100110111, which occupies only 14 bits. Therefore, it requires just one `digit`. The DATA section stores this value (number of digits required). For 9527, it's 1.

So, the `lv_tag` for 9527 is:

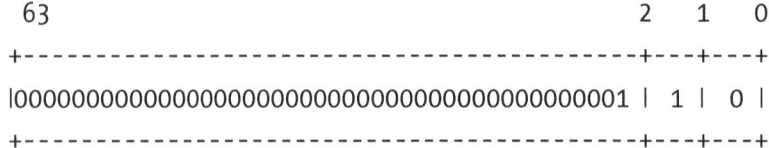

Removing the leading zeros gives you 110 in binary or 0x6 in hexadecimal. What about the actual value of 9527? It's stored in `ob_digit[0]` of _PyLongValue, resulting in:

lv_tag: 0x6
ob_digit[0]: 9527

CHAPTER 8   THE INTERNAL REPRESENTATION OF INTEGERS

If you understand this, you'll realize that any number up to 2^30 - 1 can be represented with a single digit.

Astronomical Numbers!

But what happens with even larger numbers? For example, 2 to the power of 50, which is 1,125,899,906,842,624, or a binary 1 followed by 49 zeros. Since each digit can only store 30 bits, we need another digit to hold the remaining bits. Here, the DATA section in lv_tag becomes 2 (binary = 10), indicating that two digits are needed:

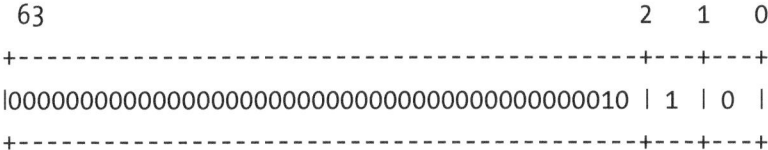

So, the lv_tag will be 1010, which is 0xA in hexadecimal. What about the ob_digit part? 2^50 in binary is 50 bits: ob_digit[0] takes the lower 30 zeros, and ob_digit[1] holds the remaining bits (1 followed by 19 zeros).

So, for 2^50, the _PyLongValue looks like this:

```
lv_tag: 0xA
ob_digit[0] = 0
ob_digit[1] = 524288
```

If you need three digits, then the DATA part of lv_tag will be 3 (binary = 11), and ob_digit will contain three elements, and so on:

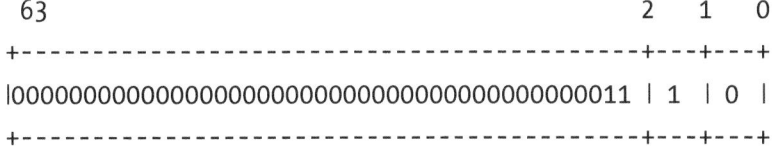

By adding more digits, you can represent even larger numbers. This is why Python can handle arbitrarily large integers—as long as your hardware has enough memory, the size of integers you can create is practically unbounded. This is how Python performs calculations with extremely large numbers.

77

While 2^50 is a huge number mathematically, in Python's internal representation, it's split into two much smaller numbers (0 and 524288). This approach allows Python to handle very large integers efficiently and bypasses the limitations typical of native CPU integer types like 2^32 or 2^64.

With this design, Python's integer limits are theoretically enormous. If you set all bits in the DATA section to 1, you could have 2^62 - 1 digits, and each digit can hold integers up to 2^30 - 1. Multiplying these two numbers gives you a value so large that, with today's hardware, there simply isn't enough memory available to store such a number.

In other words, Python's integers can be extremely large. For example, with 16 GB of memory, you could theoretically create a number with around one billion digits—such numbers are rarely encountered in everyday practice.

Small Integers

Integers are extremely common in Python programs. If a new integer object had to be created each time an integer was used, it could result in unnecessary memory waste. To address this, Python pre-allocates certain integer objects so that when you need them, you can just reuse them rather than creating new ones. Of course, since there are infinitely many integers, Python can't pre-create all of them—only the most commonly used ones are pre-allocated as a performance optimization.

Specifically, in Python, integers from -5 to 256 are particularly common. These are pre-allocated and compiled directly into the Python interpreter itself, so when you use any of these numbers, you'll actually be using the same object each time. You can verify this using the `is` keyword:

```
>>> a = 256
>>> b = 256
>>> a is b
True
>>> c = 257
>>> d = 257
>>> c is d
False
```

How is this achieved? If we look back at the `PyLong_FromLong()` function mentioned earlier, we see the following:

`// file: Objects/longobject.c`

```
if (IS_SMALL_INT(ival)) {
    return get_small_int((sdigit)ival);
}
```

The `IS_SMALL_INT()` macro checks whether a value is a small integer. Its definition is as follows:

`// file: Objects/longobject.c`

```
#define IS_SMALL_INT(ival) (-_PY_NSMALLNEGINTS <= (ival) && (ival) < _PY_NSMALLPOSINTS)
```

What are `_PY_NSMALLNEGINTS` and `_PY_NSMALLPOSINTS`?

`// file: Include/internal/pycore_global_objects.h`

```
#define _PY_NSMALLPOSINTS           257
#define _PY_NSMALLNEGINTS           5
```

That is, 5 and 257. So the `IS_SMALL_INT` macro checks for integers in the range -5 to 256. If the value falls in this range, it calls the `get_small_int()` function:

`// file: Objects/longobject.c`

```
static PyObject *
get_small_int(sdigit ival)
{
    assert(IS_SMALL_INT(ival));
    return (PyObject *)&_PyLong_SMALL_INTS[_PY_NSMALLNEGINTS + ival];
}
```

CHAPTER 8   THE INTERNAL REPRESENTATION OF INTEGERS

In the file defining Python's global objects, you'll see something like this:

```
// file: Include/internal/pycore_global_objects.h
```

```
struct _Py_static_objects {
    struct {
        /* Small integers are preallocated in this array so that they
         * can be shared.
         * The integers that are preallocated are those in the range
         * -_PY_NSMALLNEGINTS (inclusive) to _PY_NSMALLPOSINTS (exclusive).
         */
        PyLongObject small_ints[_PY_NSMALLNEGINTS + _PY_NSMALLPOSINTS];

        // ... omitted ...
    } singletons;
};
```

The `small_ints` array is a member of `static_objects`. These objects are compiled and statically included in CPython itself, meaning that when you start and run Python, these integer objects have already been created and are ready to use.

CHAPTER 9

Floating Point Numbers in CPython

What Is a "Floating Point Number"?

First, have you ever wondered why what we used to call "decimals" in math class are called "floating point numbers" in programming? What's floating about them? Will they float if you toss them in water?

Simply put, computers cannot directly handle base-10 decimals (like 3.14 or 0.001) as we see them in daily life. Instead, they need a special way to represent these numbers. The structure of floating point numbers is similar to scientific notation. For example, 3.14 can be rewritten as 3.14×10^0, and 0.001 as 1×10^{-3}. In computers, these values are represented using a "mantissa" and an "exponent".

Imagine that if we were to represent numbers like 0.0000123 or 123,000,000,000 with a fixed decimal point, the larger or smaller the number, the more zeros we would need, which could be wasteful. Using a method similar to scientific notation, they become 1.23×10^{-5} and 1.23×10^{11}, without the need for all those zeros.

So, the "floating" in "floating point" refers to the fact that the decimal point can freely move and is not fixed in one spot. This design allows computers to efficiently represent very large or very small decimal numbers, preventing overflow issues for extremely large or small values. The downside, however, is that there may be precision issues.

CHAPTER 9   FLOATING POINT NUMBERS IN CPYTHON

The Structure of Floating Point Numbers

In Python, a floating point number is also an object, and its structure is as follows:

// file: Include/cpython/floatobject.h

```
typedef struct {
    PyObject_HEAD
    double ob_fval;
} PyFloatObject;
```

Compared to the integer `PyLongObject` discussed in the previous chapter, the structure of `PyFloatObject` is simpler. It only has one member variable of type `double` called `ob_fval` to store the value of the floating point number. Some programming languages, like C, distinguish between 32-bit single precision (`float`) and 64-bit double precision (`double`) floating point numbers. However, as seen in the CPython source code, Python's floating point numbers are implemented directly using C's `double`.

Whenever you execute `a = 3.14`, CPython creates a new `PyFloatObject`. This is handled by the `PyFloat_FromDouble()` function defined in `Objects/floatobject.c`. I've omitted some less relevant conditional compilation and `{}` blocks for clarity. The essential code looks like this:

// file: Objects/floatobject.c

```
PyObject *
PyFloat_FromDouble(double fval)
{
    PyFloatObject *op;

    op = PyObject_Malloc(sizeof(PyFloatObject));
    if (!op) {
        return PyErr_NoMemory();
    }

    _PyObject_Init((PyObject*)op, &PyFloat_Type);
    op->ob_fval = fval;
    return (PyObject *) op;
}
```

The process is straightforward: first, it calls `PyObject_Malloc()` to allocate memory, then initializes the object with `_PyObject_Init()`, and finally assigns the input `fval` to the member variable `ob_fval`.

Actually, it's not quite that simple—I've omitted some code to make it look cleaner here. We'll revisit those additional details when discussing the performance aspects of floating point numbers later.

Because CPython's floating point numbers are implemented using C's `double`, the design and computation results of Python's floats align closely with those in C.

About Floating Point Numbers

As CPython's floating point type corresponds to C's `double`, it is also implemented according to the IEEE 754 standard. IEEE 754 defines that a double precision floating point number occupies 64 bits, with the following layout:

```
63  62          52                                      0
+---+-----------+---------------------------------------+
| S |     E     |                   M                   |
+---+-----------+---------------------------------------+
```

- IEEE 754: https://en.wikipedia.org/wiki/IEEE_754

Here is what the letters stand for:

- S is the sign bit, occupying 1 bit: 0 for positive, 1 for negative.
- E is the exponent, occupying 11 bits.
- M is the mantissa (also known as significant), occupying 52 bits.

For example, the binary representation of 3.14 is:

`11.00100011110101110000101000111110101...`

Although this is actually a repeating binary decimal, with the infinite part truncated due to limited storage, some inaccuracy is expected. Using a scientific notation-like format, we move the decimal point to the left by one position, resulting in:

`1.100100011110101110000101000111110101... x 2^1`

A brief note about how the exponent E is calculated: this is a bit more complex. IEEE 754 uses a "bias" for the exponent; for double, the bias is 2^10 - 1, or 1,023. As we've just seen, 3.14 in binary is expressed as `1.100100011...` x `2^1`. Here, the exponent is 1, so you add the bias to get 1,024, which is `10000000000` in binary. The bias technique allows both positive and negative exponents to be represented more easily.

So, 3.14 in IEEE 754 double precision format would be:

- S: 0, since 3.14 is positive.
- E: 10000000000, as calculated above.
- M: The sequence to the right of the decimal in `1.100100011....`

So 3.14 in IEEE 754 looks like:

`0 10000000000 1001000111101011100001010001111010111000010100011110`

From this, you can see that the M (mantissa) bit section cannot store all the digits—hence the common problem of floating point inaccuracy. Since C's `double` strictly follows IEEE 754, and CPython's floating point is implemented using C's `double`, the same imprecise behavior is to be expected.

Floating Point Arithmetic

Let's take another look at the definition of `PyFloat_Type`:

```
// file: Objects/floatobject.c

PyTypeObject PyFloat_Type = {
    PyVarObject_HEAD_INIT(&PyType_Type, 0)
    "float",
    // ... omitted ...
    &float_as_number,                       /* tp_as_number */
    0,                                      /* tp_as_sequence */
    0,                                      /* tp_clear */
    0,                                      /* tp_as_mapping */
    // ... omitted ...
};
```

Previously, we discussed the tp_as_ member variables. Arithmetic operations, such as addition, rely on the tp_as_number field, which is set to float_as_number here. Let's follow float_as_number:

// file: Objects/floatobject.c

```
static PyNumberMethods float_as_number = {
    float_add,              /* nb_add */
    float_sub,              /* nb_subtract */
    float_mul,              /* nb_multiply */
    float_rem,              /* nb_remainder */
    float_divmod,           /* nb_divmod */
    float_pow,              /* nb_power */
    (unaryfunc)float_neg,   /* nb_negative */
    float_float,            /* nb_positive */
    (unaryfunc)float_abs,   /* nb_absolute */
    (inquiry)float_bool,    /* nb_bool */
    0,                      /* nb_invert */
    // ... omitted ...
};
```

From the function names, it's clear that these operations correspond to arithmetic functions. Let's take a closer look at addition (float_add) and subtraction (float_sub):

// file: Objects/floatobject.c

```
static PyObject *
float_add(PyObject *v, PyObject *w)
{
    double a,b;
    CONVERT_TO_DOUBLE(v, a);
    CONVERT_TO_DOUBLE(w, b);
    a = a + b;
    return PyFloat_FromDouble(a);
}
```

```
static PyObject *
float_sub(PyObject *v, PyObject *w)
{
    double a,b;
    CONVERT_TO_DOUBLE(v, a);
    CONVERT_TO_DOUBLE(w, b);
    a = a - b;
    return PyFloat_FromDouble(a);
}
```

It's quite straightforward. Both values are converted to `double`, the arithmetic is performed, and the result is converted back into a `PyFloatObject`.

Infinity!

Both positive and negative infinity are represented as special floating point values in Python. When the result of a floating point operation exceeds the maximum representable value, it will be set to infinity (positive or negative as appropriate), rather than causing an overflow.

Since Python's floating point numbers are C doubles under the hood, infinity in Python is identical to infinity in C. Here's a simple C program to illustrate this:

```c
#include <stdio.h>

int main() {
    // Pick numbers close to the maximum value of double
    double positive_float = 1e308;   // Positive max value
    double negative_float = -1e308;  // Negative max value

    // Intentionally go out of range by multiplying by 10
    double result1 = positive_float * 10;
    double result2 = negative_float * 10;

    printf("Result: %f\n", result1);
    printf("Result: %f\n", result2);
}
```

The results displayed will be inf and -inf, respectively. This is the behavior of C's double when exceeding representable limits, so it's no surprise to see the same in Python.

Not a Number!

NaN (Not a Number) is a special floating point value as defined by IEEE 754, representing a value that is not a valid number. CPython defines a macro to check for NaN values:

```
// file: Include/pymath.h

#define Py_IS_NAN(X) isnan(X)
```

If you look deeper, you'll see that isnan() is simply a function or macro provided by C itself. In other words, Python just calls C's native isnan check.

If we look further at C's isnan macro:

```
#define isnan(x)                                                       \
  ( sizeof(x) == sizeof(float)  ? __inline_isnanf((float)(x))          \
  : sizeof(x) == sizeof(double) ? __inline_isnand((double)(x))         \
                                : __inline_isnanl((long double)(x)))
```

It chooses which function to use based on whether the value is a float, double, or long double. Focusing on the double version:

```
__header_always_inline int __inline_isnand(double __x) {
    return __x != __x;
}
```

It simply returns the result of comparing the value to itself. According to IEEE 754, NaN is not equal to any value, including itself. Therefore, the expression x != x is only true when x is NaN.

Comparing Floating Point Numbers

Compared to basic arithmetic operations, comparing floating point numbers is far more complicated. In fact, the comment in the code says that floating point comparisons are pretty much a nightmare:

```
// file: Objects/floatobject.c

/* Comparison is pretty much a nightmare.  When comparing float to float,
 * we do it as straightforwardly (and long-windedly) as conceivable, so
 * that, e.g., Python x == y delivers the same result as the platform
 * C x == y when x and/or y is a NaN.
 * When mixing float with an integer type, there's no good *uniform* approach.
 * Converting the double to an integer obviously doesn't work, since we
 * may lose info from fractional bits.  Converting the integer to a double
 * also has two failure modes:  (1) an int may trigger overflow (too
 * large to fit in the dynamic range of a C double); (2) even a C long may have
 * more bits than fit in a C double (e.g., on a 64-bit box long may have
 * 63 bits of precision, but a C double probably has only 53), and then
 * we can falsely claim equality when low-order integer bits are lost by
 * coercion to double.  So this part is painful too.
 */
```

Indeed, comparing floating point numbers is tricky enough, but things get even more complicated when comparing floats and integers or when dealing with special values like NaN or infinity. Let's take a look at just how complex this can get. As we have learned, comparison logic is implemented in the `tp_richcompare` member:

```
// file: Objects/floatobject.c

static PyObject*
float_richcompare(PyObject *v, PyObject *w, int op)
{
    // ... omitted ...
}
```

This function is around 170 lines long and filled with `if` and `else if` statements, including logic for handling NaN, which explains the "nightmare" comment.

Floating Point Performance

At the beginning, when discussing how floating point numbers are created—specifically the PyFloat_FromDouble() function—I initially omitted some conditional code, making it look like this:

```
// file: Objects/floatobject.c

PyObject *
PyFloat_FromDouble(double fval)
{
    PyFloatObject *op;
#if PyFloat_MAXFREELIST > 0
    struct _Py_float_state *state = get_float_state();
    op = state->free_list;
    if (op != NULL) {
        state->free_list = (PyFloatObject *) Py_TYPE(op);
        state->numfree--;
        OBJECT_STAT_INC(from_freelist);
    }
    else
#endif
    // ... omitted ...
}
```

If you look for the definition of PyFloat_MAXFREELIST, you'll find it defaults to 100. This feature is designed to optimize performance. When a floating point object is no longer in use, its memory is not immediately freed; instead, it is put into a "free list" for reuse. Here is the structure of this list:

```
// file: Include/internal/pycore_floatobject.h

struct _Py_float_state {
#if PyFloat_MAXFREELIST > 0
    /* Special free list
       free_list is a singly-linked list of available PyFloatObjects,
       linked via abuse of their ob_type members. */
```

CHAPTER 9 FLOATING POINT NUMBERS IN CPYTHON

```
    int numfree;
    PyFloatObject *free_list;
#endif
};
```

This simple structure uses `numfree` to track how many slots are available and `free_list` to point to the list of reusable floating point objects. According to the comment, it is a singly linked list, "abusing" the `ob_type` member to chain the objects together. (That "abuse" isn't my term—it's right in the comment!) In practice, the linked list looks like this:

```
+----------------+     +----------------+     +----------------+
| ob_fval = 3.14 | ->  | ob_fval = 2.71 | ->  | ob_fval = 1.41 | -> NULL
+----------------+     +----------------+     +----------------+
```

Finally, the last pointer is NULL, indicating the end of the list.

From the code in `PyFloat_FromDouble()`, you can see that Python checks the `free_list` first when creating a floating point object. If an item is available, this line is key:

```
state->free_list = (PyFloatObject *) Py_TYPE(op);
```

Syntactically, this seems to assign a new `PyFloatObject` to `free_list` after converting with the `Py_TYPE()` macro, but in fact, `Py_TYPE()` retrieves the `ob_type` of the object:

```
// file: Include/object.h

static inline PyTypeObject* Py_TYPE(PyObject *ob) {
    return ob->ob_type;
}
```

This function simply retrieves the `ob_type` from the object, so this code is not creating a new object—in effect, it's advancing the `free_list` pointer to the next item in the linked list ("popping" the list), reusing memory that's already been allocated. This technique prevents memory fragmentation and improves efficiency by recycling equally sized memory blocks.

This is quite clever! Honestly, I never would have thought to use the type pointer like this. It's truly an ingenious design!

CHAPTER 10

Inside the String Object: Part 1

In most programming languages, strings and numbers are among the most frequently used data types. Strings are primarily used to represent text data, but have you ever wondered what actually happens behind the scenes when you write a simple statement in Python like `message = "Hello, World!"`?

Creating a String

Let's start with the basics:

```
message = "Hello, World!"
```

This line of code is very common in Python. Its purpose is to create a string and assign it to the variable `message`. Let's take a look at what the bytecode for this line looks like:

```
  1           2 LOAD_CONST               0 ('Hello, World!')
              4 STORE_NAME               0 (message)
```

Once again, it uses the `LOAD_CONST` instruction to load a constant, which means that this string is already compiled into the bytecode before the bytecode even runs. When you create a string with a literal (String Literal) like this, the compiler embeds it directly into the bytecode. As for how bytecode is generated, we will cover that in detail in a later chapter. For now, let's see how a string object is created in CPython.

CHAPTER 10   INSIDE THE STRING OBJECT: PART 1

String Objects

In Python 3, strings are Unicode by default, and CPython uses the `PyUnicode_New()` function to create string objects:

```
// file: Objects/unicodeobject.c

PyObject *
PyUnicode_New(Py_ssize_t size, Py_UCS4 maxchar)
{
    // ... omitted ...
}
```

This function has a fair number of lines, so we'll go through it step by step. The first thing it does is check if it is an empty string:

```
// file: Objects/unicodeobject.c

/* Optimization for empty strings */
if (size == 0) {
    return unicode_new_empty();
}
```

There is a specific optimization for empty strings! This makes sense, since empty strings are used quite frequently. Let's see how this is implemented:

```
// file: Objects/unicodeobject.c

static inline PyObject* unicode_new_empty(void)
{
    PyObject *empty = unicode_get_empty();
    return Py_NewRef(empty);
}
```

In other words, there is only one instance of the empty string in CPython, and it is compiled directly into the Python interpreter. Every time an empty string is needed, the same empty string object is used, rather than creating a new instance. This not only saves memory but also avoids unnecessary operations in the `PyUnicode_New()` function. Next, the function determines which type of string object to create based on the encoding of the characters:

```
// file: Objects/unicodeobject.c
if (maxchar < 128) {
    kind = PyUnicode_1BYTE_KIND;
    char_size = 1;
    is_ascii = 1;
    struct_size = sizeof(PyASCIIObject);
}
else if (maxchar < 256) {
    kind = PyUnicode_1BYTE_KIND;
    char_size = 1;
}
else if (maxchar < 65536) {
    kind = PyUnicode_2BYTE_KIND;
    char_size = 2;
}
else {
    if (maxchar > MAX_UNICODE) {
        PyErr_SetString(PyExc_SystemError,
                        "invalid maximum character passed to
                        PyUnicode_New");
        return NULL;
    }
    kind = PyUnicode_4BYTE_KIND;
    char_size = 4;
}
```

Here, the value of maxchar determines which type of string object to create. CPython defines three types of string objects: PyASCIIObject is used for pure ASCII strings, where each character uses one byte. PyCompactUnicodeObject is for small Unicode strings, using two bytes per character. And PyUnicodeObject is for large Unicode strings, using four bytes per character. That is, Python chooses the most suitable type of string object for the actual content, in order to minimize unnecessary memory usage.

If you use Chinese characters or emojis, it makes sense to represent them with Unicode. But for English letters and digits, ASCII suffices. The definitions of these three string structures are also interesting—a closer look shows that they are closely related:

```
// file: Include/cpython/unicodeobject.h
typedef struct {
    PyObject_HEAD
    Py_ssize_t length;          /* Number of code points in the string */
    Py_hash_t hash;             /* Hash value; -1 if not set */
    struct {
        unsigned int interned:2;
        unsigned int kind:3;
        unsigned int compact:1;
        unsigned int ascii:1;
        unsigned int statically_allocated:1;
        unsigned int :24;
    } state;
} PyASCIIObject;

typedef struct {
    PyASCIIObject _base;
    Py_ssize_t utf8_length;     /* Number of bytes in utf8, excluding the
                                 * terminating \0. */
    char *utf8;                 /* UTF-8 representation (null-terminated) */
} PyCompactUnicodeObject;

typedef struct {
    PyCompactUnicodeObject _base;
    union {
        void *any;
        Py_UCS1 *latin1;
        Py_UCS2 *ucs2;
        Py_UCS4 *ucs4;
    } data;                     /* Canonical, smallest-form Unicode buffer */
} PyUnicodeObject;
```

CHAPTER 10   INSIDE THE STRING OBJECT: PART 1

From the source code, it's not hard to see that `PyASCIIObject` is the basic structure, `PyCompactUnicodeObject` builds upon it by adding a few members, and `PyUnicodeObject` extends `PyCompactUnicodeObject` further.

The Fundamental String Structure

Since `PyASCIIObject` is the foundational structure, let's take a closer look at its members:

```
// file: Include/cpython/unicodeobject.h
typedef struct {
    PyObject_HEAD
    Py_ssize_t length;         /* Number of code points in the string */
    Py_hash_t hash;            /* Hash value; -1 if not set */
    struct {
        unsigned int interned:2;
        unsigned int kind:3;
        unsigned int compact:1;
        unsigned int ascii:1;
        unsigned int statically_allocated:1;
        unsigned int :24;
    } state;
} PyASCIIObject;
```

- `PyObject_HEAD`: A macro required by every object, which we won't discuss here.

- `length`: As you might guess, this stores the number of characters in the string. It is set when the string object is created, so retrieving the string's length is fast and does not require recalculating every time.

- `hash`: Stores the hash value of the string. If it is `-1`, it means the hash hasn't been computed yet.

- The `state` struct contains:
  - `interned`: Indicates whether the string is "interned" (stored in an internal pool for reuse), so it doesn't have to be created again every time.

95

- **kind**: Indicates the string's encoding type, distinguishing between `PyASCIIObject`, `PyCompactUnicodeObject`, and `PyUnicodeObject`.
- **compact**: Indicates whether the string data is stored directly after the string object in memory, rather than as a separate allocation. This improves performance.
- **ascii**: Indicates whether it is a pure ASCII string.
- **statically_allocated**: Indicates whether the string is statically allocated, in which case it isn't managed by the garbage collector.
- The remaining 24 bits are reserved for future extensions, allowing new flags to be added without changing the size of the structure.

To elaborate on `compact`, imagine you have a box of clothes. You might keep clothing labels separate from the clothes, but if you use a "compact" method, the label is sewn directly onto the garment—saving space and making them easier to find.

Of course, this design isn't without drawbacks. For example, if you want to modify the string, you'll need to reallocate memory, which can be slower. However, since Python strings are immutable by design, this isn't a problem.

String Operations

Encoding Conversion

Python chooses which string object type to use based on the string's contents. Suppose you add an emoji (☺, Unicode code point = U+1F60A) to an ASCII string:

```
message = "Hello, world!"
message = message + "☺"
```

What happens here? Let's walk through it. Strings are of type `PyUnicode_Type`. As discussed in the earlier section on the `PyType_Type` structure, there are three members starting with `tp_as_`. One of them, `tp_as_sequence`, defines how the object behaves as a sequence, handling things like indexing, slicing, and concatenation. Here, joining two strings makes use of the `sq_concat` function pointer from that member:

```
// file: Objects/unicodeobject.c

PyObject *
PyUnicode_Concat(PyObject *left, PyObject *right)
{
    PyObject *result;

    // ... omitted ...
    maxchar = PyUnicode_MAX_CHAR_VALUE(left);
    maxchar2 = PyUnicode_MAX_CHAR_VALUE(right);
    maxchar = Py_MAX(maxchar, maxchar2);

    /* Concat the two Unicode strings */
    result = PyUnicode_New(new_len, maxchar);
    if (result == NULL)
        return NULL;
    _PyUnicode_FastCopyCharacters(result, 0, left, 0, left_len);
    _PyUnicode_FastCopyCharacters(result, left_len, right, 0, right_len);
    assert(_PyUnicode_CheckConsistency(result, 1));
    return result;
}
```

Here we see that the maxchar of both strings is checked and the larger value is passed to PyUnicode_New() to create the new string object. This function then determines which string object type to use based on the content. In this case, maxchar is U+1F60A, which is greater than 65536, so Python uses PyUnicodeObject to create the string.

Python strings are immutable, so message is not changed in place; instead, a brand new string object is created and assigned to message. When Python detects that the characters in the new string exceed the capabilities of the current structure, it automatically switches from using PyASCIIObject to PyUnicodeObject. We can write a small Python script to verify this:

```
import sys

def string_info(s):
    print(f"Length: {len(s)}")
    print(f"Size: {sys.getsizeof(s)} bytes")
    print(f"Is ASCII: {s.isascii()}")
```

```
message = "Hello World!"
string_info(message)

message = message + "☺"
string_info(message)
```

Output:

```
Length: 12
Size: 53 bytes
Is ASCII: True

Length: 13
Size: 112 bytes
Is ASCII: False
```

As you can see, by adding just one emoji, the size of the string jumps from 53 bytes to 112 bytes—and the `ascii` member in `state` is now 0.

Strings Are Immutable

Python strings are immutable, meaning you can read string elements, but you cannot modify them:

```
message = "Hello, World!"
print(message[0])   # prints "H"
message[0] = "h"    # This will raise an error!
```

This is implemented quite simply. When accessing or assigning by square brackets (i.e., via indexing or slicing), Python first looks for the `mp_subscript` member in the `tp_as_mapping` structure and, if not present, then checks `tp_as_sequence`.

```
// file: Objects/unicodeobject.c
static PyObject*
unicode_subscript(PyObject* self, PyObject* item)
{
    if (_PyIndex_Check(item)) {
        // ... omitted ...
        return unicode_getitem(self, i);
```

```
    } else if (PySlice_Check(item)) {
        // ... omitted ...
    } else {
        PyErr_Format(PyExc_TypeError, "string indices must be integers, 
            not '%.200s'", Py_TYPE(item)->tp_name);
        return NULL;
    }
}
```

Here, the function checks whether item is an integer or a slice. If it's an integer, it calls unicode_getitem(). If it's a slice, it creates a new string object for the slice. Reading is fine, but for assignment (modifying elements), Python checks the mp_ass_subscript member:

```
// file: Objects/unicodeobject.c

static PyMappingMethods unicode_as_mapping = {
    (lenfunc)unicode_length,          /* mp_length */
    (binaryfunc)unicode_subscript,    /* mp_subscript */
    (objobjargproc)0,                 /* mp_ass_subscript */
};
```

You can see that mp_ass_subscript is set to 0, which means this function is not implemented. As a result, attempting to use integer or slice indices to modify a string will result in an error message:

TypeError: 'str' object does not support item assignment

In summary, regarding string modification:

- Any operation that looks like it modifies a string—such as concatenation or changing case—returns a brand new string object.

- Strings are immutable simply because they do not provide any function for direct modification.

That's all there is to it.

More about string formatting, slicing, and memory-saving techniques like string interning will be covered in the next part.

CHAPTER 11

Inside the String Object: Part 2

String Operations

Copying Strings

In the previous chapter, we introduced this pattern:

```
message = "Hello, world!"
message = message + "☺"
```

Although this feels like a simple operation, similar to a = a + 1, in reality, this process creates a new string object. At the end of the function, it calls a method to concatenate the strings:

```
// file: Objects/unicodeobject.c

PyObject *
PyUnicode_Concat(PyObject *left, PyObject *right)
{
    PyObject *result;

    // ... omitted ...

    result = PyUnicode_New(new_len, maxchar);
    if (result == NULL)
        return NULL;
    _PyUnicode_FastCopyCharacters(result, 0, left, 0, left_len);
    _PyUnicode_FastCopyCharacters(result, left_len, right, 0, right_len);
```

```
    assert(_PyUnicode_CheckConsistency(result, 1));
    return result;
}
```

Here, you can see that two copy operations are performed at the end, copying the final result into the result object. Notably, the function name _PyUnicode_FastCopyCharacters includes the word Fast. Let's take a look at how fast it really is:

// file: Objects/unicodeobject.c

```
static int
_copy_characters(PyObject *to, Py_ssize_t to_start,
                 PyObject *from, Py_ssize_t from_start,
                 Py_ssize_t how_many, int check_maxchar)
{
    // ... omitted ...
}
```

This function has several parameters. The meanings of to and from are straightforward—they represent the objects to copy from and to. to_start and from_start indicate the starting positions in the destination and source objects, respectively. how_many specifies how many characters to copy, while check_maxchar determines whether to check the maximum character value.

Let's look further down:

// file: Objects/unicodeobject.c

```
from_kind = PyUnicode_KIND(from);
from_data = PyUnicode_DATA(from);
to_kind   = PyUnicode_KIND(to);
to_data   = PyUnicode_DATA(to);

if (from_kind == to_kind) {
    if (check_maxchar
        && !PyUnicode_IS_ASCII(from) && PyUnicode_IS_ASCII(to))
    {
        Py_UCS4 max_char;
        max_char = ucs1lib_find_max_char(from_data,
```

```
                                    (const Py_UCS1*)from_data +
                                    how_many);
        if (max_char >= 128)
            return -1;
    }
    memcpy((char*)to_data + to_kind * to_start,
           (const char*)from_data + from_kind * from_start,
           to_kind * how_many);
}
else if (from_kind == PyUnicode_1BYTE_KIND
        && to_kind == PyUnicode_2BYTE_KIND)
{
    // ... omitted ...
}
```

The PyUnicode_KIND macro simply checks the kind property inside the string object's state structure. If the kind property of both string objects is the same, the function uses the memcpy() function to copy the memory directly. This memcpy() operates at the memory level, without any extra checks or processing; it simply copies data from one memory region to another, which is much faster than copying characters one by one.

If the encodings are the same, the operation is a memory-level copy. But what if the string objects have different encodings? Next, you'll see a series of else if conditions:

```
// file: Objects/unicodeobject.c

if (from_kind == to_kind) {
    // Fast copy
}
else if (from_kind == PyUnicode_1BYTE_KIND
        && to_kind == PyUnicode_2BYTE_KIND)
{
    // ... omitted ...
}
else if (from_kind == PyUnicode_1BYTE_KIND
        && to_kind == PyUnicode_4BYTE_KIND)
```

```
{
    // ... omitted ...
}
else if (from_kind == PyUnicode_2BYTE_KIND
        && to_kind == PyUnicode_4BYTE_KIND)
{
    // ... omitted ...
}
else
{
    // ... omitted ...
}
```

This section does the heavy lifting. Whenever the encodings differ, the string is first converted to the matching encoding before being copied character by character. Naturally, this isn't as fast as `memcpy()`. In summary, if two string objects have the same encoding, concatenation operates very quickly.

String Slicing

In Python, you can extract a portion of a string using the slice operation. For example:

```
text = "Hello, World!"
print(text[0:5])   # Output: "Hello"
```

How does this work? Previously, we introduced that at the top level, the `PyType_Type` structure contains three members with names starting with `tp_as_`. When using square brackets (`[]`) for operations, Python first tries to access the `mp_subscript` member inside `tp_as_mapping`.

```
// file: Objects/unicodeobject.c
```

```
static PyObject*
unicode_subscript(PyObject* self, PyObject* item)
{
    if (_PyIndex_Check(item)) {
        Py_ssize_t i = PyNumber_AsSsize_t(item, PyExc_IndexError);
        // ... omitted ...
        return unicode_getitem(self, i);
```

```
    } else if (PySlice_Check(item)) {
        Py_ssize_t start, stop, step, slicelength, i;
        // ... omitted ...
    }
}
```

From here, you can see that if the incoming item is a number, the function calls unicode_getitem() to handle single-character access. If the incoming item is a slice object, it proceeds with the slice operation.

What is a slice object? It's actually a type called PySlice_Type:

// file: Objects/sliceobject.c

```
PyTypeObject PySlice_Type = {
    PyVarObject_HEAD_INIT(&PyType_Type, 0)
    "slice",                    /* Name of this type */
    sizeof(PySliceObject),      /* Basic object size */
    0,                          /* Item size for varobject */
    // ... omitted ...
    (destructor)slice_dealloc,  /* tp_dealloc */
    0,                          /* tp_iternext */
    slice_methods,              /* tp_methods */
    slice_members,              /* tp_members */
    0,                          /* tp_init */
    0,                          /* tp_alloc */
    slice_new,                  /* tp_new */
};
```

Compared to numbers or strings, the slice type is relatively simple. Slice objects in Python are used like this:

```
reverse = slice(None, None, -1)
all = slice(None, None, None)
last_five = slice(-5, None)

message = "hellokitty"
print(message[reverse])     # Output: yttikolleh
print(message[all])         # Output: hellokitty
print(message[last_five])   # Output: kitty
```

CHAPTER 11　INSIDE THE STRING OBJECT: PART 2

Returning to the unicode_subscript() function, let's look further:

```
// file: Objects/sliceobject.c
slicelength = PySlice_AdjustIndices(PyUnicode_GET_LENGTH(self),
                                    &start, &stop, step);
if (slicelength <= 0) {
    _Py_RETURN_UNICODE_EMPTY();
} else if (start == 0 && step == 1 &&
           slicelength == PyUnicode_GET_LENGTH(self)) {
    return unicode_result_unchanged(self);
} else if (step == 1) {
    return PyUnicode_Substring(self, start, start + slicelength);
}
```

The PySlice_AdjustIndices() function calculates the length of the slice. If the length is less than or equal to 0, it returns an empty string. If the slice spans the entire original string, it returns the original string directly. The slicing syntax in Python is similar to indexing. Both use square brackets, but the slice syntax has up to three fields separated by colons (:): "start position", "stop position", and "step". Each field is optional.

In fact, calculating the slice length can get a bit complicated, which is why the PySlice_AdjustIndices() function contains this comment:

```
// file: Objects/sliceobject.c
Py_ssize_t
PySlice_AdjustIndices(Py_ssize_t length,
                      Py_ssize_t *start, Py_ssize_t *stop, Py_ssize_t step)
{
    /* this is harder to get right than you might think */

    assert(step != 0);
    assert(step >= -PY_SSIZE_T_MAX);
    // ... omitted ...
}
```

Comments nowadays certainly speak their mind!

Performance

String Interning

String interning is one of Python's memory management techniques for strings. By storing strings that meet certain criteria in the "string pool," Python ensures that strings with identical contents share the same memory. This not only saves memory space but also improves performance.

As seen in the state structure of PyASCIIObject, there is an interned property that marks whether the string has been interned:

```
// file: Include/cpython/unicodeobject.h
typedef struct {
    PyObject_HEAD
    Py_ssize_t length;          /* Number of code points in the string */
    Py_hash_t hash;             /* Hash value; -1 if not set */
    struct {
        unsigned int interned:2;
        unsigned int kind:3;
        unsigned int compact:1;
        unsigned int ascii:1;
        unsigned int statically_allocated:1;
        unsigned int :24;
    } state;
} PyASCIIObject;
```

The interned field can have several states:

```
// file: Include/cpython/unicodeobject.h

#define SSTATE_NOT_INTERNED 0
#define SSTATE_INTERNED_MORTAL 1
#define SSTATE_INTERNED_IMMORTAL 2
#define SSTATE_INTERNED_IMMORTAL_STATIC 3
```

Descriptions:

- SSTATE_NOT_INTERNED: The string hasn't been interned yet. This is the default state for most dynamically created strings.

- SSTATE_INTERNED_MORTAL: The string has been interned, but will be garbage collected if no objects reference it (i.e., reference count drops to 0). For example, strings manually interned in Python code with sys.intern() fall into this category.

- SSTATE_INTERNED_IMMORTAL: The string has been interned and will not be collected by the garbage collector; as long as Python is running, it stays alive. Python keywords such as "def", "class", and "if" are examples.

- SSTATE_INTERNED_IMMORTAL_STATIC: The string is interned and also statically allocated, meaning it's created at Python startup and never freed or created again. This is used for extremely common strings, such as the empty string "", or single ASCII characters like "a" or "A".

```
# file: Tools/build/generate_global_objects.py
def main() -> None:
    identifiers, strings = get_identifiers_and_strings()

    generate_global_strings(identifiers, strings)
    generated_immortal_objects = generate_runtime_init(identifiers,
    strings)
    generate_static_strings_initializer(identifiers, strings)
    generate_global_object_finalizers(generated_immortal_objects)

if __name__ == '__main__':
    main()
```

From the function names in this Python script, you can infer that it generates global or identifier strings, including some of the "immortal" objects we mentioned earlier. Running this script writes to files such as Include/internal/pycore_unicodeobject_generated.h and Include/internal/pycore_runtime_init_generated.h, and these are compiled directly into the Python interpreter during the build process. If you're interested, you can take a look at these files:

// file: Include/internal/pycore_runtime_init_generated.h

```
#define _Py_small_ints_INIT { \
    _PyLong_DIGIT_INIT(-5), \
    _PyLong_DIGIT_INIT(-4), \
    _PyLong_DIGIT_INIT(-3), \
    // ... omitted ...
    _PyLong_DIGIT_INIT(255), \
    _PyLong_DIGIT_INIT(256), \
}

#define _Py_str_ascii_INIT { \
    _PyASCIIObject_INIT("\x00"), \
    _PyASCIIObject_INIT("\x01"), \
    // ... omitted ...
    _PyASCIIObject_INIT("\x04"), \
    _PyASCIIObject_INIT("\x7f"), \
}
```

You'll find that not only are ASCII characters compiled in, but even the "small integers" (from -5 to 256) we introduced earlier are included here.

CHAPTER 12

What Happens When Python Starts

Let's say you wrote a Python program like this:

```
# file: hello.py

def greeting(name):
    return f"Hello, {name}!"

print(greeting("Kitty"))
```

When you enter the command `python hello.py` in your terminal, you happily see "Hello Kitty" printed out. But do you know what the Python interpreter actually does behind the scenes? Or if you want to try tracing CPython's source code, where should you start? The built-in Python debugger `pdb` can set breakpoints or step through your Python code line by line. However, if you want to trace the interpreter itself, `pdb` won't help—you'll need a debugger designed for C programs.

Using a Debugger

The C language debuggers most commonly used in the industry are GDB and LLDB. Their functionality and commands are quite similar, but since my environment is macOS, LLDB is a bit more straightforward for me. I'll use it as an example here. Normally, to run your program, you'd execute:

```
$ ./python.exe hello.py
```

Here, python.exe is my self-compiled CPython interpreter. To have LLDB help me run this command, I simply prefix it with lldb:

```
$ lldb ./python.exe hello.py
(lldb) target create "./python.exe"
Current executable set to '/Users/kaochenlong/sources/python/cpython/python.exe' (arm64).
(lldb) settings set -- target.run-args  "hello.py"
(lldb) breakpoint set --name main
Breakpoint 1: 13 locations.
(lldb)
```

Here, the command breakpoint set --name main sets a breakpoint at the main function, which is the entry point of the entire program. This allows us to halt execution just as the program starts and step through its operation. If you think this command is a bit verbose, you can simply write b main for the same effect.

Once the breakpoint is set, you can begin execution.

Program Entry Point

```
(lldb) run
Process 77203 launched: '/Users/kaochenlong/sources/python/cpython/python.exe' (arm64)
Process 77203 stopped
* thread #1, queue = 'com.apple.main-thread', stop reason = breakpoint 1.1
    frame #0: 0x0000000100003d1c python.exe`main(argc=2, argv=0x000000016fdfe128) at python.c:15:12 [opt]
   12   int
   13   main(int argc, char **argv)
   14   {
-> 15       return Py_BytesMain(argc, argv);
   16   }
   17   #endif
Target 0: (python.exe) stopped.
warning: python.exe was compiled with optimization - stepping may behave oddly; variables may not be available.
(lldb)
```

CHAPTER 12   WHAT HAPPENS WHEN PYTHON STARTS

By entering run in LLDB, the program starts execution and halts at the main function. According to the output, we are currently at line 15 of python.c, preparing to execute the function Py_BytesMain().

Tracing into Py_BytesMain():

```
// file: Modules/main.c

int
Py_BytesMain(int argc, char **argv)
{
    _PyArgv args = {
        .argc = argc,
        .use_bytes_argv = 1,
        .bytes_argv = argv,
        .wchar_argv = NULL};
    return pymain_main(&args);
}
```

It appears that this function primarily performs argument conversion and then calls pymain_main():

```
// file: Modules/main.c

static int
pymain_main(_PyArgv *args)
{
    // ... omitted ...
    return Py_RunMain();
}
```

Tracing further to the Py_RunMain() function:

```
// file: Modules/main.c

int
Py_RunMain(void)
{
    int exitcode = 0;
```

113

CHAPTER 12   WHAT HAPPENS WHEN PYTHON STARTS

```
    pymain_run_python(&exitcode);

    // ... omitted ...
}
```

The pymain_run_python() function here is quite crucial:

```c
// file: Modules/main.c

static void
pymain_run_python(int *exitcode)
{
    // ... omitted ...

    if (config->run_command) {
        *exitcode = pymain_run_command(config->run_command);
    }
    else if (config->run_module) {
        *exitcode = pymain_run_module(config->run_module, 1);
    }
    else if (main_importer_path != NULL) {
        *exitcode = pymain_run_module(L"__main__", 0);
    }
    else if (config->run_filename != NULL) {
        *exitcode = pymain_run_file(config);
    }
    else {
        *exitcode = pymain_run_stdin(config);
    }

    // ... omitted ...
}
```

Because we are running python hello.py, execution will follow the config->run_filename branch and invoke the pymain_run_file() function:

```c
// file: Modules/main.c

static int
pymain_run_file(const PyConfig *config)
```

```
{
    // ... omitted ...
    int res = pymain_run_file_obj(program_name, filename,
                                  config->skip_source_first_line);
    // ... omitted ...
}
```

Reading the Program File

Up to this point, the program hasn't actually executed our code—it has only just read the file hello.py. The real action is about to start in the following pymain_run_file_obj() function.

```
// file: Modules/main.c
static int
pymain_run_file_obj(PyObject *program_name, PyObject *filename,
                    int skip_source_first_line)
{
    // ... omitted ...
    FILE *fp = _Py_fopen_obj(filename, "rb");

    // ... omitted ...

    PyCompilerFlags cf = _PyCompilerFlags_INIT;
    int run = _PyRun_AnyFileObject(fp, filename, 1, &cf);
    return (run != 0);
}
```

The key line of this function is the call to _PyRun_AnyFileObject():

```
// file: Python/pythonrun.c
int
_PyRun_AnyFileObject(FILE *fp, PyObject *filename, int closeit,
                     PyCompilerFlags *flags)
```

```
{
    // ... omitted ...
    int res;
    if (_Py_FdIsInteractive(fp, filename)) {
        res = _PyRun_InteractiveLoopObject(fp, filename, flags);
        if (closeit) {
            fclose(fp);
        }
    }
    else {
        res = _PyRun_SimpleFileObject(fp, filename, closeit, flags);
    }
    // ... omitted ...
}
```

Here, the _Py_FdIsInteractive() function checks whether Python should run in interactive mode. But why might a .py file run in interactive mode? For example, if your script uses the input() function, it's running in an interactive context. In our hello.py example, there's no interactive component, so execution proceeds to the _PyRun_SimpleFileObject() function:

// file: Python/pythonrun.c

```
int
_PyRun_SimpleFileObject(FILE *fp, PyObject *filename, int closeit,
                        PyCompilerFlags *flags)
{
    // ... omitted ...

    m = PyImport_AddModule("__main__");
    // ... omitted ...

    int pyc = maybe_pyc_file(fp, filename, closeit);
    // ... omitted ...

    if (pyc) {
        FILE *pyc_fp;
        // ... omitted ...
```

```
        pyc_fp = _Py_fopen_obj(filename, "rb");
        // ... omitted ...

        v = run_pyc_file(pyc_fp, d, d, flags);
    } else {
        // ... omitted ...

        v = pyrun_file(fp, filename, Py_file_input, d, d,
                    closeit, flags);
    }
    // ... omitted ...
}
```

Within this function, Python first creates a module named __main__, which is where your program will execute. Next, it checks whether a corresponding .pyc file (compiled bytecode) exists. If so, it reads the .pyc file as binary and calls run_pyc_file(); otherwise, it calls pyrun_file(). Since our hello.py doesn't have a .pyc file yet, it proceeds to pyrun_file().

Typically, running a project will generate a .pyc file so that the next execution can skip recompilation and go straight to running the bytecode. If you want to manually generate a .pyc file, you can use the py_compile module:

```
$ python -m py_compile hello.py
```

Building the Abstract Syntax Tree

Now, let's look at the pyrun_file() function:

```
// file: Python/pythonrun.c

static PyObject *
pyrun_file(FILE *fp, PyObject *filename, int start, PyObject *globals,
          PyObject *locals, int closeit, PyCompilerFlags *flags)
{
    PyArena *arena = _PyArena_New();
    // ... omitted ...

    mod_ty mod;
```

```
    mod = _PyParser_ASTFromFile(fp, filename, NULL, start, NULL, NULL,
                                flags, NULL, arena);
    // ... omitted ...
    PyObject *ret;
    if (mod != NULL) {
        ret = run_mod(mod, filename, globals, locals, flags, arena);
    }
    else {
        ret = NULL;
    }
    _PyArena_Free(arena);
    return ret;
}
```

Here, an "arena" object is created for memory management. When the program completes, releasing the entire arena simplifies memory cleanup (essentially running a loop and calling `PyMem_Free()` on each object).

Next, as the name suggests, the `_PyParser_ASTFromFile()` function reads the Python code and parses it into an Abstract Syntax Tree (AST). The details of AST conversion will be covered in a later chapter—at this stage, just know that this is where the source file is read and transformed into an AST.

Creating the Code Object

Once the transformation is complete, we proceed to the `run_mod()` function:

```
// file: Python/pythonrun.c

static PyObject *
run_mod(mod_ty mod, PyObject *filename, PyObject *globals, PyObject
*locals, PyCompilerFlags *flags, PyArena *arena)
{
    PyThreadState *tstate = _PyThreadState_GET();
    PyCodeObject *co = _PyAST_Compile(mod, filename, flags, -1, arena);
```

```
// ... omitted ...

PyObject *v = run_eval_code_obj(tstate, co, globals, locals);
Py_DECREF(co);
return v;
}
```

The main action here is `_PyAST_Compile()`, which compiles the AST into a Code Object. The concept and implementation of Code Objects will also be described in detail in a later chapter.

Ready for Liftoff!

The next step is to execute the compiled Code Object, which is handled by the `run_eval_code_obj()` function:

```
// file: Python/pythonrun.c

static PyObject *
run_eval_code_obj(PyThreadState *tstate, PyCodeObject *co, PyObject *globals, PyObject *locals)
{
    PyObject *v;
    _PyRuntime.signals.unhandled_keyboard_interrupt = 0;

    // ... omitted ...

    v = PyEval_EvalCode((PyObject*)co, globals, locals);
    if (!v && _PyErr_Occurred(tstate) == PyExc_KeyboardInterrupt) {
        _PyRuntime.signals.unhandled_keyboard_interrupt = 1;
    }
    return v;
}
```

Finally, the `PyEval_EvalCode()` function is where your `hello.py` code is actually executed. After this entire journey, we've arrived at the final step. This function runs your Code Object and returns the result. If all goes well, you'll see "Hello Kitty" printed on your screen.

Mission accomplished! This covers the steps taken by the Python interpreter to execute the `hello.py` script you wrote. There are many details, such as ASTs, Code Objects, the execution environment, and more. We will explore these aspects chapter by chapter in the following sections.

CHAPTER 13

From Source to Bytecode: How .py Becomes .pyc

Although Python is often classified as an interpreted language, Python code is actually compiled to bytecode before execution, as we've mentioned several times in previous chapters. The `.pyc` file is the file generated from this compilation process, and its main purpose is to boost program execution speed. In this chapter, we'll take a closer look at how these `.pyc` files are generated and what interesting things they contain.

Having a .pyc Is All You Need

To experiment, I prepared a rather (not really) impressive `hello` module:

```
# file: hello.py

def greeting(name):
    print(f"Hello, {name}!")
```

And a main script, `app.py`:

```
# file: app.py

from hello import greeting
greeting("Kitty")
```

These codes are trivial, serving purely for demonstration. After running the `python app.py` command, you should notice a new `__pycache__` directory in your folder, containing a file named `hello.cpython-312.pyc`:

```
├── __pycache__
│   └── hello.cpython-312.pyc
├── app.py
└── hello.py
```

The encoding of the filename `hello.cpython-312.pyc` is straightforward—it's based on the version of Python used for compilation.

This file is the bytecode file produced after Python compiles the code. Note that only a `.pyc` file for `hello.py` is generated at this point. If you also want to produce a `.pyc` file for `app.py`, you can use the built-in `py_compile` module:

```
$ python -m py_compile app.py
```

Or use the even more convenient `compileall` module:

```
$ python -m compileall .
```

This will compile all `.py` files in the directory to `.pyc` files at once.

Next, you can delete the `.py` source files, go into the `__pycache__` directory, and rename `app.cpython-312.pyc` and `hello.cpython-312.pyc` to `app.pyc` and `hello.pyc`, respectively. Then, by running `python app.pyc`, you'll find that your program still runs perfectly fine.

```
$ python app.pyc
Hello, Kitty!
```

There's nothing mysterious here. As mentioned in the previous chapter, during Python's process of reading program files, the `maybe_pyc_file()` function checks if the file is a `.pyc`; if so, the file is read in binary and executed accordingly.

Sometimes you may not want to distribute source code for various reasons, and providing only the `.pyc` files is enough for execution. Why someone would choose not to distribute source code is not my concern here; what I am curious about is why running `python app.py` does not produce a `.pyc` for the main script, while modules imported by the main script, such as `hello`, do.

This is related to Python's import mechanism.

"Maybe" a .pyc File?

We've covered Python's import mechanism in earlier chapters. The first part takes place in Python/import.c, and the latter is handled by Lib/importlib/_bootstrap.py.

However, as seen in the previous chapter, when executing the main script, if you trace from the initial Py_BytesMain() down to the final run_eval_code_obj() function, you'll notice that there's no process generating a .pyc file. Although Python first checks for an existing .pyc during execution (reading it in binary if it exists), otherwise running pyrun_file(), in most cases, scripts are run only once. So, while saving a .pyc for faster future runs is possible, it's generally unnecessary—hence Python doesn't bother generating a .pyc for the main script. On the other hand, modules imported into various scripts are likely to be reused across different programs, so compiling them to .pyc does make sense for performance.

But then, why is the function called maybe_pyc_file()—why the doubt? Isn't programming mostly black and white, 0 or 1? Let's see what's happening:

```
// file: Python/pythonrun.c

static int
maybe_pyc_file(FILE *fp, PyObject *filename, int closeit)
{
    PyObject *ext = PyUnicode_FromString(".pyc");
    if (ext == NULL) {
        return -1;
    }
    Py_ssize_t endswith = PyUnicode_Tailmatch(filename, ext, 0, PY_SSIZE_T_MAX, +1);
    Py_DECREF(ext);
    if (endswith) {
        return 1;
    }
    // ... snipped ...

    /* Read only two bytes of the magic. If the file was opened in
       text mode, the bytes 3 and 4 of the magic (\r\n) might not
       be read as they are on disk. */
```

```
    unsigned int halfmagic = PyImport_GetMagicNumber() & 0xFFFF;
    unsigned char buf[2];
    /* Mess:  In case of -x, the stream is NOT at its start now,
        and ungetc() was used to push back the first newline,
        which makes the current stream position formally undefined,
        and a x-platform nightmare.
        Unfortunately, we have no direct way to know whether -x
        was specified.  So we use a terrible hack:  if the current
        stream position is not 0, we assume -x was specified, and
        give up.  Bug 132850 on SourceForge spells out the
        hopelessness of trying anything else (fseek and ftell
        don't work predictably x-platform for text-mode files).
    */
    int ispyc = 0;
    if (ftell(fp) == 0) {
        if (fread(buf, 1, 2, fp) == 2 &&
            ((unsigned int)buf[1]<<8 | buf[0]) == halfmagic)
            ispyc = 1;
        rewind(fp);
    }
    return ispyc;
}
```

This function checks:

- Whether the filename ends with .pyc.

- If it doesn't, it checks whether the first two bytes of the file match Python's "magic number."

We'll discuss this magic number soon, but there's also a comment in the middle about a complicated condition stemming from platform-specific issues, as detailed in a SourceForge bug report. Due to difficulties predicting stream positions across platforms (especially when the -x option is involved), in certain cases, the function simply gives up—possibly explaining the cautious naming with maybe_.

Magic Number, Magic!

So, what is this "magic number"? Let's see how PyImport_GetMagicNumber() retrieves it:

// *file: Python/import.c*

```
long
PyImport_GetMagicNumber(void)
{
    long res;
    PyInterpreterState *interp = _PyInterpreterState_GET();
    PyObject *external, *pyc_magic;

    external = PyObject_GetAttrString(IMPORTLIB(interp), "_bootstrap_
    external");
    if (external == NULL)
        return -1;
    pyc_magic = PyObject_GetAttrString(external, "_RAW_MAGIC_NUMBER");
    Py_DECREF(external);
    if (pyc_magic == NULL)
        return -1;
    res = PyLong_AsLong(pyc_magic);
    Py_DECREF(pyc_magic);
    return res;
}
```

This fetches the _RAW_MAGIC_NUMBER attribute from the Python module importlib._bootstrap_external. Let's keep digging:

file: Lib/importlib/_bootstrap_external.py

```
MAGIC_NUMBER = (3531).to_bytes(2, 'little') + b'\r\n'
_RAW_MAGIC_NUMBER = int.from_bytes(MAGIC_NUMBER, 'little')  # For import.c
```

Here's some familiar Python code again. The .to_bytes() method with argument 'little' means little-endian order (as opposed to big-endian). For example, using the number 9527:

- 9527 in hexadecimal is 0x2537.
- In big-endian, the most significant byte (MSB) comes first: \x25\x37.
- In little-endian, the least significant byte (LSB) comes first: \x37\x25.

Back to the code: the number 3531 is converted into two bytes (little-endian), and then \r\n is appended, forming the "magic number." Scrolling up a bit in the source, you'll find the meaning of 3531:

```
# file: Lib/importlib/_bootstrap.py

# Known values:
#  Python 1.5:    20121
#  Python 1.5.1:  20121
#      Python 1.5.2: 20121
#      Python 1.6:   50428
#      Python 2.0:   50823
#      ... snipped ...
#      Python 2.7a0  62211 (introduce MAP_ADD and SET_ADD)
#      Python 3000:    3000
#                      3010 (removed UNARY_CONVERT)
#                      3020 (added BUILD_SET)
#      ... snipped ...
#      Python 3.12b1 3530 (Shrink the LOAD_SUPER_ATTR caches)
#      Python 3.12b1 3531 (Add PEP 695 changes)
#
#      Python 3.13 will start with 3550
```

This shows that each Python version has a corresponding magic number. We can check it in the REPL; different Python versions have different magic numbers:

```
# Python 3.11.9
>>> from importlib._bootstrap_external import MAGIC_NUMBER
>>> MAGIC_NUMBER
b'\xa7\r\r\n'
```

```
# Python 3.12.6
>>> from importlib._bootstrap_external import MAGIC_NUMBER
>>> MAGIC_NUMBER
b'\xcb\r\r\n'
```

Here, using Python 3.11 and 3.12, you can see the magic numbers are different. Recall that we used the py_compile module to generate a .pyc. Let's see how it works internally:

```
# file: Lib/py_compile.py

def compile(file, cfile=None, dfile=None, doraise=False, optimize=-1,
            invalidation_mode=None, quiet=0):
    # ... snipped ...

    if invalidation_mode == PycInvalidationMode.TIMESTAMP:
        source_stats = loader.path_stats(file)
        bytecode = importlib._bootstrap_external._code_to_timestamp_pyc(
            code, source_stats['mtime'], source_stats['size'])
    else:
        source_hash = importlib.util.source_hash(source_bytes)
        bytecode = importlib._bootstrap_external._code_to_hash_pyc(
            code,
            source_hash,
            (invalidation_mode == PycInvalidationMode.CHECKED_HASH),
        )
    # ... snipped ...
```

In the compile function, you'll see it decides whether to use _code_to_timestamp_pyc() or _code_to_hash_pyc() based on certain conditions. Let's check these two functions:

```
# file: Lib/importlib/_bootstrap_external.py

def _code_to_timestamp_pyc(code, mtime=0, source_size=0):
    data = bytearray(MAGIC_NUMBER)
    data.extend(_pack_uint32(0))
    data.extend(_pack_uint32(mtime))
    data.extend(_pack_uint32(source_size))
```

```
    data.extend(marshal.dumps(code))
    return data

def _code_to_hash_pyc(code, source_hash, checked=True):
    data = bytearray(MAGIC_NUMBER)
    flags = 0b1 | checked << 1
    data.extend(_pack_uint32(flags))
    assert len(source_hash) == 8
    data.extend(source_hash)
    data.extend(marshal.dumps(code))
    return data
```

Although the contents packed in the middle differ, both start with the magic number, which is stored at the very beginning of the ByteArray during compilation. In other words, bytecode compiled by different Python versions will be different.

I did a simple experiment: compile app.pyc with Python 3.11 and hello.pyc with Python 3.12, then run:

```
$ python app.pyc
RuntimeError: Bad magic number in .pyc file
```

This demonstrates that bytecode compiled by different Python versions is incompatible.

As for the compileall module, looking into its source, you'll see it's just a loop that calls py_compile.compile() for each file. Now that we get the mechanism, we can also directly call py_compile.compile() to generate a .pyc:

```
$ python
>>> from py_compile import compile
>>> compile("hello.py")
'__pycache__/hello.cpython-312.pyc'
```

It works!

By now, you might believe that Python translates source to AST, then to bytecode, and possibly saves it as a .pyc file; thus, a .pyc is just bytecode. That's correct in general, but let's open a .pyc and see what's really inside.

Unpacking a .pyc File

Earlier, we saw that during creation, bytecode is serialized with `marshal.dumps()`, so theoretically we can use `marshal.loads()` to recover it. Let's write a small program:

```
with open("hello.pyc", "rb") as f:
    print(f.read())
```

Assuming you have a `hello.pyc` file, this just loads it in binary. The result will look like:

`b'\xcb\r\r\n\x00\x00\x00\x00S\xac\xf6f1\x00\...`

Notice the first few familiar bytes? Yes—the magic number. The real contents are after these bytes, so let's skip the first four bytes and use `marshal.loads()` to see what's inside:

```
import marshal

with open("hello.pyc", "rb") as f:
    f.read(16)
    content = marshal.load(f)
    print(type(content))
```

You'll see that this is a Code Object. We'll explore Code Objects in more detail in later chapters, but for now, note that the `.co_code` attribute shows the bytecode contained inside. Printing it gives:

`b'\x97\x00d\x00\x84\x00Z\x00y\x01'`

Is this ByteArray code? Not exactly. Let's convert it to a list for clarity:

```
>>> list(b'\x97\x00d\x00\x84\x00Z\x00y\x01')
[151, 0, 100, 0, 132, 0, 90, 0, 121, 1]
```

What do these numbers mean? Remember how we sometimes use the `dis` module to decompile code into bytecode? Look at the opcode definitions:

`// file: Include/opcode.h`

```
#define CACHE                        0
#define POP_TOP                      1
```

CHAPTER 13 FROM SOURCE TO BYTECODE: HOW .PY BECOMES .PYC

```
#define PUSH_NULL                        2
#define INTERPRETER_EXIT                 3
// ... snipped ...
#define SWAP                            99
#define LOAD_CONST                     100
#define LOAD_NAME                      101
// ... snipped ...
#define YIELD_VALUE                    150
#define RESUME                         151
#define MATCH_CLASS                    152
#define FORMAT_VALUE                   155
// ... snipped ...
```

Each instruction corresponds to a number; these are defined in opcode.h. Opcode stands for Operation Code, and Python's Virtual Machine reads and executes these. Let's try using the dis module to map the list of numbers to opcode names:

```
>>> ops = [151, 0, 100, 0, 132, 0, 90, 0, 121, 1]
>>> for op in ops:
...     print(dis.opname[op])
...
RESUME
CACHE
LOAD_CONST
CACHE
MAKE_FUNCTION
CACHE
STORE_NAME
CACHE
RETURN_CONST
POP_TOP
```

Now, let's disassemble hello.py using dis:

```
$ python -m dis hello.py
  0           0 RESUME                   0
  1           2 LOAD_CONST               0 (<code object greeting>)
```

130

```
              4 MAKE_FUNCTION           0
              6 STORE_NAME              0 (greeting)
              8 RETURN_CONST            1 (None)
```
`... snipped ...`

The opcode value for CACHE is 0. If you remove CACHE, the instructions look like this:

```
RESUME
LOAD_CONST
MAKE_FUNCTION
STORE_NAME
RETURN_CONST
POP_TOP
```

This matches what the `dis` module shows.

So, to be more precise, the bytecode stored in a `.pyc` file is actually a ByteArray composed of a sequence of opcodes, and Python's VM executes them one by one.

CHAPTER 14

The List Object and Its Internal Management

Some programming languages, such as C, require arrays to store only one type of data and to have their size defined in advance. The advantage of this approach is high performance and efficient memory usage, but it can feel restrictive if you are used to dynamically adding or removing elements in your code. In contrast, Python's list has none of these constraints: you can store elements of different types, insert and remove items at any time, and don't need to worry about whether they are numbers, strings, or any other kind—just put them in the list. This design is extremely convenient.

But how does CPython implement this kind of data structure? How does it dynamically increase its capacity? In this chapter, we will see how lists work under the hood.

Internal Structure of Lists

In previous chapters, we briefly looked at the structure of list objects, which looks roughly like this:

```
// file: Include/cpython/listobject.h
```

```
typedef struct {
    PyObject_VAR_HEAD
    PyObject **ob_item;
    Py_ssize_t allocated;
} PyListObject;
```

For integers, floats, and strings introduced previously, the structure begins with PyObject_HEAD, whereas lists use PyObject_VAR_HEAD. What's the difference between these two?

```
// file: Include/object.h
#define PyObject_HEAD          PyObject ob_base;
#define PyObject_VAR_HEAD      PyVarObject ob_base;
```

Both macros define an ob_base member, but PyObject_HEAD sets its type as PyObject, while PyObject_VAR_HEAD uses PyVarObject. We've already seen PyObject; here's the definition of PyVarObject:

```
// file: Include/object.h
typedef struct {
    PyObject ob_base;
    Py_ssize_t ob_size; /* Number of items in variable part */
} PyVarObject;
```

Aside from the basic structure of PyObject, PyVarObject adds an ob_size field, which records the number of elements in the list. When you execute len(["a", "b", "c"]) and get 3, that's because Python reads the value of this ob_size member. Back in the PyListObject structure, ob_item is a pointer to an array of PyObject*, storing pointers to all elements in the list.

The allocated member records the amount of memory currently allocated for the ob_item array. It is usually greater than or equal to ob_size (the actual number of elements), and we will soon see how this number changes.

Creating and Initializing a List

When you create a new list in Python, CPython looks for the tp_new member in PyList_Type, which points to the PyType_GenericNew() function:

```
// file: Objects/typeobject.c
PyObject *
PyType_GenericNew(PyTypeObject *type, PyObject *args, PyObject *kwds)
```

```
{
    return type->tp_alloc(type, 0);
}
```

This function merely calls the function pointed to by the tp_alloc member. For lists, tp_alloc points to the PyType_GenericAlloc() function:

```
// file: Objects/typeobject.c

PyObject *
PyType_GenericAlloc(PyTypeObject *type, Py_ssize_t nitems)
{
    PyObject *obj = _PyType_AllocNoTrack(type, nitems);
    if (obj == NULL) {
        return NULL;
    }

    if (_PyType_IS_GC(type)) {
        _PyObject_GC_TRACK(obj);
    }
    return obj;
}
```

The _PyType_AllocNoTrack() function requests sufficient memory from the system based on the type and the number of requested items (nitems). But how is the required memory calculated?

```
// file: Objects/object.c

PyObject *
_PyType_AllocNoTrack(PyTypeObject *type, Py_ssize_t nitems)
{
    PyObject *obj;
    const size_t size = _PyObject_VAR_SIZE(type, nitems+1);

    const size_t presize = _PyType_PreHeaderSize(type);
    char *alloc = PyObject_Malloc(size + presize);
    // ... omitted ...
```

CHAPTER 14   THE LIST OBJECT AND ITS INTERNAL MANAGEMENT

```
    if (type->tp_itemsize == 0) {
        _PyObject_Init(obj, type);
    }
    else {
        _PyObject_InitVar((PyVarObject *)obj, type, nitems);
    }
    return obj;
}
```

First, the macro _PyObject_VAR_SIZE() computes the size of memory to allocate. How is it calculated?

```
// file: Include/cpython/objimpl.h
```

```
static inline size_t _PyObject_VAR_SIZE(PyTypeObject *type, Py_ssize_t nitems) {
    size_t size = _Py_STATIC_CAST(size_t, type->tp_basicsize);
    size += _Py_STATIC_CAST(size_t, nitems) * _Py_STATIC_CAST(size_t, type->tp_itemsize);
    return _Py_SIZE_ROUND_UP(size, SIZEOF_VOID_P);
}
```

As the function name suggests, this calculation applies to any object with a variable size, not just lists. The calculation is straightforward: tp_basicsize is the base size of the type, tp_itemsize is the size of each individual element, and nitems is the number of elements required. The formula is simply:

size = tp_basicsize + (tp_itemsize x nitems)

At the end, _Py_SIZE_ROUND_UP() ensures memory alignment. The macro expands to:

```
// file: Include/pymacro.h
```

```
#define _Py_SIZE_ROUND_UP(n, a) (((size_t)(n) + \
        (size_t)((a) - 1)) & ~(size_t)((a) - 1))
```

While this formula appears complex, it simply rounds n up to the nearest multiple of a. In CPython, SIZEOF_VOID_P is defined as 8, so all allocations are to 8-byte boundaries. For example, if size is computed as 61, it is rounded up to 64; if it is 65, it becomes 72.

Why do this? Memory alignment ensures efficient and correct access of elements in memory.

Next, `_PyType_PreHeaderSize()` checks whether additional memory is needed (e.g., to store garbage collection metadata). If so, a fixed amount of extra memory is allocated, regardless of the number of elements. For reference, in Python, some objects (like small integers from -5 to 256, or the immortal references for `True`, `False`, and `None`) never release their memory back to the system.

Finally, `PyObject_Malloc()` requests the memory from the system based on the computation.

Once the memory has been allocated, either `_PyObject_Init()` or `_PyObject_InitVar()` is called depending on `tp_itemsize`. The main difference is that `_PyObject_InitVar()` additionally initializes the `ob_size` field.

For `PyList_Type`, `tp_itemsize` is 0, so `_PyObject_Init()` is called. But why is `tp_itemsize` zero? Wasn't the formula `tp_basicsize + (tp_itemsize x nitems)`? If `tp_itemsize` is 0, doesn't this mean the list doesn't need to store any elements? In reality, the elements are stored elsewhere; the memory in the list object stores only pointers to the elements, not the elements themselves. This design allows lists to store objects of varying types.

At this point, list initialization is complete, and elements can now be added to the list.

Memory Management

A core feature of Python lists is dynamic resizing. If memory were reallocated every time an element was added, performance would be poor. To avoid this, Python over-allocates: when it needs more memory, it requests extra space in anticipation of future growth, thus reducing frequent reallocations. Think of it as asking your parents for extra allowance in advance so you don't need to ask too often. This strategy is called "over-allocation".

The logic for this operation is defined in the `list_resize()` function:

```
// file: Objects/listobject.c

static int
list_resize(PyListObject *self, Py_ssize_t newsize)
```

```
{
    PyObject **items;
    size_t new_allocated, num_allocated_bytes;
    Py_ssize_t allocated = self->allocated;

    if (allocated >= newsize && newsize >= (allocated >> 1)) {
        assert(self->ob_item != NULL || newsize == 0);
        Py_SET_SIZE(self, newsize);
        return 0;
    }
    // ... omitted ...
    new_allocated = ((size_t)newsize + (newsize >> 3) + 6) & ~(size_t)3;
    if (newsize - Py_SIZE(self) > (Py_ssize_t)(new_allocated - newsize))
        new_allocated = ((size_t)newsize + 3) & ~(size_t)3;

    // ... omitted ...
    self->ob_item = items;
    Py_SET_SIZE(self, newsize);
    self->allocated = new_allocated;
    return 0;
}
```

When Is More Memory Needed?

First, the function checks whether resizing is really necessary. If the current allocation suffices, it merely updates the ob_size value. What does "enough" mean?

1. The currently allocated space (allocated) is greater than or equal to the new required size (newsize).

2. The new required size is greater than or equal to half the current allocation (allocated >> 1, which is allocated / 2).

Both conditions must be true to avoid a reallocation. Some examples are as follows.

1. Adding Elements, But Within Current Capacity

If 8 slots are allocated and 5 are used, adding 2 more elements brings `newsize` to 7. Since 8 >= 7 and 7 >= 4, no reallocation is needed—just update `ob_size` to 7.

2. Adding Elements, Now Exceeding Capacity

If 10 slots are allocated and all are used, adding 1 more element sets `newsize` to 11. Since 10 >= 11 is false, reallocation is required.

3. Removing Some Elements, But Still Above Half the Capacity

If 16 slots are allocated and all used, deleting 5 elements brings `newsize` to 11. Because 16 >= 11 and 11 >= 8, no reallocation occurs—just update `ob_size` to 11.

4. Sharply Decreasing Size

If 100 slots were allocated and all used, deleting 80 elements leaves `newsize` at 20. While 100 >= 20 is true, 20 < 50 is false, so memory will be reallocated.

5. Clearing the List

If 10 slots are allocated and 5 are used, clearing the list sets `newsize` to 0. Though 10 >= 0 is true, 0 < 5 is not, prompting a reallocation.

By the way, Python provides several ways to clear a list:

```
numbers = [9, 5, 2, 7]

# Method 1
numbers.clear()

# Method 2
numbers = []
```

Calling the `.clear()` method directly invokes the C-implemented `list_resize()` and is very efficient. The second method creates a new empty list and points the variable to it; if the original list has no other references, it will eventually be garbage collected. This approach is a bit less efficient.

The Over-allocation Formula

The formula for over-allocation is written directly in `list_resize()`:

```
// file: Objects/listobject.c
static int
list_resize(PyListObject *self, Py_ssize_t newsize)
{
    // ... omitted ...

    new_allocated = ((size_t)newsize + (newsize >> 3) + 6) & ~(size_t)3;
    if (newsize - Py_SIZE(self) > (Py_ssize_t)(new_allocated - newsize))
        new_allocated = ((size_t)newsize + 3) & ~(size_t)3;

    // ... omitted ...
}
```

`new_allocated` is calculated differently under certain conditions, but let's look at the main line first. In addition to allocating space for `newsize`, Python adds a bit more: `newsize >> 3` (which is `newsize / 8`), plus 6. The purpose of adding 6 is to ensure enough spare capacity for small lists, avoiding frequent reallocations. The operation `& ~(size_t)3` aligns the size to a multiple of 4.

For example, if `newsize` is 1, the calculation is:

```
1 + (1 >> 3) + 6 = 1 + 0 + 6 = 7
```

After alignment, it becomes 8 (next multiple of 4).
If `newsize` is 5:

```
5 + (5 >> 3) + 6 = 5 + 0 + 6 = 11
```

After alignment, it becomes 12.

Due to this formula, the resulting allocation sizes are always multiples of 4: 0, 4, 8, 12, 16, 20, etc. If you remove the "+ 6", small lists would be reallocated for every new element, hurting performance. Adding a little extra might waste some memory, but it greatly improves performance.

What about the `if` statement that follows? This is to avoid severe over-allocation when the list suddenly grows by a large amount. For example, if the current size is 100 and you want to extend it to 1,000, `newsize` is 1,000. Without this check, reallocation would result in 1,000 + 125 + 6 = 1,131, rounded up to 1,132 for alignment. With this check, only 1,003 elements are allocated (1,000 + 3), rounded up to 1,004.

Common List Operations

Now, let's look at how some of the main list operations are implemented. The methods available on list objects are defined in the `tp_methods` member of `PyList_Type`. Here, we'll review the implementation of `append`, `insert`, and `remove`.

Appending Elements

At the C level, the list's `.append()` method corresponds to the `list_append` function:

```
// file: Objects/listobject.c

static PyObject *
list_append(PyListObject *self, PyObject *object)
{
    if (_PyList_AppendTakeRef(self, Py_NewRef(object)) < 0) {
        return NULL;
    }
    Py_RETURN_NONE;
}
```

The real logic is inside `_PyList_AppendTakeRef()`:

```
// file: Include/internal/pycore_list.h

static inline int
_PyList_AppendTakeRef(PyListObject *self, PyObject *newitem)
{
    assert(self != NULL && newitem != NULL);
    assert(PyList_Check(self));
    Py_ssize_t len = PyList_GET_SIZE(self);
    Py_ssize_t allocated = self->allocated;
```

```
    assert((size_t)len + 1 < PY_SSIZE_T_MAX);
    if (allocated > len) {
        PyList_SET_ITEM(self, len, newitem);
        Py_SET_SIZE(self, len + 1);
        return 0;
    }
    return _PyList_AppendTakeRefListResize(self, newitem);
}
```

Here, `allocated` is the current allocation, and `len` is obtained from `ob_size` (the number of elements). If there is enough space, the new element is appended directly and the list length is updated, which is very fast. If not, `_PyList_AppendTakeRefListResize()` is called, which reallocates memory by calling the `list_resize()` function described earlier.

Inserting Elements

The list's `.insert()` method corresponds to the `list_insert` function:

```
// file: Objects/listobject.c

static PyObject *
list_insert(PyListObject *self, PyObject *const *args, Py_ssize_t nargs)
{
    // ... omitted ...
    return_value = list_insert_impl(self, index, object);

    // ... omitted ...
}
```

The main logic resides in `list_insert_impl()`:

```
// file: Objects/listobject.c

static int
ins1(PyListObject *self, Py_ssize_t where, PyObject *v)
{
    // ... omitted ...
    if (list_resize(self, n+1) < 0)
        return -1;
```

```
    if (where < 0) {
        where += n;
        if (where < 0)
            where = 0;
    }
    if (where > n)
        where = n;
    items = self->ob_item;
    for (i = n; --i >= where; )
        items[i+1] = items[i];
    items[where] = Py_NewRef(v);
    return 0;
}
```

This function also calls `list_resize()` since inserting an element increases the list's size and could require memory reallocation. The actual insertion involves moving each element after the insertion point one slot to the right and placing the new element into the desired position—a straightforward approach.

Removing Elements

Finally, let's look at the `.remove()` method, which corresponds to the `list_remove` function:

```
// file: Objects/listobject.c
static PyObject *
list_remove(PyListObject *self, PyObject *value)
{
    Py_ssize_t i;

    for (i = 0; i < Py_SIZE(self); i++) {
        PyObject *obj = self->ob_item[i];
        Py_INCREF(obj);
        int cmp = PyObject_RichCompareBool(obj, value, Py_EQ);
        Py_DECREF(obj);
        if (cmp > 0) {
```

```
            if (list_ass_slice(self, i, i+1,
                               (PyObject *)NULL) == 0)
                Py_RETURN_NONE;
            return NULL;
        }
        else if (cmp < 0)
            return NULL;
    }
    PyErr_SetString(PyExc_ValueError, "list.remove(x): x not in list");
    return NULL;
}
```

This function runs a for loop that compares each element to the target value. If no element matches, it raises an error:

```
>>> numbers = [9, 5, 2, 7]
>>> numbers.remove(100)
Traceback (most recent call last):
  File "<stdin>", line 1, in <module>
ValueError: list.remove(x): x not in list
```

If a match is found, list_ass_slice() is called to remove the element at that position by slicing. Here, ass stands for "assign". In Python terms, the equivalent operation is self[i:i+1] = [], which deletes the element at index i.

CHAPTER 15

The Dictionary Object: Part 1

Just like lists, dictionaries (dict) are one of the most frequently used data types in Python. Dictionaries allow data access through key/value pairs, providing excellent performance. In this chapter, we'll explore how dictionaries are implemented in Python.

The Internal Structure of Dictionaries

By now, you might have guessed—without even looking at the source code—that the dictionary object in CPython is called `PyDictObject`. Let's take a look at its structure:

In CPython, the internal structure of a dictionary is defined in the file `Include/dictobject.h`. I've removed some conditional compilations for clarity; it looks like this:

```
// file: Include/cpython/dictobject.h
```

```c
typedef struct {
    PyObject_HEAD
    Py_ssize_t ma_used;
    uint64_t ma_version_tag;
    PyDictKeysObject *ma_keys;
    PyDictValues *ma_values;
} PyDictObject;
```

Leaving aside the uses of these fields for now, you'll notice that several members in this structure start with ma_. What does this mean? In Python's naming conventions, ma stands for Mapping—a general term in Python representing data structures accessible by key/value pairs, such as dictionaries and sets. We've actually seen similar conventions before:

- ob_: Used for members in PyObject, such as ob_refcnt, ob_size, etc.
- tp_: Used for members in PyTypeObject, such as tp_name, tp_init, etc.
- sq_: Used for sequence members, such as sq_length, sq_item, etc.
- nb_: Used for numeric type members, such as nb_add, nb_subtract, etc.
- co_: Used for code object members, such as co_argcount, co_consts, etc.

Back to the PyDictObject structure, here are a few important members:

- ma_used: The number of elements currently in the dictionary
- ma_keys: A PyDictKeysObject instance
- ma_values: A PyDictValues instance

Hmm…at a glance, it appears that the keys and values of a dictionary are stored as separate objects. This seems a bit odd—why not store them together in a single object? Let's dig deeper into what these two structures actually contain, starting with PyDictKeysObject:

// file: Include/internal/pycore_dict.h

```
struct _dictkeysobject {
    Py_ssize_t dk_refcnt;
    uint8_t dk_log2_size;
    uint8_t dk_log2_index_bytes;
    uint8_t dk_kind;
    uint32_t dk_version;
```

```
    Py_ssize_t dk_usable;
    Py_ssize_t dk_nentries;
    char dk_indices[];
};
```

This contains fields like the reference count and some members whose purposes aren't immediately apparent. Let's proceed to look at the `PyDictValues` structure:

// file: Include/internal/pycore_dict.h

```
struct _dictvalues {
    PyObject *values[1];
};
```

This is just a straightforward `values` member—very simple. But then, if the structure is so basic, why not put it directly inside the `PyDictKeysObject`? Let's look at how Python creates a new dictionary object.

Creating a Dictionary

Following the process we've learned before, we should look for the `tp_new` member of the `PyDict_Type` type:

// file: Objects/dictobject.c

```
static PyObject *
dict_new(PyTypeObject *type, PyObject *args, PyObject *kwds)
{
    // ... omitted ...
    PyObject *self = type->tp_alloc(type, 0);
    if (self == NULL) {
        return NULL;
    }
    // ... omitted ...
    return self;
}
```

CHAPTER 15   THE DICTIONARY OBJECT: PART 1

As expected, it first calls tp_alloc, which—for dictionaries—also points to the _PyType_AllocNoTrack() function. This is the same as what we saw for list objects in the previous chapter: although lists and dictionaries have different structures, their memory calculation and allocation strategies are the same. Let's look further down in dict_new:

```
// file: Objects/dictobject.c

static PyObject *
dict_new(PyTypeObject *type, PyObject *args, PyObject *kwds)
{
    // ... omitted ...
    PyDictObject *d = (PyDictObject *)self;

    d->ma_used = 0;
    d->ma_version_tag = DICT_NEXT_VERSION(
            _PyInterpreterState_GET());
    dictkeys_incref(Py_EMPTY_KEYS);
    d->ma_keys = Py_EMPTY_KEYS;
    d->ma_values = NULL;

    // ... omitted ...
}
```

This is about initialization: setting ma_used to 0 means the dictionary has no elements yet, and setting ma_values to NULL means there are no values yet. These are pretty clear. But what is ma_keys pointing to—what is Py_EMPTY_KEYS?

```
// file: Objects/dictobject.c

static PyDictKeysObject empty_keys_struct = {
        _Py_IMMORTAL_REFCNT, /* dk_refcnt */
        0, /* dk_log2_size */
        0, /* dk_log2_index_bytes */
        DICT_KEYS_UNICODE, /* dk_kind */
        1, /* dk_version */
        0, /* dk_usable (immutable) */
        0, /* dk_nentries */
        {DKIX_EMPTY, DKIX_EMPTY, DKIX_EMPTY, DKIX_EMPTY,
         DKIX_EMPTY, DKIX_EMPTY, DKIX_EMPTY, DKIX_EMPTY}, /* dk_indices */
};
```

Py_EMPTY_KEYS is actually a PyDictKeysObject instance, but with a twist: this empty dictionary is immutable and immortal (cannot be destroyed). This means all empty dictionaries can share this object, saving memory and avoiding repeated creation of empty key objects.

Additionally, the last part of this empty keys object contains eight DKIX_EMPTY values. DKIX_EMPTY is -1, indicating an empty slot. If you get this value during a lookup, it means the slot is empty and you can stop searching.

So, even an empty dictionary is allocated some space. This may seem wasteful, but from a performance standpoint, for dictionaries with fewer than eight key/value pairs, you can use this pre-allocated space and save on memory allocation time—a trade-off of space for speed.

Now I'm starting to understand why the keys and values in a dictionary are stored in separate objects.

Adding Elements

Now that we have a general idea of the dictionary's structure, let's look at the process of adding an element. Suppose we have an empty dictionary, and we add a key with the value "Kitty":

```
hero = {}
hero["name"] = "Kitty"
```

Accessing or assigning items using square brackets in a dictionary is (as we've seen so far) implemented via the tp_as_mapping member in PyDict_Type:

```
// file: Objects/dictobject.c

static PyMappingMethods dict_as_mapping = {
    (lenfunc)dict_length,          /*mp_length*/
    (binaryfunc)dict_subscript,    /*mp_subscript*/
    (objobjargproc)dict_ass_sub,   /*mp_ass_subscript*/
};
```

CHAPTER 15   THE DICTIONARY OBJECT: PART 1

So the operation hero["name"] = "Kitty" triggers the dict_ass_sub method:

// file: Objects/dictobject.c

```
static int
dict_ass_sub(PyDictObject *mp, PyObject *v, PyObject *w)
{
    if (w == NULL)
        return PyDict_DelItem((PyObject *)mp, v);
    else
        return PyDict_SetItem((PyObject *)mp, v, w);
}
```

This is straightforward. The next call is to PyDict_SetItem(), which, upon inspection, actually calls _PyDict_SetItem_Take2(). The _Take2 in the name likely means they couldn't think of a better name.

// file: Objects/dictobject.c

```
int
_PyDict_SetItem_Take2(PyDictObject *mp, PyObject *key, PyObject *value)
{
    // ... omitted ...
    Py_hash_t hash;
    if (!PyUnicode_CheckExact(key) || (hash = unicode_get_hash(key))
        == -1) {
        hash = PyObject_Hash(key);
        if (hash == -1) {
            Py_DECREF(key);
            Py_DECREF(value);
            return -1;
        }
    }
    // ... omitted ...
}
```

First, it checks if the key is a Unicode string—if yes, it uses unicode_get_hash() to compute the hash; otherwise, it uses PyObject_Hash(). Personally, I don't particularly like such "concise" code, but maybe that's just me. Let's see how unicode_get_hash() computes the hash:

// file: Objects/dictobject.c

```
static inline Py_hash_t
unicode_get_hash(PyObject *o)
{
    assert(PyUnicode_CheckExact(o));
    return _PyASCIIObject_CAST(o)->hash;
}
```

This function is declared as inline, meaning it will be inserted directly at the call site. The compiled file might be slightly larger, but this saves a function call and is faster—a typical space/speed trade-off. The function simply returns the hash member of the PyASCIIObject; this hash is calculated when the Unicode object is created. What about the PyObject_Hash() function?

// file: Objects/object.c

```
Py_hash_t
PyObject_Hash(PyObject *v)
{
    PyTypeObject *tp = Py_TYPE(v);
    if (tp->tp_hash != NULL)
        return (*tp->tp_hash)(v);

    // ... omitted ...
    return PyObject_HashNotImplemented(v);
}
```

Basically, it just returns the tp_hash member of the object's type. Now that we've seen how the hash is calculated, let's move on:

// file: Objects/dictobject.c

```
int
_PyDict_SetItem_Take2(PyDictObject *mp, PyObject *key, PyObject *value)
```

CHAPTER 15   THE DICTIONARY OBJECT: PART 1

```
{
    // ... omitted ...
    PyInterpreterState *interp = _PyInterpreterState_GET();
    if (mp->ma_keys == Py_EMPTY_KEYS) {
        return insert_to_emptydict(interp, mp, key, hash, value);
    }

    return insertdict(interp, mp, key, hash, value);
}
```

If the dictionary is empty (i.e., ma_keys is Py_EMPTY_KEYS), it calls insert_to_emptydict(); otherwise, it uses insertdict(). These two functions are the core of this process. Let's look at insert_to_emptydict(), focusing on its first part:

```
// file: Objects/dictobject.c
static int
insert_to_emptydict(PyInterpreterState *interp, PyDictObject *mp,
                    PyObject *key, Py_hash_t hash, PyObject *value)
{
    // ... omitted ...
    PyDictKeysObject *newkeys = new_keys_object(
            interp, PyDict_LOG_MINSIZE, unicode);

    // ... omitted ...
    mp->ma_keys = newkeys;
    mp->ma_values = NULL;

    MAINTAIN_TRACKING(mp, key, value);

    size_t hashpos = (size_t)hash & (PyDict_MINSIZE-1);
    dictkeys_set_index(mp->ma_keys, hashpos, 0);
}
```

Here, it creates a new PyDictKeysObject using new_keys_object() and assigns this to the ma_keys member and sets ma_values to NULL.

CHAPTER 15   THE DICTIONARY OBJECT: PART 1

Remember how we just calculated a hash value for the key? Here, this hash value determines its "position." `PyDict_MINSIZE` has a value of 8, so `& (PyDict_MINSIZE-1)` is equivalent to `% 8`, but faster in binary operations. What position? It's which slot in the `dk_indices` array of the `newkeys` object (the `PyDictKeysObject` we just made).

If we're taking the remainder of division by 8, the possible results are 0 through 7—a total of eight slots. What if that's not enough? We'll see how to enlarge this later. But what if multiple keys hash to the same value? Of course, collisions are possible—this is known as a hash collision. Python uses a technique called "open addressing" to resolve this, which, simply put, means finding the next available empty spot. For example, if all eight slots are empty:

```
dk_indices:
   0    1    2    3    4    5    6    7
+----+----+----+----+----+----+----+----+
|    |    |    |    |    |    |    |    |
+----+----+----+----+----+----+----+----+
```

Suppose `hero["aa"] = "Hello"`; assume the hash for `"aa"` is 81761723, so `hashpos` is 81761723 % 8, or 3. The key is placed at index 3:

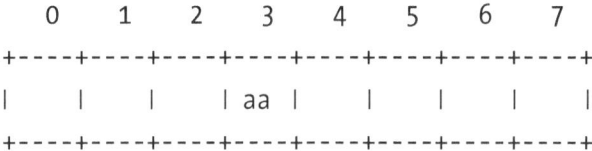

Similarly, for `hero["bb"] = "World"`, suppose the hash for `"bb"` is 28716210, which gives `hashpos` 2. So "bb" goes into index 2:

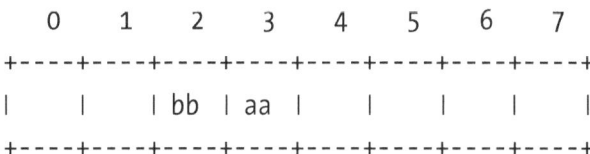

This works fine—but what if the computed index already has something there?

153

CHAPTER 15   THE DICTIONARY OBJECT: PART 1

Handling Hash Collisions

Let's add `hero["cc"] = "Kitty"`. Assume the hash for `"cc"` is 14500523, which gives a `hashpos` of 3, but position 3 is already occupied; this is a collision.

When a collision occurs, Python tries to find the next available spot. The simplest approach is `i + 1` (linear probing)—if that's taken, try `i + 2`, and so on. However, this "linear probing" can cause clustering, where later positions get filled up and searches slow down. Honestly, I wouldn't have thought of this if I hadn't looked at the source—there's a lot to consider for performance.

Python doesn't use linear probing (`i + 1`) but instead uses this formula:

```
i = ((5 * i) + 1) % 8
```

Not only that, but to increase randomness, Python also shifts the key's hash value to the right by five bits and uses this result as `p` in the formula:

```
i = ((5 * i) + p + 1) % 8
```

Here, `p` is `hash >> 5`, to make collision resolution more uniform. Of course, as `p` keeps shifting right, it eventually becomes 0, returning to the original formula. If you see the following in the source code:

```
perturb >>= PERTURB_SHIFT;
i = mask & (i*5 + perturb + 1);
```

That's what this is doing: `PERTURB_SHIFT` is 5 in CPython. Let's substitute the hash for `"cc"` (14500523):

```
i = ((5 * 3) + (14500523 >> 5) + 1) % 8
```

Calculate that, and you get 5, so `"cc"` is placed at index 5:

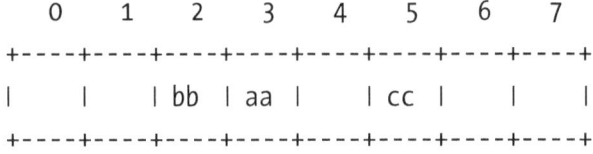

Using this method, as long as there's enough space, the average search time approaches O(1), since in most cases you'll find the right spot directly from `hashpos`. Once you know where a key goes, the next step is to insert the key and value:

154

CHAPTER 15   THE DICTIONARY OBJECT: PART 1

// file: Objects/dictobject.c

```
static int
insert_to_emptydict(PyInterpreterState *interp, PyDictObject *mp,
                    PyObject *key, Py_hash_t hash, PyObject *value)
{
    // ... omitted ...
    if (unicode) {
        PyDictUnicodeEntry *ep = DK_UNICODE_ENTRIES(mp->ma_keys);
        ep->me_key = key;
        ep->me_value = value;
    }
    else {
        PyDictKeyEntry *ep = DK_ENTRIES(mp->ma_keys);
        ep->me_key = key;
        ep->me_hash = hash;
        ep->me_value = value;
    }
    mp->ma_used++;
    mp->ma_version_tag = new_version;
    mp->ma_keys->dk_usable--;
    mp->ma_keys->dk_nentries++;
    return 0;
}
```

This chooses a structure based on whether the key is a Unicode string: either PyDictKeyEntry or PyDictUnicodeEntry:

// file: Include/internal/pycore_dict.h

```
typedef struct {
    Py_hash_t me_hash;
    PyObject *me_key;
    PyObject *me_value;
} PyDictKeyEntry;
```

```
typedef struct {
    PyObject *me_key;
    PyObject *me_value;
} PyDictUnicodeEntry;
```

These are just key/value combinations. At the end, it updates ma_used, ma_version_tag, dk_usable, and dk_nentries, thus completing the key/value addition.

But where are these entries stored? They are contiguous with the newkeys (the PyDictKeysObject we created). You can locate them using the DK_ENTRIES() or DK_UNICODE_ENTRIES() macros, which compute their location based on the memory position of ma_keys. How do we know this? In the last part of the new_keys_object() function, you'll see:

```
// file: Objects/dictobject.c
dk = PyObject_Malloc(sizeof(PyDictKeysObject)
                     + ((size_t)1 << log2_bytes)
                     + entry_size * usable);
```

Normally, you'd only allocate as much memory as needed, but here, it allocates extra space—entry_size * usable—to hold these entries.

How are the objects linked? Remember how we computed the remainder of 8 to get an index and placed the key in a designated slot?

```
dk_indices:
   0    1    2    3    4    5    6    7
+----+----+----+----+----+----+----+----+
|    |    | bb | aa |    | cc |    |    |
+----+----+----+----+----+----+----+----+
```

But it's not the key itself ("aa", "bb", "cc") that's stored in the slot. Instead, the slot stores the index of the entry corresponding to that key. What does that mean? Let me draw it out:

```
dk_indices:
  0   1   2   3   4   5   6   7
+---+---+---+---+---+---+---+---+
|   |   | 2 | 1 |   | 3 |   |   |
+---+---+---+---+---+---+---+---+
```

dk_entries:
```
+---+----------------------------+
| 0 | DKIX_DUMMY                 |
+---+----------------------------+
| 1 | {81761723, "aa", "Hello"}  |
+---+----------------------------+
| 2 | {28716210, "bb", "World"}  |
+---+----------------------------+
| 3 | {14500523, "cc", "Kitty"}  |
+---+----------------------------+
```

Entries are filled in order of addition. The `dk_indices` array stores only the index of each entry, allowing the lookup to quickly reach the entry.

Although a little complex, it matches up. Wait, earlier we mentioned that if collisions occur and the search moves to another spot, won't the indexes get mixed up? Good question—let's look at the lookup process.

Looking Up Elements

When you look up a key (e.g., `hero["aa"]`) in a Python dictionary, the process goes like this:

- A. The key `"aa"` is a string object; its hash is calculated—say, `81761723`.
- B. Compute the array index using the hash (modulo 8); the result is 3.
- C. Use index 3 to access `dk_indices`, which yields 1.
- D. Use index 1 to access `dk_entries`, finding the corresponding entry. You get the value `"Hello"`.

If the key is not present, you'll find a `DKIX_EMPTY` at step C, indicating the key doesn't exist, resulting in a `KeyError`.

But what if there was a collision, for example, with `hero["cc"]`?

- A. Calculate the hash for `"cc"`; it's `14500523`.
- B. Modulo 8, index is 3.
- C. Use index 3 in `dk_indices` to get value 1.

- D. Use index 1 in dk_entries to find the entry, but the hashes don't match—this is not the wanted entry.
- E. Go back to step C, but this time use the collision resolution formula (5 * 3 + perturb + 1) % 8, which gives 5.
- F. Use index 5 in dk_entries, and now you find the correct entry.
- G. If not found in F, keep cycling: recalculate the next index with the formula, check that slot, and so on.
- H. If no match is found, or a DKIX_EMPTY is encountered, the key doesn't exist—raise KeyError.

The lookup process may seem complex, but the computations are fast, enabling dictionaries to perform near O(1) lookup in most cases. Of course, if collisions increase, performance deteriorates—meaning dk_indices isn't big enough and needs to be resized. In the next chapter, we'll explore how much space is needed for dictionary resizing.

CHAPTER 16

The Dictionary Object: Part 2

In the previous chapter, we explored how to create dictionary objects. However, as a dictionary's `dk_indices` array becomes increasingly filled, the frequency of collisions rises, leading to a decline in performance. To address this, Python automatically expands the dictionary's capacity when it's nearly full. As end users, we typically do not need to worry about these details—but how is this accomplished?

If the available space is too small, the system will allocate more memory for the dictionary. However, if too much memory is allocated at once, the risk of collisions decreases, but this may also lead to wasted space. Therefore, the questions arise: "When" should more memory be requested, and "how much" should be allocated each time, in order to balance performance and memory usage? In this chapter, we will take a closer look at how Python manages these issues.

Dictionary Memory Management Techniques

Adding More Elements

Previously, we saw that for a brand-new dictionary object, adding the first element calls the `insert_to_emptydict()` function. However, if you wish to add an element to an existing dictionary (i.e., not empty), the `insertdict()` function is called when inserting the second and subsequent items. This function is longer and more complex, so let's go through it in sections:

```
// file: Objects/dictobject.c
```
```
static int
insertdict(PyInterpreterState *interp, PyDictObject *mp,
           PyObject *key, Py_hash_t hash, PyObject *value)
```

CHAPTER 16   THE DICTIONARY OBJECT: PART 2

```
{
    PyObject *old_value;

    if (DK_IS_UNICODE(mp->ma_keys) && !PyUnicode_CheckExact(key)) {
        if (insertion_resize(interp, mp, 0) < 0)
            goto Fail;
        assert(mp->ma_keys->dk_kind == DICT_KEYS_GENERAL);
    }
    // ... omitted ...
}
```

The macro DK_IS_UNICODE() checks if this dictionary's ma_keys member uses an optimized state specifically for Unicode strings. If so, but the new key to be added is not a Unicode string—for example, if you assign hero[42] = "Kitty"—Python will convert the dictionary from the optimized Unicode format to the general-purpose format in order to accommodate different types of keys. This conversion is essentially a capacity change, which is why insertion_resize() is called here. We'll discuss the specifics of resizing later, but here's a quick example:

```
import sys

fruits1 = {"apple": "Apple", "banana": "Banana"}
fruits2 = {"apple": "Apple", "banana": "Banana"}

print(sys.getsizeof(fruits1))
print(sys.getsizeof(fruits2))

fruits1["pineapple"] = "Pineapple"
fruits2[42] = "Pineapple"

print(sys.getsizeof(fruits1))
print(sys.getsizeof(fruits2))
```

In Python, not only strings can be used as dictionary keys—any hashable object is allowed. In this example, I use the string "pineapple" and the number 42 as keys. As a result, these otherwise identical dictionaries become different in size. When run on my computer, this code prints:

184
184
184
352

Why does `fruits2` become larger? Because a non-Unicode key (42) was added to `fruits2`, Python converts its `dk_kind` from the Unicode-specialized format `DICT_KEYS_UNICODE` to the general-purpose format `DICT_KEYS_GENERAL`. This format conversion increases memory usage. In summary, although any hashable object can be used as a key, using strings provides the best performance.

Returning to the `insertdict()` function, let's look further down:

```
// file: Objects/dictobject.c

static int
insertdict(PyInterpreterState *interp, PyDictObject *mp,
           PyObject *key, Py_hash_t hash, PyObject *value)
{
   // ... omitted ...
   Py_ssize_t ix = _Py_dict_lookup(mp, key, hash, &old_value);

   // ... omitted ...
   if (ix == DKIX_EMPTY) {
       assert(old_value == NULL);
       if (mp->ma_keys->dk_usable <= 0) {
           if (insertion_resize(interp, mp, 1) < 0)
               goto Fail;
       }
       // ... omitted ...
   }
}
```

We encounter `insertion_resize()` again. If `ix` is `DKIX_EMPTY`, it means that the key is new and needs to be added. At this point, the code checks if the dictionary has available space. This is the primary checkpoint for triggering capacity changes in this function. If there isn't enough room, `insertion_resize()` is called to expand capacity.

The check `dk_usable <= 0` appears straightforward, but it's not as simple as it looks.

CHAPTER 16   THE DICTIONARY OBJECT: PART 2

Should We Request More Capacity?

dk_usable is a member variable of the PyDictKeysObject structure. Judging from the name, you might guess it tracks the number of free slots available in the dictionary. However, that's not exactly the case. If it did, waiting until dk_usable <= 0 to increase capacity would be too conservative. Earlier, we mentioned that waiting until the dictionary is nearly full would increase collisions and hurt performance. So, clearly, dk_usable is not so literal.

Let's take another look at the PyDictKeysObject structure, as introduced previously:

```
// file: Include/internal/pycore_dict.h
struct _dictkeysobject {
    Py_ssize_t dk_refcnt;
    uint8_t dk_log2_size;
    uint8_t dk_log2_index_bytes;
    uint8_t dk_kind;
    uint32_t dk_version;
    Py_ssize_t dk_usable;
    Py_ssize_t dk_nentries;
    char dk_indices[];
};
```

Let's also borrow an example from earlier:

```
dk_indices:
   0   1   2   3   4   5   6   7
 +---+---+---+---+---+---+---+---+
 |   |   | 2 | 1 |   | 3 |   |   |
 +---+---+---+---+---+---+---+---+
```

Let me explain the PyDictKeysObject members for this case:

- dk_log2_size: The size of the dictionary is 2^3 = 8, meaning it can hold eight elements, so this field's value is 3 (i.e., log2(8)).

- dk_nentries: Also 3, indicating this dictionary currently stores three keys (entries).

The member dk_log2_index_bytes is a little special. Let me explain further. In the previous chapter, we covered the new_keys_object() function, which creates a new PyDictKeysObject. Part of that function is as follows:

```
// file: Objects/dictobject.c
static PyDictKeysObject*
new_keys_object(PyInterpreterState *interp, uint8_t log2_size, bool unicode)
{
    // ... omitted ...
    if (log2_size < 8) {
        log2_bytes = log2_size;
    }
    else if (log2_size < 16) {
        log2_bytes = log2_size + 1;
    }
    else {
        log2_bytes = log2_size + 2;
    }
    // ... omitted ...
}
```

Based on this, the value of dk_log2_index_bytes depends on the size of the dictionary.

- For small dictionaries (log2_size from 0 to 7, i.e., up to 128 elements), this value equals dk_log2_size.
- For medium dictionaries ($2^8 = 256$ to $2^{15} = 32,768$ elements), it's dk_log2_size + 1.
- For large dictionaries ($2^{16} = 65,536$ slots and above), it's dk_log2_size + 2.

Now let's introduce a term called "load factor," denoted here as α (alpha). Its calculation is:

α = used space / total available space

CHAPTER 16 THE DICTIONARY OBJECT: PART 2

In our earlier example, we are using three slots out of eight, so α is 3/8 = 0.375. Python dictionaries generally maintain a relatively low α to ensure high performance. As more elements are added, when α exceeds 2/3, adding a new element will trigger capacity expansion.

But what exactly is dk_usable? How does it relate to α? Let's have a look:

// file: Objects/dictobject.c

```
static PyDictKeysObject*
new_keys_object(PyInterpreterState *interp, uint8_t log2_size, bool unicode)
{
    PyDictKeysObject *dk;
    Py_ssize_t usable;
    // ... omitted ...

    usable = USABLE_FRACTION((size_t)1<<log2_size);
    // ... omitted ...
}
```

Let's expand the USABLE_FRACTION macro:

// file: Objects/dictobject.c

```
#define USABLE_FRACTION(n) (((n) << 1)/3)
```

<< 1 shifts bits to the left by one (i.e., multiplies by 2), and / 3 divides by 3. Thus, this macro calculates 2/3 of the total capacity. Applying this back to our example:

```
  0   1   2   3   4   5   6   7
+---+---+---+---+---+---+---+---+
|   |   | 2 | 1 |   | 3 |   |   |
+---+---+---+---+---+---+---+---+
```

The total space is eight slots, so dk_usable is USABLE_FRACTION(8), calculated as 8 x 2 / 3 = 5. That is, for a newly created dictionary, dk_usable equals 5. Each time a new key is added via insert_to_emptydict() or insertdict(), dk_usable decreases by 1. In our example with three keys, dk_usable is 5 - 3 = 2, indicating that there is room for two more elements before a resize is required.

Thus, dk_usable is essentially a counter that tells you how many more elements you can add without resizing. When dk_usable drops to 0 or below, the load factor has exceeded 2/3, and it's time to allocate more memory.

But why 2/3? Where does this value come from? It's not explicit in the code, but since Python's dictionary has a long history, it's likely that 2/3 was empirically determined by the core developers via experimentation and performance testing.

Now that we understand these relationships, let's look at how these values change as elements are added:

dk_size	dk_entries	dk_usable	α
8	3	2	0.375
8	4	1	0.5
8	5	0	0.625

Originally eight slots, now five are used, and dk_usable is 0; it's almost time to expand. If you add another element:

dk_size	dk_entries	dk_usable	α
8	3	2	0.375
8	4	1	0.5
8	5	0	0.625
16	6	4	0.375

The overall dictionary size increases to 16 slots. Why 16? We'll calculate that in a moment. Since one more element was added, dk_entries increases from 5 to 6. As dk_size has grown, dk_usable increases as well, and the load factor (α) drops. By expanding capacity, α is kept below 2/3, thus reducing collision risk.

CHAPTER 16   THE DICTIONARY OBJECT: PART 2

How Much Space to Allocate?

Now we know that when more than roughly 2/3 of the dictionary is filled, Python will request more memory when new elements are added. But by how much should it grow each time? If the allocation is too large, you end up wasting memory; if too small, frequent expansions hurt performance. Not only does expanding allocate new memory, but it must also rehash and relocate all elements, which is computationally expensive.

So what's Python's resizing strategy? The insertion_resize() function provides a clue:

// file: Objects/dictobject.c

```
static int
insertion_resize(PyInterpreterState *interp, PyDictObject *mp, int unicode)
{
    return dictresize(interp, mp, calculate_log2_keysize(GROWTH_RATE(mp)),
      unicode);
}
```

The macro GROWTH_RATE(mp) is self-descriptive—let's see how it's defined:

// file: Objects/dictobject.c

```
#define GROWTH_RATE(d) ((d)->ma_used*3)
```

This multiplies the number of used slots by 3. Let's use our earlier example:

dk_size	dk_entries	dk_usable	α
8	4	1	0.5
8	5	0	0.625

Assume five elements are currently used. Then, GROWTH_RATE() yields 5 x 3 = 15, meaning that on resizing, the requested capacity is 15. But since Python dictionary sizes must be powers of 2, this is rounded up to 16 slots.

Now with 16 slots, as you continue adding elements, when dk_entries reaches 10, dk_usable once again hits 0. On resizing, you'd request 10 x 3 = 30 slots, but this will be rounded up to 2^5 = 32 slots.

With this logic, each expansion increases capacity at roughly a twofold pace. If you reviewed the source code, you'd notice that the GROWTH_RATE has changed over Python versions:

- GROWTH_RATE was set to used*4 up to version 3.2.
- GROWTH_RATE was set to used*2 in version 3.3.0
- GROWTH_RATE was set to used*2 + capacity/2 in 3.4.0–3.6.0.

Initially, it was times 4, then 2, then 2 plus half the previous capacity, and currently it's times 3. These heuristics are undoubtedly informed by extensive experimentation and performance testing. This is where the value of mathematics and algorithms becomes crystal clear!

Returning Memory: Does It Happen?

Now we know that Python requests more memory as the dictionary capacity is exceeded. But what if elements are removed—Will Python hand back the spare memory? In real life, when fuel prices rise, commodity prices often go up too, but do they fall when fuel becomes cheaper? Well, you know the answer.

For example, if the dictionary expands from 8 to 16 slots and then you delete all elements, will it shrink back to 8? The answer is no. A Python dictionary will not release extra space just because the number of elements drops. If it did, this would require recalculating capacity with every deletion, which would impact performance. Here's a code sample to illustrate:

```python
from sys import getsizeof

heroes = {
    "Frieren": "Frieren",
    "Himmel": "Himmel",
    "Heiter": "Heiter",
    "Fern": "Fern",
    "Stark": "Stark",
}
```

```
print(getsizeof(heroes))

# Add one-this will trigger capacity expansion
heroes["Eisen"] = "Eisen"
print(getsizeof(heroes))

# Delete three
del heroes["Eisen"]
del heroes["Stark"]
del heroes["Fern"]
print(getsizeof(heroes))
```

After originally adding five elements, inserting one more causes the dictionary to expand from 8 to 16 slots. However, deleting three elements does not reduce the allocated memory. On my machine, it outputs:

```
184
272
272
```

If you really want to shrink a dictionary's capacity, there are a couple of ways. You can call the .clear() method, which will release the memory. For details, you can check the PyDict_Clear() function in Objects/dictobject.c, where you'll see that after clearing elements, memory is also freed.

Alternatively, you can reassign with heroes = {}—this makes the variable point to a brand-new empty dictionary, and the original will be garbage-collected in due course. However, use cases where you need to be so strict about space are rare, and with Python's heavy use of small dictionaries, writing code this way can become unnecessarily verbose.

CHAPTER 17

The Tuple Object and Its Immutability

In Python, a tuple is an immutable data structure designed to store multiple elements, which can be accessed using index values. Tuples are similar to lists, but with one key difference: once a tuple is created, its elements cannot be added, deleted, or modified. This chapter explores how tuples are implemented and highlights some of their interesting characteristics.

Tuple Design

// file: Include/cpython/tupleobject.h

```
typedef struct {
    PyObject_VAR_HEAD
    PyObject *ob_item[1];
} PyTupleObject;
```

If you've been following along, this structure should look familiar. The `PyTupleObject` structure starts with a `PyObject_VAR_HEAD`, much like lists, and includes an `ob_item` member used to store the tuple's elements. But why is this member defined as `ob_item[1]` instead of the `**ob_items` seen in `PyListObject`? What does this [1] signify?

This is a C programming technique known as a "Flexible Array Member." With this approach, the final member of the structure can be an array of unknown size. While it is written as if there were only one element, it can actually accommodate any number of elements in contiguous memory. This design allows tuples to occupy continuous blocks in memory, making element access more efficient. Visually, it looks something like this:

```
+-------------------+
| PyObject_VAR_HEAD |
+-------------------+
| ob_item[0]        |
+-------------------+
| ob_item[1]        |
+-------------------+
| ob_item[2]        |
+-------------------+
| ...               |
+-------------------+
| ob_item[size-1]   |
+-------------------+
```

Unlike lists, which use **ob_items, tuples do not require dynamic resizing, so this simpler design improves execution efficiency.

Creating a Tuple

To create a tuple, look for the tp_new member in PyTuple_Type, which points to the tuple_new() function:

```
// file: Objects/clinic/tupleobject.c.h

static PyObject *
tuple_new(PyTypeObject *type, PyObject *args, PyObject *kwargs)
{
    PyObject *return_value = NULL;
    PyTypeObject *base_tp = &PyTuple_Type;
    PyObject *iterable = NULL;
```

```
    // ... omitted ...
    if (PyTuple_GET_SIZE(args) < 1) {
        goto skip_optional;
    }
    iterable = PyTuple_GET_ITEM(args, 0);
skip_optional:
    return_value = tuple_new_impl(type, iterable);

exit:
    return return_value;
}
```

After skipping some parameter checks, the first highlight is the PyTuple_GET_ITEM() macro, which expands to:

```
// file: Include/cpython/tupleobject.h

#define PyTuple_GET_ITEM(op, index) (_PyTuple_CAST(op)->ob_item[(index)])
```

This macro is used to access elements within a tuple. It directly accesses the ob_item array and returns the element at the requested index. This macro is commonly used wherever tuple elements are accessed and forms a core part of tuple operations.

The next key function is tuple_new_impl(), which actually creates the tuple:

```
// file: Objects/tupleobject.c

static PyObject *
tuple_new_impl(PyTypeObject *type, PyObject *iterable)
{
    if (type != &PyTuple_Type)
        return tuple_subtype_new(type, iterable);

    if (iterable == NULL) {
        return tuple_get_empty();
    }
    else {
        return PySequence_Tuple(iterable);
    }
}
```

There are two main branches here. The first checks if the type is a subclass of tuple. In Python, you might see:

```python
class HelloTuple(tuple):
    pass
```

If this is the case, the function calls `tuple_subtype_new()`. This function ultimately still calls `tuple_new_impl()`, just with different parameters. This setup allows subclasses of tuple to modify or extend tuple creation behavior as needed.

If you're creating a standard tuple, the function checks whether to create an empty tuple or one with elements. Let's first look at how empty tuples are created in `tuple_get_empty()`.

Empty Tuples

```c
// file: Objects/tupleobject.c
static inline PyObject *
tuple_get_empty(void)
{
    return Py_NewRef(&_Py_SINGLETON(tuple_empty));
}
```

Here, the `_Py_SINGLETON()` macro defines a global singleton object that is never collected by the garbage collector. This ensures that every request for an empty tuple returns the same object, avoiding redundant creation. Therefore, comparing two empty tuples using the `is` keyword in Python yields True:

```python
>>> a = ()
>>> b = ()
>>> a is b
True
```

Both variables point to the same object, which is initialized when the Python interpreter starts.

Non-empty Tuples

Here, "non-empty" means creating a tuple with elements, such as passing data when calling the tuple() class:

```
>>> t1 = tuple([1, 2, 3])
>>> t1
(1, 2, 3)
>>> t2 = tuple("hello")
>>> t2
('h', 'e', 'l', 'l', 'o')
>>>
```

As long as an iterable is passed, Python will convert it into a tuple. Let's look at how PySequence_Tuple() achieves this. Since the function is lengthy, we'll review it in parts:

```
// file: Objects/abstract.c

PyObject *
PySequence_Tuple(PyObject *v)
{
    // ... omitted ...
    if (PyTuple_CheckExact(v)) {
        return Py_NewRef(v);
    }
    if (PyList_CheckExact(v))
        return PyList_AsTuple(v);

    // ... omitted ...
}
```

Two checks are performed here. If the incoming object is already a tuple, it simply returns a new reference to it rather than creating a new tuple. So:

```
>>> a = (1, 2, 3)
>>> b = tuple(a)
>>> a is b
True
```

CHAPTER 17 THE TUPLE OBJECT AND ITS IMMUTABILITY

If the object is a list, PyList_AsTuple() is called, converting the list to a tuple. The key implementation happens in _PyTuple_FromArray():

```
// file: Objects/tupleobject.c
PyObject *
_PyTuple_FromArray(PyObject *const *src, Py_ssize_t n)
{
    if (n == 0) {
        return tuple_get_empty();
    }

    PyTupleObject *tuple = tuple_alloc(n);
    if (tuple == NULL) {
        return NULL;
    }
    PyObject **dst = tuple->ob_item;
    for (Py_ssize_t i = 0; i < n; i++) {
        PyObject *item = src[i];
        dst[i] = Py_NewRef(item);
    }
    _PyObject_GC_TRACK(tuple);
    return (PyObject *)tuple;
}
```

Conversion here is simply a loop that copies references from the source to the ob_item array, thus creating the tuple.

Deallocation Mechanism

When a tuple is no longer needed—for example, when its reference count drops to zero—the system should reclaim its memory. This is managed by the function referenced by the tp_dealloc member of PyTuple_Type, namely, tupledealloc():

```
// file: Objects/tupleobject.c
static void
tupledealloc(PyTupleObject *op)
```

CHAPTER 17 THE TUPLE OBJECT AND ITS IMMUTABILITY

```
{
    if (Py_SIZE(op) == 0) {
        if (op == &_Py_SINGLETON(tuple_empty)) {
            return;
        }
    }

    PyObject_GC_UnTrack(op);
    Py_TRASHCAN_BEGIN(op, tupledealloc)

    Py_ssize_t i = Py_SIZE(op);
    while (--i >= 0) {
        Py_XDECREF(op->ob_item[i]);
    }
    if (!maybe_freelist_push(op)) {
        Py_TYPE(op)->tp_free((PyObject *)op);
    }

    Py_TRASHCAN_END
}
```

There are two notable points here. First, when the tuple to be deallocated is the singleton empty tuple, it skips memory reclamation, as this tuple is global and never destroyed. The second point is the call to the maybe_freelist_push() function:

// file: Objects/tupleobject.c

```
static inline int
maybe_freelist_push(PyTupleObject *op)
{
    PyInterpreterState *interp = _PyInterpreterState_GET();
    if (Py_SIZE(op) == 0) {
        return 0;
    }
    Py_ssize_t index = Py_SIZE(op) - 1;
    if (index < PyTuple_NFREELISTS
        && STATE.numfree[index] < PyTuple_MAXFREELIST
        && Py_IS_TYPE(op, &PyTuple_Type))
```

175

CHAPTER 17   THE TUPLE OBJECT AND ITS IMMUTABILITY

```
    {
        op->ob_item[0] = (PyObject *) STATE.free_list[index];
        STATE.free_list[index] = op;
        STATE.numfree[index]++;
        OBJECT_STAT_INC(to_freelist);
        return 1;
    }

    return 0;
}
```

Recall from the chapter on floats that Python uses a "Free List" mechanism for memory optimization. The `maybe_freelist_push()` function manages such reuse for tuples. If the tuple is empty, it is not managed by the free list.

If:

1. The number of elements in the tuple is less than `PyTuple_NFREELISTS` (usually set to 20),

2. The object is indeed a tuple,

3. The available space in the free list is not yet over `PyTuple_MAXFREELIST` (commonly 2,000),

then the tuple is added to the free list for possible reuse. In other words, for tuples with fewer than 20 elements, Python does not immediately free their memory; instead, it places them in a free list.

Here's some code to demonstrate this behavior:

```
>>> t1 = tuple(range(20))
>>> id(t1)
4339988768

>>> del t1
>>> t2 = tuple(range(20))
>>> id(t2)
4339988768

>>> t3 = tuple(range(21))
>>> id(t3)
4306827552
```

```
>>> del t3
>>> t4 = tuple(range(21))
>>> id(t4)
4306827552
```

As shown, when the tuple has 20 or fewer elements, deleting it and then creating another tuple with the same size and values gives the same `id`, indicating Python reused the same tuple from the free list. If the tuple has more than 20 elements, Python creates a new object instead.

Common Tuple Operations

Modifying Tuples

Tuples are immutable, meaning you cannot modify their elements. This is similar to strings. The reason is straightforward: the `tuple_as_mapping` member related to modification is set to `NULL` in `PyTuple_Type`:

// file: Objects/tupleobject.c

```
static PyMappingMethods tuple_as_mapping = {
    (lenfunc)tuplelength,
    (binaryfunc)tuplesubscript,
    0
};
```

Reading via `tuplesubscript()` is fine, but since the modification function is `NULL`, attempts at item assignment will result in an error:

```
>>> t = (9, 5, 2, 7)
>>> t[0] = "x"
Traceback (most recent call last):
  File "<stdin>", line 1, in <module>
TypeError: 'tuple' object does not support item assignment
```

CHAPTER 17   THE TUPLE OBJECT AND ITS IMMUTABILITY

Tuple Unpacking

In Python, you can "unpack" a tuple, assigning its elements to multiple variables at once:

```
t = (9, 5, 2, 7)
a, b, c, d = t
```

How does this work? Looking at the bytecode for this snippet, tuple unpacking corresponds to the UNPACK_SEQUENCE opcode. Here is the relevant code:

```
// file: Python/bytecodes.c
inst(UNPACK_SEQUENCE, (unused/1, seq -- unused[oparg])) {
    #if ENABLE_SPECIALIZATION
    _PyUnpackSequenceCache *cache = (_PyUnpackSequenceCache *)next_instr;
    if (ADAPTIVE_COUNTER_IS_ZERO(cache->counter)) {
        next_instr--;
        _Py_Specialize_UnpackSequence(seq, next_instr, oparg);
        DISPATCH_SAME_OPARG();
    }
    STAT_INC(UNPACK_SEQUENCE, deferred);
    DECREMENT_ADAPTIVE_COUNTER(cache->counter);
    #endif  /* ENABLE_SPECIALIZATION */
    PyObject **top = stack_pointer + oparg - 1;
    int res = unpack_iterable(tstate, seq, oparg, -1, top);
    DECREF_INPUTS();
    ERROR_IF(res == 0, error);
}
```

Both tuples and lists use UNPACK_SEQUENCE, but distinguishing between them is handled in _Py_Specialize_UnpackSequence():

```
// file: Python/specialize.c
void
_Py_Specialize_UnpackSequence(PyObject *seq, _Py_CODEUNIT *instr,
int oparg)
{
    // ... omitted ...
```

```
    _PyUnpackSequenceCache *cache = (_PyUnpackSequenceCache *)(instr + 1);
    if (PyTuple_CheckExact(seq)) {
        // ... omitted ...
        if (PyTuple_GET_SIZE(seq) == 2) {
            instr->op.code = UNPACK_SEQUENCE_TWO_TUPLE;
            goto success;
        }
        instr->op.code = UNPACK_SEQUENCE_TUPLE;
        goto success;
    }
    if (PyList_CheckExact(seq)) {
        // ... omitted ...
        instr->op.code = UNPACK_SEQUENCE_LIST;
        goto success;
    }
    // ... omitted ...
}
```

Here, you can see that different opcodes are chosen. Specifically, if the tuple has exactly two elements, the specialized UNPACK_SEQUENCE_TWO_TUPLE opcode is used; otherwise, UNPACK_SEQUENCE_TUPLE is used for other tuple lengths. This raises the question: Has Python optimized unpacking for two-element tuples? Let's compare the two opcodes:

// file: Python/bytecodes.c

```
inst(UNPACK_SEQUENCE_TUPLE, (unused/1, seq -- values[oparg])) {
    // ... omitted ...
    PyObject **items = _PyTuple_ITEMS(seq);
    for (int i = oparg; --i >= 0; ) {
        *values++ = Py_NewRef(items[i]);
    }
    DECREF_INPUTS();
}
```

For general tuple unpacking, the code loops (in reverse order) over the tuple's ob_item array, copying each element. The loop is reversed, matching the stack's "last in, first out" behavior; for example, for t = (9, 5, 2, 7):

CHAPTER 17   THE TUPLE OBJECT AND ITS IMMUTABILITY

```
+-----+-----+-----+-----+-----+
|  t  |  9  |  5  |  2  |  7  |
+-----+-----+-----+-----+-----+
^
|
PyTupleObject itself
```

The reversed loop ensures elements are placed correctly on the stack. For two-element tuples, the code becomes even simpler:

// file: Python/bytecodes.c

```c
inst(UNPACK_SEQUENCE_TWO_TUPLE, (unused/1, seq -- values[oparg])) {
    // ... omitted ...
    values[0] = Py_NewRef(PyTuple_GET_ITEM(seq, 1));
    values[1] = Py_NewRef(PyTuple_GET_ITEM(seq, 0));
    DECREF_INPUTS();
}
```

With just two elements, Python skips the loop and assigns both values directly, illustrating a targeted optimization.

A quick look at list unpacking:

// file: Python/bytecodes.c

```c
inst(UNPACK_SEQUENCE_LIST, (unused/1, seq -- values[oparg])) {
    // ... omitted ...
    PyObject **items = _PyList_ITEMS(seq);
    for (int i = oparg; --i >= 0; ) {
        *values++ = Py_NewRef(items[i]);
    }
    DECREF_INPUTS();
}
```

The process is nearly the same, except it uses the list's `ob_item` array instead of the tuple's.

If you need any further clarification or see sections that reference or depend on earlier context, please let me know so I can ensure the translation stays faithful to your intended meaning.

CHAPTER 18

Inside the Python VM: Code Objects

The Python Virtual Machine (PVM) is the core that runs behind Python code. It is responsible for interpreting and executing every line of code we write. Everything from converting bytecode to actual operations, creating and destroying objects, to memory management falls under its domain. In the following chapters, I will use simple programs to explore the operating principles of the Python Virtual Machine.

Previously, we introduced the process of starting the interpreter—from reading files into memory, converting to AST, then to bytecode, and finally handing over to the virtual machine for execution. So, let's begin with functions!

In Python, functions are defined using the def keyword. This chapter will focus on how functions are defined in CPython, what interesting things are hidden inside function objects, and what actually happens when a function is executed.

Functions Are Also Objects

In Python, functions are also objects. Since they are objects, we should be able to find their corresponding type structure:

```
PyTypeObject PyFunction_Type = {
    PyVarObject_HEAD_INIT(&PyType_Type, 0)
    "function",
    // ... omitted ...
    (reprfunc)func_repr,              /* tp_repr */
    0,                                /* tp_as_number */
    0,                                /* tp_as_sequence */
    0,                                /* tp_as_mapping */
```

```
    0,                                            /* tp_hash */
    PyVectorcall_Call,                            /* tp_call */
    0,                                            /* tp_str */
    // ... omitted ...
    0,                                            /* tp_dict */
    func_descr_get,                               /* tp_descr_get */
    0,                                            /* tp_descr_set */
    offsetof(PyFunctionObject, func_dict),        /* tp_dictoffset */
    0,                                            /* tp_init */
    0,                                            /* tp_alloc */
    func_new,                                     /* tp_new */
};
```

It can be seen that this type does not implement many functionalities. For instance, the three tp_as_ member variables are all zero, which means it cannot be operated as a number, sequence, or mapping type. This is reasonable—functions neither have nor need behaviors like strings, lists, dictionaries, or tuples. They are only responsible for their core job: accepting arguments, executing the function, and returning the appropriate value.

That said, the PyFunctionObject type structure contains quite a few members:

```
// file: Include/cpython/funcobject.h
typedef struct {
    PyObject_HEAD
    _Py_COMMON_FIELDS(func_)
    PyObject *func_doc;         /* The __doc__ attribute, can be
                                   anything */
    PyObject *func_dict;        /* The __dict__ attribute, a dict
                                   or NULL */
    PyObject *func_weakreflist; /* List of weak references */
    PyObject *func_module;      /* The __module__ attribute, can be
                                   anything */
    PyObject *func_annotations; /* Annotations, a dict or NULL */
    PyObject *func_typeparams;  /* Tuple of active type variables
                                   or NULL */
```

```
    vectorcallfunc vectorcall;
    uint32_t func_version;
} PyFunctionObject;
```

If you expand _Py_COMMON_FIELDS(func_), the complete PyFunctionObject looks like this:

```
// file: Include/cpython/funcobject.h
typedef struct {
    PyObject_HEAD

    // Py_COMMON_FIELDS
    PyObject *func_globals;
    PyObject *func_builtins;
    PyObject *func_name;
    PyObject *func_qualname;
    PyObject *func_code;        /* A code object, the __code__ attribute */
    PyObject *func_defaults;    /* NULL or a tuple */
    PyObject *func_kwdefaults;  /* NULL or a dict */
    PyObject *func_closure;     /* NULL or a tuple of cell objects */

    PyObject *func_doc;         /* The __doc__ attribute, can be
                                   anything */
    PyObject *func_dict;        /* The __dict__ attribute, a dict
                                   or NULL */
    PyObject *func_weakreflist; /* List of weak references */
    PyObject *func_module;      /* The __module__ attribute, can be
                                   anything */
    PyObject *func_annotations; /* Annotations, a dict or NULL */
    PyObject *func_typeparams;  /* Tuple of active type variables
                                   or NULL */
    vectorcallfunc vectorcall;
    uint32_t func_version;
} PyFunctionObject;
```

Some members are easy to guess just by their names. Notably, the `func_code` member is annotated as a code object; we've seen this several times already, and it is indeed the core of the function. In Python, you can think of a function as a named box: when you invoke the function using its name, essentially, you are handing over the code object inside the function object to the virtual machine for execution. The question is, how and when is this code object created? Let's try writing a simple function to find out.

Preparing to Create a Function

Let's start with a simple greeting function:

```python
def greeting(name):
    print(f"Hello, {name}")
```

The corresponding bytecode looks like this:

```
1             2 LOAD_CONST              0 (<code object>)
              4 MAKE_FUNCTION           0
              6 STORE_NAME              0 (greeting)
              8 RETURN_CONST            1 (None)
```

It seems that the `MAKE_FUNCTION` instruction is responsible for creating the function. The name of the instruction is pretty self-explanatory. However, right before `MAKE_FUNCTION`, there is a `LOAD_CONST` instruction that loads a code object. We've seen similar instructions before, indicating that this code object is created during the compilation phase—that is, in the process of converting the AST into bytecode. Only then can it be "loaded" here and passed into the function via the `MAKE_FUNCTION` instruction. In our earlier discussion of the process from AST to bytecode, we traced the `_PyAST_Compile()` function, whose return value is indeed a code object.

It looks like to understand functions, we first need to spend some time studying this code object. So, let's temporarily set functions aside and take a look at what a code object actually is.

Code Object

The name "code object" already tells us that it is an object. Following CPython's naming conventions, it's not hard to guess that this object is called PyCodeObject. Checking the source code, we find it is defined as a macro:

```
// file: Include/cpython/code.h

#define _PyCode_DEF(SIZE) {                                              \
    PyObject_VAR_HEAD                                                    \
                                                                         \
    // ... omitted ...                                                   \
    /* The hottest fields (in the eval loop) are grouped here at the top. */ \
    PyObject *co_consts;         /* list (constants used) */             \
    PyObject *co_names;          /* list of strings (names used) */      \
    PyObject *co_exceptiontable; /* Byte string encoding exception handling \
                                    table */                             \
    // ... omitted ...                                                   \
}
```

It doesn't really matter whether it is a structure or macro, but this structure is quite large. At the beginning of the Python/compile.c file, there is a comment that reads:

```
The primary entry point is _PyAST_Compile(), which returns a
PyCodeObject.  The compiler makes several passes to build the code
object:
   1. Checks for future statements.  See future.c
   2. Builds a symbol table.  See symtable.c.
   3. Generate an instruction sequence. See compiler_mod() in this file.
   4. Generate a control flow graph and run optimizations on it.  See
      flowgraph.c.
   5. Assemble the basic blocks into final code.  See optimize_and_
      assemble() in this file, and assembler.c.
```

First, it checks for "future statements," i.e., lines like from __future__ import .... The so-called "future module" mainly exists to allow Python 2 code to run on Python 3. This step ensures code compatibility. Next, it builds the symbol table, which records information about variables, functions, classes, etc., used in the program.

Then, the AST is converted to intermediate code, followed by control flow analysis and optimization, which gets a bit more complicated. However, the final assembly process happens in the optimize_and_assemble() function in Python/compile.c. The code object is probably put together at this stage, so let's start tracing from here:

```
// file: Python/compile.c

static PyCodeObject *
optimize_and_assemble(struct compiler *c, int addNone)
{
    struct compiler_unit *u = c->u;
    PyObject *const_cache = c->c_const_cache;
    PyObject *filename = c->c_filename;

    int code_flags = compute_code_flags(c);

    // ... omitted ...

    return optimize_and_assemble_code_unit(u, const_cache, code_flags,
    filename);
}
```

As expected, this function creates and returns a PyCodeObject. Let's continue following optimize_and_assemble_code_unit():

```
// file: Python/compile.c

static PyCodeObject *
optimize_and_assemble_code_unit(struct compiler_unit *u, PyObject
*const_cache,
                    int code_flags, PyObject *filename)
{
   // ... omitted ...
   co = _PyAssemble_MakeCodeObject(&u->u_metadata, const_cache, consts,
                                   maxdepth, &optimized_instrs,
                                   nlocalsplus,
                                   code_flags, filename);

   // ... omitted ...
}
```

CHAPTER 18   INSIDE THE PYTHON VM: CODE OBJECTS

This function is quite lengthy, but most of the initial part is preparatory work. Finally, the _PyAssemble_MakeCodeObject() function assembles the gathered information and creates the code object:

// file: Python/assemble.c

```
PyCodeObject *
_PyAssemble_MakeCodeObject(_PyCompile_CodeUnitMetadata *umd, PyObject *const_cache,
                           PyObject *consts, int maxdepth, instr_sequence
                           *instrs, int nlocalsplus, int code_flags,
                           PyObject *filename)
{
    PyCodeObject *co = NULL;

    struct assembler a;
    int res = assemble_emit(&a, instrs, umd->u_firstlineno, const_cache);
    if (res == SUCCESS) {
        co = makecode(umd, &a, const_cache, consts, maxdepth, nlocalsplus,
                      code_flags, filename);
    }
    assemble_free(&a);
    return co;
}
```

This is it! The makecode() function is where the code object is actually created:

// file: Python/assemble.c

```
static PyCodeObject *
makecode(_PyCompile_CodeUnitMetadata *umd, struct assembler *a, PyObject *const_cache,
         PyObject *constslist, int maxdepth, int nlocalsplus, int
         code_flags, PyObject *filename)
{
    PyCodeObject *co = NULL;
    PyObject *names = NULL;
    PyObject *consts = NULL;
```

CHAPTER 18   INSIDE THE PYTHON VM: CODE OBJECTS

```
    PyObject *localsplusnames = NULL;
    // ... omitted ...
    consts = PyList_AsTuple(constslist); /* PyCode_New requires a tuple */
    // ... omitted ...
    localsplusnames = PyTuple_New(nlocalsplus);

    struct _PyCodeConstructor con = {
        // ... omitted ...
        .consts = consts,
        .names = names,
        .localsplusnames = localsplusnames,
    };

    // ... omitted ...
    co = _PyCode_New(&con);

    // ... omitted ...
    return co;
}
```

There are a few key points in this function: constants and local variables used here are stored as tuples, and _PyCode_New() is called to create the code object:

```
// file: Objects/codeobject.c

PyCodeObject *
_PyCode_New(struct _PyCodeConstructor *con)
{
    // ... omitted ...
    Py_ssize_t size = PyBytes_GET_SIZE(con->code) / sizeof(_Py_CODEUNIT);
    PyCodeObject *co = PyObject_NewVar(PyCodeObject, &PyCode_Type, size);
    if (co == NULL) {
        Py_XDECREF(replacement_locations);
        PyErr_NoMemory();
        return NULL;
    }
```

```
    init_code(co, con);
    Py_XDECREF(replacement_locations);
    return co;
}
```

You can see that this function creates a PyCodeObject and initializes it with the previously collected information using the init_code() function:

// file: Objects/codeobject.c

```
static void
init_code(PyCodeObject *co, struct _PyCodeConstructor *con)
{
    // ... omitted ...
    co->co_filename = Py_NewRef(con->filename);
    co->co_name = Py_NewRef(con->name);
    co->co_qualname = Py_NewRef(con->qualname);
    co->co_flags = con->flags;

    // ... omitted ...
    co->co_consts = Py_NewRef(con->consts);
    co->co_names = Py_NewRef(con->names);

    // ... omitted ...
}
```

That completes the creation of the code object. Let's try inspecting it in the REPL:

```
$ python -i hi.py
>>> greeting.__code__
<code object greeting>
>>> greeting.__code__.co_name
'greeting'
>>> greeting.__code__.co_consts
(None, 'Hello, ')
```

CHAPTER 18   INSIDE THE PYTHON VM: CODE OBJECTS

In Python, you can use __code__ to access a function's code object. The values initialized earlier, such as co_name and co_consts, are all accessible through this code object. In this example, we can see that the function's name is greeting and the constants used in the function are None and 'Hello, '.

The constant 'Hello, ' is easy enough to understand, but can you guess where None is used inside the function?

CHAPTER 19

Inside the Python VM: Function Objects

In the previous chapter, we got a general overview of Code Objects wrapped inside functions. Code Objects are created during the compilation process—when a program runs, they are loaded via the `LOAD_CONST` instruction and wrapped into functions. However, unlike Code Objects, functions are not pre-built; they are created during runtime through the `MAKE_FUNCTION` instruction. In this chapter, let's take a closer look at how Python function objects work.

Creating Function Objects

A function object in Python is defined as follows:

// file: Include/cpython/funcobject.h

```
typedef struct {
    PyObject_HEAD

    // Py_COMMON_FIELDS
    PyObject *func_globals;
    PyObject *func_builtins;
    PyObject *func_name;
    PyObject *func_qualname;
    PyObject *func_code;        /* A code object, the __code__ attribute */
    PyObject *func_defaults;    /* NULL or a tuple */
    PyObject *func_kwdefaults;  /* NULL or a dict */
    PyObject *func_closure;     /* NULL or a tuple of cell objects */

    PyObject *func_doc;         /* The __doc__ attribute, can be
                                   anything */
```

```
    PyObject *func_dict;          /* The __dict__ attribute, a dict
                                     or NULL */
    PyObject *func_weakreflist;   /* List of weak references */
    PyObject *func_module;        /* The __module__ attribute, can be
                                     anything */
    PyObject *func_annotations;   /* Annotations, a dict or NULL */
    PyObject *func_typeparams;    /* Tuple of active type variables
                                     or NULL */
    vectorcallfunc vectorcall;
    uint32_t func_version;
} PyFunctionObject;
```

Among these, func_code is already familiar to us as the Code Object. To access it directly in Python, you can use the __code__ attribute. So, how are function objects actually created? As we saw in the previous chapter, function objects are produced by the MAKE_FUNCTION instruction. The function object contains the function's name, parameters, default values, and code. Let's see what happens under the hood with this instruction:

```
// file: Python/bytecodes.c

inst(MAKE_FUNCTION, (defaults     if (oparg & 0x01),
                     kwdefaults   if (oparg & 0x02),
                     annotations  if (oparg & 0x04),
                     closure      if (oparg & 0x08),
                     codeobj -- func)) {

    PyFunctionObject *func_obj = (PyFunctionObject *)
        PyFunction_New(codeobj, GLOBALS());

    // ... omitted ...
    if (oparg & 0x08) {
        assert(PyTuple_CheckExact(closure));
        func_obj->func_closure = closure;
    }
    // ... omitted ...
}
```

We can see that this instruction creates a `PyFunctionObject`, but what about the series of bitwise operations with `oparg` that follow? What exactly is `oparg`?

What Do the Parameters Look Like?

Actually, `oparg` is determined at compile time. Let's look again at the compiled bytecode instructions:

```
1           2 LOAD_CONST               0 (<code object>)
            4 MAKE_FUNCTION            0
            6 STORE_NAME               0 (greeting)
            8 RETURN_CONST             1 (None)
```

The 0 after the `MAKE_FUNCTION` instruction is the `oparg`. Its main purpose is to let the virtual machine know what attributes this function object possesses. `oparg` is an eight-bit integer, but only the lowest four bits are currently in use. Different functions may have different attributes. For example, in the original example with simple parameters, the `oparg` is 0. If we change the function to:

```python
def greeting(name="Kitty"):
    print(f"Hello, {name}")
```

This function has a default parameter, so its `oparg` is 1 (i.e., 0001). If the function is further modified to:

```python
def greeting(name: str):
    print(f"Hello, {name}")
```

Here, we've added a type annotation, so the `oparg` becomes 4 (i.e., 0100). If we combine both:

```python
def greeting(name: str = "Kitty"):
    print(f"Hello, {name}")
```

Now, `oparg` is 5 (i.e., 0101), which is the result of a bitwise operation between 0001 and 0100. Using `oparg`, the virtual machine can determine what kind of attributes this function object should have.

The series of bitwise operations in the latter half of the `MAKE_FUNCTION` instruction handles exactly this.

CHAPTER 19   INSIDE THE PYTHON VM: FUNCTION OBJECTS

Accessing Function Attributes

Why is it that accessing __name__ on a function returns its name, __code__ gives us the internal Code Object, and __annotations__ provides the type annotations? How are these attributes mapped to the underlying function object?

Recall in the previous chapter, we looked at the PyFunction_Type. Although it doesn't have members like tp_as_, to access properties via attributes, we need to look at the tp_getset member, which corresponds to func_getsetlist:

// file: Objects/funcobject.c

```
static PyGetSetDef func_getsetlist[] = {
    {"__code__", (getter)func_get_code, (setter)func_set_code},
    {"__defaults__", (getter)func_get_defaults,
     (setter)func_set_defaults},
    {"__kwdefaults__", (getter)func_get_kwdefaults,
     (setter)func_set_kwdefaults},
    {"__annotations__", (getter)func_get_annotations,
     (setter)func_set_annotations},
    {"__dict__", PyObject_GenericGetDict, PyObject_GenericSetDict},
    {"__name__", (getter)func_get_name, (setter)func_set_name},
    {"__qualname__", (getter)func_get_qualname, (setter)func_set_qualname},
    {"__type_params__", (getter)func_get_type_params,
     (setter)func_set_type_params},
    {NULL} /* Sentinel */
};
```

Here, the getter and setter functions are used to retrieve and set these attributes. Let's look up the func_get_code function corresponding to __code__:

// file: Objects/funcobject.c

```
static PyObject *
func_get_code(PyFunctionObject *op, void *Py_UNUSED(ignored))
{
    if (PySys_Audit("object.__getattr__", "Os", op, "__code__") < 0) {
        return NULL;
    }
```

```c
    return Py_NewRef(op->func_code);
}
```

It's straightforward: it simply returns the func_code member of the PyFunctionObject structure. Other attributes follow a similar pattern. For example, the __name__ attribute:

```c
// file: Objects/funcobject.c
static PyObject *
func_get_name(PyFunctionObject *op, void *Py_UNUSED(ignored))
{
    return Py_NewRef(op->func_name);
}
```

Given that there's a setter here as well, does this mean we can dynamically change the Code Object inside a function during runtime, thereby altering its behavior? Let's give it a try:

```python
def greeting(name):
    print(f"Hello, {name}")

greeting("Kitty")   # Hello, Kitty

secret_object = compile('print("Hey Hey!")', __name__, "exec")
greeting.__code__ = secret_object
greeting()
```

However, not just anything can be assigned to __code__. If you're interested, check out the func_set_code function, which contains some checks. Nevertheless, running the code above will indeed print Hey Hey!—so it is possible to do this, though it's hard to think of a practical use case where you'd actually need it.

Calling a Function

Previously, when examining the PyType_Type structure, we saw a tp_call member. Attempting to use parentheses () on an object triggers this member. Function objects also have this member. Let's take a look at the tp_call member of PyFunction_Type; it points to the `PyVectorcall_Call()` function. Even before looking at the source code, let's consider the name: "Vector" typically means an array or sequence, but what does this have to do with calling functions?

What Is "Vectorcall"?

In earlier versions of Python, calling a function required packing positional arguments into a tuple and keyword arguments into a dictionary. This process incurred overhead from extra memory and operations. Starting from Python 3.9, PEP 590 introduced a new calling mechanism called "Vectorcall," described as "a fast calling protocol for CPython." The Changelog of version 3.9 notes that this change improves performance for common built-in types such as lists, tuples, dictionaries, and sets. In current versions, most objects already support Vectorcall, though some third-party packages may still use the old `tp_call` approach.

- **PEP 590**: https://peps.python.org/pep-0590/
- **Changelog**: https://docs.python.org/3.9/whatsnew/changelog.html

From the official documentation:

> Changed in version 3.12:
>
> The `Py_TPFLAGS_HAVE_VECTORCALL` flag is now removed from a class when the class's **call**() method is reassigned. (This internally sets tp_call only and thus may make it behave differently than the vectorcall function.) In earlier Python versions, vectorcall should only be used with immutable or static types.

This means if you implement a `__call__` method in your own class, the `Py_TPFLAGS_HAVE_VECTORCALL` setting will be removed, causing the class to revert to the traditional `tp_call` approach rather than using Vectorcall.

So, what exactly makes Vectorcall faster? Let's take a look at the `PyVectorcall_Call()` function:

```
// file: Objects/call.c

PyObject *
PyVectorcall_Call(PyObject *callable, PyObject *tuple, PyObject *kwargs)
```

CHAPTER 19 INSIDE THE PYTHON VM: FUNCTION OBJECTS

```c
{
    PyThreadState *tstate = _PyThreadState_GET();

    Py_ssize_t offset = Py_TYPE(callable)->tp_vectorcall_offset;

    // ... omitted ...

    vectorcallfunc func;
    memcpy(&func, (char *) callable + offset, sizeof(func));
    if (func == NULL) {
        _PyErr_Format(tstate, PyExc_TypeError,
                      "'%.200s' object does not support vectorcall",
                      Py_TYPE(callable)->tp_name);
        return NULL;
    }

    return _PyVectorcall_Call(tstate, func, callable, tuple, kwargs);
}
```

We can see that the function to execute is located by calculating the tp_vectorcall_offset member variable. This method improves performance because it directly computes the location from PyObject_HEAD by adding the offset. Essentially, this is just pointer arithmetic, avoiding costly lookups via hash tables or other complex data structures, which is much faster. Then, memcpy() is used to copy the function pointer, and finally, it calls the internal API _PyVectorcall_Call():

```c
// file: Objects/call.c

static PyObject *
_PyVectorcall_Call(PyThreadState *tstate, vectorcallfunc func,
                   PyObject *callable, PyObject *tuple, PyObject *kwargs)
{
    assert(func != NULL);

    Py_ssize_t nargs = PyTuple_GET_SIZE(tuple);

    if (kwargs == NULL || PyDict_GET_SIZE(kwargs) == 0) {
        return func(callable, _PyTuple_ITEMS(tuple), nargs, NULL);
    }
```

```
    PyObject *const *args;
    PyObject *kwnames;

    // ... omitted ...
    PyObject *result = func(callable, args,
                            nargs | PY_VECTORCALL_ARGUMENTS_OFFSET,
                            kwnames);
    _PyStack_UnpackDict_Free(args, nargs, kwnames);

    return _Py_CheckFunctionResult(tstate, callable, result, NULL);
}
```

It first checks if there are keyword arguments. If not, it takes a "fast path" and calls func directly. If keyword arguments are present, it prepares them and then invokes func.

For most Python developers, these kinds of low-level optimizations are transparent. In other words, we can just trust that Python keeps improving performance behind the scenes. In most programming languages, when a function is called, it is pushed onto a stack known as the call stack. Python has a similar mechanism, which we will cover in more detail in the next chapter.

CHAPTER 20

Inside the Python VM: Frame Objects

In previous chapters, we briefly examined the structure of Code Objects and function objects. We learned that each function contains a Code Object, which serves as the smallest executable unit. Having traced from the lowest-level Code Object up to the function, we will now continue this journey upward to see what happens during the execution of a function.

In most programming languages, when a function is called, a new execution environment is created. This environment contains all the essential information for that function, such as local variables, global variables, and more. In some languages, this execution environment is referred to as the "call stack," while in Python, it is known as the Frame Object. Every time a function is called, a new Frame is created. The Frame is pushed onto a stack, and when the function completes execution, the Frame is removed.

Let's take a look at what a Frame looks like in CPython, as well as the process of its creation and destruction.

Frame Object

```
// file: Include/internal/pycore_frame.h
struct _frame {
    PyObject_HEAD
    PyFrameObject *f_back;
    struct _PyInterpreterFrame *f_frame;
    PyObject *f_trace;
    int f_lineno;
    char f_trace_lines;
```

```
    char f_trace_opcodes;
    char f_fast_as_locals;
    PyObject *_f_frame_data[1];
};
```

Aside from the common PyObject_HEAD, there are several members worth mentioning. The f_back member points to the previous Frame Object in the stack, forming a linked list structure. The f_frame member is a pointer to a _PyInterpreterFrame type—more on this in a bit. There are also some members that appear to be related to line numbers and, at the end, the _f_frame_data[1] member. We encountered a similar design in earlier chapters—this is a Flexible Array Member used for storing additional frame-related data.

Let's take a look at the definition of _PyInterpreterFrame:

```
// file: Include/internal/pycore_frame.h
typedef struct _PyInterpreterFrame {
    PyCodeObject *f_code;
    struct _PyInterpreterFrame *previous;
    PyObject *f_funcobj;
    PyObject *f_globals;
    PyObject *f_builtins;
    PyObject *f_locals;
    PyFrameObject *frame_obj;
    _Py_CODEUNIT *prev_instr;
    int stacktop;
    uint16_t return_offset;
    char owner;
    PyObject *localsplus[1];
} _PyInterpreterFrame;
```

Here, we see the familiar Code Object f_code, and there is also a previous pointer, linking to the previous structure and forming the execution stack. The f_funcobj member points to the function object associated with this Frame.

You can also find f_globals, f_builtins, and f_locals in this structure. As their names suggest, these are used to store global variables, built-in variables, and local variables, respectively.

Finally, there's `localsplus`, which is also a flexible array member. In fact, this is where the local variables are actually stored. The `f_locals` member typically refers to a dictionary structure, but most of the time, it remains NULL. The dictionary is only created when there's an explicit need to access local variables as a dictionary (e.g., when calling the `locals()` function). When this happens, the values from `localsplus` are copied into or populate the `f_locals` dictionary.

The Life Cycle of a Frame Object

When a Python function is called, it creates a new `PyFrameObject` and a `_PyInterpreterFrame`. The `f_frame` member of `PyFrameObject` points to the `_PyInterpreterFrame`, and the `frame_obj` member of `_PyInterpreterFrame` points back to the `PyFrameObject`.

To track how Frames are created, we usually start from the `_PyEval_EvalFrameDefault` function. However, even before digging into the implementation, there's a warning comment at the very beginning:

`_PyEval_EvalFrameDefault()` is a *big* function

And indeed, it's not small—it spans roughly 350 lines:

```
// file: Python/ceval.c

PyObject* _Py_HOT_FUNCTION
_PyEval_EvalFrameDefault(PyThreadState *tstate, _PyInterpreterFrame *frame,
int throwflag)
{
    // ... omitted ...
}
```

Here are some key points extracted from within:

```
// file: Python/ceval.c

PyObject* _Py_HOT_FUNCTION
_PyEval_EvalFrameDefault(PyThreadState *tstate, _PyInterpreterFrame *frame,
int throwflag)
```

```c
{
    _PyInterpreterFrame  entry_frame;
    _PyCFrame *prev_cframe = tstate->cframe;
    // ... omitted ...

    entry_frame.f_code = tstate->interp->interpreter_trampoline;
    entry_frame.prev_instr =
        _PyCode_CODE(tstate->interp->interpreter_trampoline);
    entry_frame.stacktop = 0;
    entry_frame.owner = FRAME_OWNED_BY_CSTACK;
    entry_frame.return_offset = 0;

    entry_frame.previous = prev_cframe->current_frame;
    frame->previous = &entry_frame;
}
```

When entering, a new entry_frame is created, and the current stack is obtained through PyThreadState. Along the way, several members of entry_frame are initialized. By assigning the previous pointer of entry_frame to the Frame in the stack, entry_frame is effectively pushed onto the stack. Finally, the previous member of frame is set to point to this new entry_frame. It's a bit complicated, but this is how a new Frame is created.

Next, there's a code segment with rather complex formatting:

```c
// file: Python/ceval.c

PyObject* _Py_HOT_FUNCTION
_PyEval_EvalFrameDefault(PyThreadState *tstate, _PyInterpreterFrame *frame,
int throwflag)
{
    /* Start instructions */
#if !USE_COMPUTED_GOTOS
    dispatch_opcode:
        switch (opcode)
#endif
        {
```

```
#include "generated_cases.c.h"

    // ... omitted ...
#if USE_COMPUTED_GOTOS
        TARGET_INSTRUMENTED_LINE:
#else
        case INSTRUMENTED_LINE:
#endif
    // ... omitted ...

        } /* End instructions */
}
```

From /* Start instructions */ to /* End instructions */, this is a large switch statement, with many different case branches, each representing an instruction. Take note of #include "generated_cases.c.h", which pulls in a massive number of generated opcodes. Tracing into this generated file, you'll see it's nearly 4,800 lines long. The comment at the beginning states how the file was produced:

```
// This file is generated by Tools/cases_generator/generate_cases.py
// from:
//    Python/bytecodes.c
// Do not edit!
```

It explicitly says not to edit this file manually. If interested, you can further explore how generate_cases.py creates it.

Finally, let's look at how the Frame Object is destroyed:

```
// file: Python/ceval.c

PyObject* _Py_HOT_FUNCTION
_PyEval_EvalFrameDefault(PyThreadState *tstate, _PyInterpreterFrame *frame,
int throwflag)
{
    // ... omitted ...
exit_unwind:
    assert(_PyErr_Occurred(tstate));
    _Py_LeaveRecursiveCallPy(tstate);
    assert(frame != &entry_frame);
    // GH-99729: We need to unlink the frame *before* clearing it:
```

```
    _PyInterpreterFrame *dying = frame;
    frame = cframe.current_frame = dying->previous;
    _PyEvalFrameClearAndPop(tstate, dying);
    frame->return_offset = 0;
    if (frame == &entry_frame) {
        /* Restore previous cframe and exit */
        tstate->cframe = cframe.previous;
        assert(tstate->cframe->current_frame == frame->previous);
        tstate->c_recursion_remaining += PY_EVAL_C_STACK_UNITS;
        return NULL;
    }
    // ... omitted ...
}
```

The exit_unwind label handles cleanup during the function's exit. There's also an inline comment:

// GH-99729: We need to unlink the frame *before* clearing it:

This means that before breaking the link to a Frame, we must first detach it from the Frame chain. These two lines:

// file: Python/ceval.c

_PyInterpreterFrame *dying = frame;

create a new _PyInterpreterFrame pointer, named dying, because it's about to be released. Next:

// file: Python/ceval.c

frame = cframe.current_frame = dying->previous;

Frames are originally linked together; this line updates the subsequent Frame to point to the Frame preceding dying, thereby removing dying from the chain.

Finally, the _PyEvalFrameClearAndPop() function is called for cleanup.

From the moment a Frame is born, its fate is to lead a busy and brief life. Each time you call a function, there's an unseen Frame managing variables, executing instructions, and handling unexpected situations, all so your program can run smoothly. Next time you make a function call, don't forget to thank these unsung heroes working behind the scenes!

CHAPTER 21

Inside the Python VM: Namespaces and Scopes

In Python, there are four types of scopes: LEGB (Local, Enclosing, Global, Built-in). In this chapter, we will explore how these scopes are implemented within CPython.

Variable Scope

Let's start with a simple example:

```
a = 9527
b = 1450

def hello():
    x = 520
    y = 1314
    print(a, b, x, y)
hello()
```

Here, we have two global variables, a and b, and two local variables, x and y. When the `hello()` function is called, the values of these variables will be printed. This behavior is straightforward. However, let's take a look at the bytecode instructions generated when this code is executed:

```
// ... omitted ...
5           0 RESUME                   0
6           2 LOAD_CONST               1 (520)
            4 STORE_FAST               0 (x)
```

```
7           6 LOAD_CONST             2 (1314)
            8 STORE_FAST             1 (y)
8          10 LOAD_GLOBAL            1 (NULL + print)
           20 LOAD_GLOBAL            2 (a)
           30 LOAD_GLOBAL            4 (b)
           40 LOAD_FAST              0 (x)
           42 LOAD_FAST              1 (y)
           44 CALL                   4
// ... omitted ...
```

Notice that reading global variables like a uses LOAD_GLOBAL, while local variables such as x and y are accessed using LOAD_FAST. This indicates that Python employs different mechanisms for accessing global and local variables.

Local Variables (L)

First, let's see what the LOAD_FAST instruction does when reading local variables:

// file: Python/bytecodes.c

```
inst(LOAD_FAST, (-- value)) {
    value = GETLOCAL(oparg);
    assert(value != NULL);
    Py_INCREF(value);
}
```

This is quite straightforward. Now let's look at how the GETLOCAL macro is defined:

// file: Python/ceval_macros.h

```
#define GETLOCAL(i)     (frame->localsplus[i])
```

We talked about localsplus in the previous chapter. It is a member of the Frame structure—a flexible array used to store local variables. Here, i is the index of the variable, allowing us to fetch the value of the corresponding local variable. Thus, in the lines above:

```
           40 LOAD_FAST              0 (x)
           42 LOAD_FAST              1 (y)
```

LOAD_FAST 0 fetches the value of x, and LOAD_FAST 1 fetches the value of y. But when are these local variables stored? It appears that the preceding STORE_FAST instruction handles this, so let's trace it:

// file: Python/bytecodes.c

```
inst(STORE_FAST, (value --)) {
    SETLOCAL(oparg, value);
}
```

Now, let's see the definition of the SETLOCAL macro:

// file: Python/ceval_macros.h

```
#define SETLOCAL(i, value)      do { PyObject *tmp = GETLOCAL(i); \
                                    GETLOCAL(i) = value; \
                                    Py_XDECREF(tmp); } while (0)
```

Also straightforward. This uses the GETLOCAL macro to fetch the original value from localsplus, saves the new value at the designated index, and finally releases the old value. This way, storing and retrieving local variables is accomplished. The pattern do { ... } while (0) may look odd at first, but it allows multiple statements to be placed safely without causing syntax errors.

Therefore, STORE_FAST 0 stores the value of x in position 0 of localsplus, and STORE_FAST 1 stores the value of y in position 1, and so on. Later, when local variables need to be read, LOAD_FAST with the correct index can quickly fetch their values.

Local variables are handled quite simply. Next, let's look at global variables.

Global and Built-in Variables (G, B)

Let's start with the storage of global variables:

```
1         2 LOAD_CONST            0 (9527)
          4 STORE_NAME            0 (a)
2         6 LOAD_CONST            1 (1450)
          8 STORE_NAME            1 (b)
```

The instruction used here is STORE_NAME. Let's look into what this instruction does:

```
// file: Python/bytecodes.c

inst(STORE_NAME, (v -- )) {
    PyObject *name = GETITEM(frame->f_code->co_names, oparg);
    PyObject *ns = LOCALS();
    int err;
    // ... omitted ...
    if (PyDict_CheckExact(ns))
        err = PyDict_SetItem(ns, name, v);
    else
        err = PyObject_SetItem(ns, name, v);
    DECREF_INPUTS();
    ERROR_IF(err, error);
}
```

name is fetched from the current Frame's Code Object's co_names member, which is typically a tuple. With the GETITEM() macro and oparg, it fetches the item at the specific index.

Next, ns is acquired using the LOCALS() macro, which gets the f_locals member of the Frame—typically a dictionary. When you call Python's locals() function, it returns this object. It is called ns here as an abbreviation for "namespace".

With the desired variable name and the namespace, the value is saved using either PyDict_SetItem() or PyObject_SetItem(). Thus, for the lines below:

```
  2 LOAD_CONST               0 (9527)
  4 STORE_NAME               0 (a)

  6 LOAD_CONST               1 (1450)
  8 STORE_NAME               1 (b)
```

It's clear that 9527 is stored as a and 1450 as b. These variable-value pairs are stored in the Frame's f_locals dictionary. With an understanding of how these are stored, let's now see how global variables are read. Reading global variables is done via the LOAD_GLOBAL instruction, which is more complex than LOAD_FAST:

// file: Python/bytecodes.c

CHAPTER 21   INSIDE THE PYTHON VM: NAMESPACES AND SCOPES

```
inst(LOAD_GLOBAL, (unused/1, unused/1, unused/1, unused/1 -- null if
(oparg & 1), v)) {
    #if ENABLE_SPECIALIZATION
    _PyLoadGlobalCache *cache = (_PyLoadGlobalCache *)next_instr;
    if (ADAPTIVE_COUNTER_IS_ZERO(cache->counter)) {
        PyObject *name = GETITEM(frame->f_code->co_names, oparg>>1);
        next_instr--;
        _Py_Specialize_LoadGlobal(GLOBALS(), BUILTINS(), next_instr, name);
        DISPATCH_SAME_OPARG();
    }
    STAT_INC(LOAD_GLOBAL, deferred);
    DECREMENT_ADAPTIVE_COUNTER(cache->counter);
    #endif   /* ENABLE_SPECIALIZATION */
    // ... omitted ...
}
```

Let's break this down, starting with:

`PyObject *name = GETITEM(frame->f_code->co_names, oparg>>1);`

This should look familiar. It retrieves the relevant item from the Frame's Code Object's co_names tuple, using oparg>>1 to get the index. For example:

```
10  LOAD_GLOBAL              1 (NULL + print)
20  LOAD_GLOBAL              2 (a)
30  LOAD_GLOBAL              4 (b)
```

At this point, co_names might look like (NULL + print, a, b), so LOAD_GLOBAL 2 shifts 2 right by one bit to get 1, fetching co_names[1], which is a. Similarly, LOAD_GLOBAL 4 gets index 2, corresponding to b.

Next:

`_Py_Specialize_LoadGlobal(GLOBALS(), BUILTINS(), next_instr, name);`

This _Py_Specialize_LoadGlobal() function is quite complex internally, but what it does is interesting. Suppose we have the following Python code:

`print(x)`

On the first execution, Python will normally use the LOAD_GLOBAL instruction to look up both print and x. This lookup checks the global and built-in namespaces, which is a bit slower. When _Py_Specialize_LoadGlobal intervenes, it records the result of this lookup:

For example, it might record that the variable x was found in a particular position in the global namespace, or note that the lookup succeeded in the built-in namespace. This information is stored in the memory following this bytecode instruction, allowing the VM to skip the full lookup process on subsequent encounters and fetch the value directly from the cached information.

In other words, if a variable is repeatedly looked up (like the built-in function print()), Python will "remember" its location, so next time it doesn't have to search from scratch.

The arguments, such as next_instr, indicate the next bytecode instruction, while GLOBALS() and BUILTINS() are macros for the Frame's f_globals (global variables) and f_builtins (built-in variables) members:

// file: Python/ceval_macros.h

```
#define GLOBALS() frame->f_globals
#define BUILTINS() frame->f_builtins
```

Now, let's look at the lower part of the LOAD_GLOBAL instruction:

// file: Python/bytecodes.c

```
inst(LOAD_GLOBAL, (unused/1, unused/1, unused/1, unused/1 -- null if (oparg & 1), v)) {
    // ... omitted ...
    PyObject *name = GETITEM(frame->f_code->co_names, oparg>>1);
    if (PyDict_CheckExact(GLOBALS())
        && PyDict_CheckExact(BUILTINS()))
    {
        v = _PyDict_LoadGlobal((PyDictObject *)GLOBALS(),
                               (PyDictObject *)BUILTINS(),
                               name);
        // ... omitted ...
        Py_INCREF(v);
    }
```

```
    else {
        v = PyObject_GetItem(GLOBALS(), name);
        if (v == NULL) {
            // ... omitted ...
            v = PyObject_GetItem(BUILTINS(), name);
            // ... omitted ...
        }
    }
    null = NULL;
}
```

I've omitted some error handling for clarity. Python first checks if `GLOBALS()` and `BUILTINS()` are both dictionaries. If so, `_PyDict_LoadGlobal()` is used to fetch the variable; otherwise, it falls back to `PyObject_GetItem()`.

Regardless of the path taken, you can see that the search for a global variable begins with the global namespace (G) and, if not found, proceeds to the built-in namespace (B). This completes the process of reading a global variable.

Enclosing Variables (E)

Finally, let's examine enclosing variables, which are those found in nested functions, for example:

```
def outer():
    x = 520

    def inner():
        print(x)

    inner()
```

Here, x is an enclosing variable. Inspecting the bytecode for this example, the instruction for `x = 520` is:

```
       4 LOAD_CONST               1 (520)
       6 STORE_DEREF              1 (x)
```

And the instruction for print(x) is:

```
 4 LOAD_GLOBAL            1 (NULL + print)
14 LOAD_DEREF             0 (x)
16 CALL                   1
```

It seems STORE_DEREF and LOAD_DEREF deal with enclosing variables. Let's view STORE_DEREF:

// file: Python/bytecodes.c

```c
inst(STORE_DEREF, (v --)) {
    PyObject *cell = GETLOCAL(oparg);
    PyObject *oldobj = PyCell_GET(cell);
    PyCell_SET(cell, v);
    Py_XDECREF(oldobj);
}
```

Here, PyCellObject is related to closures. We'll discuss closures in detail in the next chapter. For now, you can think of it as a container for storing enclosing variables. What about LOAD_DEREF?

// file: Python/bytecodes.c

```c
inst(LOAD_DEREF, ( -- value)) {
    PyObject *cell = GETLOCAL(oparg);
    value = PyCell_GET(cell);
    if (value == NULL) {
        format_exc_unbound(tstate, frame->f_code, oparg);
        ERROR_IF(true, error);
    }
    Py_INCREF(value);
}
```

As expected, this fetches the value from the PyCellObject. This completes storage and retrieval for enclosing variables.

A brief summary:

- **Local variables (L)** are stored in the Frame's f_localsplus via STORE_FAST and read using LOAD_FAST.

- **Enclosing variables (E)** are stored in a PyCellObject via STORE_DEREF and read using LOAD_DEREF.

- **Global variables (G)** are found in the Frame's f_globals member; **built-ins (B)** are in f_builtins. Both are set via STORE_NAME and read using LOAD_GLOBAL.

Although the LEGB lookup order is determined at runtime, whether x = 520 is local or global is decided at compile time. That means that, when you write and run your Python code, the Python compiler translates your code to bytecode and that bytecode has already determined which lookup method should be used for each variable.

If you want to understand how Python decides LEGB scopes at compile time, you'll need to dive deeper into how Python compiles code to bytecode.

CHAPTER 22

Inside the Python VM: Cells and Closures

In the previous chapter, we discussed the LEGB scope design and encountered a special object called the Cell Object. In Python, this object is used to implement the concept of "closure." Many programming languages feature closures, and in this chapter, we will explore what a Cell Object is and how closures are designed by looking directly at the CPython source code.

Creating a Cell Object

Let's first take a look at the structure of a Cell:

// file: Include/cpython/cellobject.h

```
typedef struct {
    PyObject_HEAD
    PyObject *ob_ref;
} PyCellObject;
```

Compared to other types, the structure of `PyCellObject` is much simpler. Aside from the standard `PyObject_HEAD`, it only has one member: `ob_ref`. This member is of type `PyObject*`, which allows the `PyCellObject` to store a pointer to any kind of Python object. Let's see how it is created, using the following example:

```
def hi():
    a = 1
    b = 2

    def hey():
        print(a)
```

First, let's examine the bytecode for the definition part of the hi() function:

```
// ... omitted ...
            0 MAKE_CELL               2 (a)

2           4 LOAD_CONST              1 (1)
            6 STORE_DEREF             2 (a)

3           8 LOAD_CONST              2 (2)
           10 STORE_FAST              0 (b)
// ... omitted ...
```

Before creating the hey() function, several new instructions appear. Let's go through them line by line, starting with MAKE_CELL 2:

```
// file: Python/bytecodes.c

inst(MAKE_CELL, (--)) {
    PyObject *initial = GETLOCAL(oparg);
    PyObject *cell = PyCell_New(initial);
    if (cell == NULL) {
        goto resume_with_error;
    }
    SETLOCAL(oparg, cell);
}
```

As seen in the previous chapter, GETLOCAL(oparg) retrieves a value from the localsplus array of the current frame, based on the value of oparg. This value is then passed to the PyCell_New() function:

```
// file: Objects/cellobject.c

PyObject *
PyCell_New(PyObject *obj)
{
    PyCellObject *op;

    op = (PyCellObject *)PyObject_GC_New(PyCellObject, &PyCell_Type);
    if (op == NULL)
        return NULL;
    op->ob_ref = Py_XNewRef(obj);
```

```
    _PyObject_GC_TRACK(op);
    return (PyObject *)op;
}
```

This function creates a `PyCellObject` and assigns the passed-in `obj` to the Cell's `ob_ref` member. The Cell is then placed back into the local variables—specifically, at a designated position in the frame's `localsplus` array—using the `SETLOCAL(oparg, cell)` macro. In other words, before the assignment `a = 1` takes place, a Cell has already been prepared in the `localsplus` array for the variable a.

The next instruction, `STORE_DEREF 2`, has been discussed in the previous chapter. Here, the argument 2—identical to `MAKE_CELL 2`—indicates the value should be stored in the Cell just created. As for variable b, this does not receive the same handling; it is simply a regular local variable and is thus managed with a `STORE_FAST 0` instruction.

Closures

Let's proceed and review the next section:

```
// ... omitted ...
  5         12 LOAD_CLOSURE           2 (a)
            14 BUILD_TUPLE            1
            16 LOAD_CONST             3 (<code object)
            18 MAKE_FUNCTION          8 (closure)
            20 STORE_FAST             1 (hey)
            22 RETURN_CONST           0 (None)
// ... omitted ...
```

From the compiled bytecode, you can see that although the inner `hey()` function is created with the familiar `MAKE_FUNCTION` instruction, there is a new instruction beforehand called `LOAD_CLOSURE 2`. What does this do?

// file: Python/bytecodes.c

```
inst(LOAD_CLOSURE, (-- value)) {
    value = GETLOCAL(oparg);
    ERROR_IF(value == NULL, unbound_local_error);
    Py_INCREF(value);
}
```

This simply retrieves a value from the frame's `localsplus` array; no additional action is taken. Next, what does BUILD_TUPLE 1 do?

// file: Python/bytecodes.c

```
inst(BUILD_TUPLE, (values[oparg] -- tup)) {
    tup = _PyTuple_FromArraySteal(values, oparg);
    ERROR_IF(tup == NULL, error);
}
```

As its name suggests, it constructs a tuple and places the value fetched by LOAD_CLOSURE inside. Next is MAKE_FUNCTION 8, which we've discussed earlier. This instruction creates a function object, but the argument 8 here means the function is a closure:

// file: Python/bytecodes.c

```
inst(MAKE_FUNCTION, (defaults     if (oparg & 0x01),
                    kwdefaults   if (oparg & 0x02),
                    annotations  if (oparg & 0x04),
                    closure      if (oparg & 0x08),
                    codeobj -- func)) {
    // ... omitted ...

    if (oparg & 0x08) {
        assert(PyTuple_CheckExact(closure));
        func_obj->func_closure = closure;
    }
    // ... omitted ...
}
```

Because `oparg` is 8, a tuple is assigned to the function object's `func_closure` member. With this step, the hey() function is now fully created. Let's continue by examining what happens when the inner hey() function is executed.

Free Variables

```
              0 COPY_FREE_VARS           1

6             4 LOAD_GLOBAL              1 (NULL + print)
             14 LOAD_DEREF               0 (a)
             16 CALL                     1
             24 POP_TOP
             26 RETURN_CONST             0 (None)
```

Here, we see a new instruction: COPY_FREE_VARS 1. What does this do?

// file: Python/bytecodes.c

```c
inst(COPY_FREE_VARS, (--)) {
    PyCodeObject *co = frame->f_code;
    assert(PyFunction_Check(frame->f_funcobj));
    PyObject *closure = ((PyFunctionObject *)frame->f_funcobj)->func_closure;
    assert(oparg == co->co_nfreevars);
    int offset = co->co_nlocalsplus - oparg;
    for (int i = 0; i < oparg; ++i) {
        PyObject *o = PyTuple_GET_ITEM(closure, i);
        frame->localsplus[offset + i] = Py_NewRef(o);
    }
}
```

This code is quite straightforward. Here, closure refers to the tuple that was created earlier and stored in the function object's func_closure member. The code copies the values inside that tuple into the current frame's localsplus array, appending them after the existing local variables. As a result, the inner function hey() gains access to the outer function's local variables.

Thus, a "free variable" refers to a variable used by an inner function that is not defined or declared in its own scope but instead comes from the enclosing function. If you understand the workflow above, the idea of free variables becomes much less mysterious.

CHAPTER 22   INSIDE THE PYTHON VM: CELLS AND CLOSURES

From the Python Perspective

So far, we've looked at these mechanisms from the perspective of CPython internals. But if you want to view them from Python itself, that's possible too:

```
>>> hi.__code__.co_varnames
('b', 'hey')
>>> hi.__code__.co_cellvars
('a',)
```

Every function has a `__code__` attribute, which points to its code object. This code object has the `co_varnames` attribute, which lists the variables defined in the function's local scope. As you can see, currently, only `'b'` and `'hey'` are present. What about variable `'a'`? From Python's perspective, it's no longer a simple local variable, but instead can be found via `co_cellvars`, indicating it has become a Cell Object.

So how are these `co_*` attributes implemented? The answer lies within the `tp_getset` and `tp_members` members in the `PyCode_Type` structure:

// file: Objects/codeobject.c

```c
static PyGetSetDef code_getsetlist[] = {
    {"co_lnotab",         (getter)code_getlnotab,       NULL, NULL},
    {"_co_code_adaptive", (getter)code_getcodeadaptive, NULL, NULL},
    {"co_varnames",       (getter)code_getvarnames,     NULL, NULL},
    {"co_cellvars",       (getter)code_getcellvars,     NULL, NULL},
    {"co_freevars",       (getter)code_getfreevars,     NULL, NULL},
    {"co_code",           (getter)code_getcode,         NULL, NULL},
    {0}
};

static PyMemberDef code_memberlist[] = {
    {"co_argcount",        T_INT,    OFF(co_argcount),        READONLY},
    {"co_posonlyargcount", T_INT,    OFF(co_posonlyargcount), READONLY},
    {"co_kwonlyargcount",  T_INT,    OFF(co_kwonlyargcount),  READONLY},
    {"co_stacksize",       T_INT,    OFF(co_stacksize),       READONLY},
    {"co_flags",           T_INT,    OFF(co_flags),           READONLY},
    {"co_nlocals",         T_INT,    OFF(co_nlocals),         READONLY},
    {"co_consts",          T_OBJECT, OFF(co_consts),          READONLY},
```

```
    {"co_names",          T_OBJECT, OFF(co_names),         READONLY},
    {"co_filename",       T_OBJECT, OFF(co_filename),      READONLY},
    {"co_name",           T_OBJECT, OFF(co_name),          READONLY},
    {"co_qualname",       T_OBJECT, OFF(co_qualname),      READONLY},
    {"co_firstlineno",    T_INT,    OFF(co_firstlineno),   READONLY},
    {"co_linetable",      T_OBJECT, OFF(co_linetable),     READONLY},
    {"co_exceptiontable", T_OBJECT, OFF(co_exceptiontable),READONLY},
    {NULL}      /* Sentinel */
};
```

All these co_* attributes are implemented here. Attributes in tp_members are typically more "static" and map directly to structure members with fixed memory offsets, resulting in faster access with less computational overhead. In contrast, tp_getset uses getter and setter functions, allowing for greater flexibility, but often with a performance trade-off compared to direct member access.

If you want to observe these operations more closely, you can use Python's built-in breakpoint to investigate:

```
def hi():
    a = 1
    b = 2

    def hey():
        print(a)

breakpoint()
```

After running, you'll enter interactive mode, where you can inspect some properties of the hey function:

```
$ python -i hi.py
>>> hi()
--Return--
> /Users/kaochenlong/projects/products/books/pythonbook.cc/hi.py(8)
hi()->None
-> breakpoint()
(Pdb) hey
<function hi.<locals>.hey>
```

```
(Pdb) hey.__closure__
(<cell: int object>,)
(Pdb) hey.__closure__[0]
<cell: int object>
(Pdb) hey.__closure__[0].cell_contents
1
```

Through the function's `__closure__` attribute, you can obtain all Cells belonging to the inner hey() function. Every Cell has a `cell_contents` attribute, which lets you see what the Cell contains. Additionally, Python has a built-in module called `inspect` that enables you to access the current frame:

```
(Pdb) import inspect
(Pdb) f = inspect.currentframe()
(Pdb) f
<frame>
(Pdb) f.f_code
<code object <module>>
(Pdb) f.f_locals
{
  'b': 2,
  'hey': <function hi.<locals>.hey>,
  'a': 1,
  '__return__': None,
  'inspect': <module 'inspect'>,
  'f': <frame>
}
(Pdb) f.f_locals['hey']
<function hi.<locals>.hey>
```

With `inspect.currentframe()`, you can access the current frame and experiment with the attributes we previously examined. By following the progression from the beginning of this series to this chapter, you should have a better understanding of where to start in the source code if you're interested in how a particular feature is implemented.

CHAPTER 23

Classes and Where They Come From

When people talk about object-oriented programming, classes are usually the first thing that comes up. A class can create "instances," which we commonly refer to as objects. But in the Python world, where everything is an object, a class itself is also an object. If a class is an object, then what class creates the class object itself? Let's use a simple class as an example:

```python
class Cat:
    def __init__(self, name):
        self.name = name

    def meow(self):
        print(f"Hello, {self.name}")
kitty = Cat("Kitty")
kitty.meow()
```

In this chapter, we'll look at what happens during the execution of this code from the perspective of CPython's source code and see how the class itself is created.

Creating a Class

Since classes are also objects, based on our understanding from previous chapters, you might expect something like `PyClassObject` to exist in CPython. However, you'll soon realize no such thing exists. Instead, let's start from the bytecode to see how the `class` statement creates a class:

CHAPTER 23   CLASSES AND WHERE THEY COME FROM

```
1             2 PUSH_NULL
              4 LOAD_BUILD_CLASS
              6 LOAD_CONST                0 (<code object Cat>)
              8 MAKE_FUNCTION             0
             10 LOAD_CONST                1 ('Cat')
             12 CALL                      2
             20 STORE_NAME                0 (Cat)
// ... omitted ...
```

The only unfamiliar instruction here is LOAD_BUILD_CLASS. From the name, we can guess that it's involved in creating the class. Let's see what this actually does:

```
// file: Python/bytecodes.c
inst(LOAD_BUILD_CLASS, ( -- bc)) {
    if (PyDict_CheckExact(BUILTINS())) {
        bc = _PyDict_GetItemWithError(BUILTINS(),
                                     &_Py_ID(__build_class__));
        // ... error handling omitted ...
        Py_INCREF(bc);
    }
    else {
        bc = PyObject_GetItem(BUILTINS(), &_Py_ID(__build_class__));
        // ... error handling omitted ...
    }
}
```

This checks whether BUILDINS() is a dictionary. If so, it uses _PyDict_GetItemWithError(); otherwise it calls PyObject_GetItem(). We've seen PyObject_GetItem() before—it has a slightly longer execution path and therefore worse performance compared to _PyDict_GetItemWithError().

But when would BUILDINS() not be a dictionary? Most of the time it is, unless you manually modify the __builtins__ variable. __builtins__ is Python's built-in module containing many of the built-in functions, but you are technically able to change it manually:

```
>>> __builtins__
<module 'builtins' (built-in)>
```

```
>>> __builtins__ = "Hello Kitty"
>>> __builtins__
'Hello Kitty'
```

At this point, BUILDINS() is no longer a dictionary. But doing this may make your program behave unexpectedly or throw errors, so unless you know exactly what you're doing, don't change it. So what is __build_class__? It's actually a built-in Python function:

```
>>> __build_class__
<built-in function __build_class__>
```

In other words, the LOAD_BUILD_CLASS instruction fetches the __build_class__ function, which will be used shortly to create the class. You probably don't use this function directly very often, but let me demonstrate using it to create a simple Cat class. First, I'll define a function:

```python
def cat_body():
    def __init__(self, name):
        self.name = name

    def meow(self):
        print(f"Hello, {self.name}")

    return locals()
```

This function defines two inner functions, __init__() and meow(). Since they are local variables within cat_body(), calling locals() at the end will return a dictionary that includes these functions. Next, we use the __build_class__() function to construct the class:

```python
MyCat = __build_class__(cat_body, "Cat")
kitty = MyCat("Kitty")
kitty.meow()
```

This allows us to create a Cat class. In the Python world, class is just syntactic sugar—under the hood, it's the __build_class__() built-in function doing the actual work.

CHAPTER 23   CLASSES AND WHERE THEY COME FROM

The Mastermind Behind the Scenes

So, how is the __build_class__() built-in function defined?

```
// file: Python/bltinmodule.c
static PyObject *
builtin___build_class__(PyObject *self, PyObject *const *args, Py_ssize_t nargs,
                        PyObject *kwnames)
{
   // ... omitted ...
}
```

This function is about 150 lines long; let's go through it step by step:

```
if (nargs < 2) {
   PyErr_SetString(PyExc_TypeError,
                   "__build_class__: not enough arguments");
   return NULL;
}
func = args[0];   /* Better be callable */
if (!PyFunction_Check(func)) {
   PyErr_SetString(PyExc_TypeError,
                   "__build_class__: func must be a function");
   return NULL;
}
name = args[1];
if (!PyUnicode_Check(name)) {
   PyErr_SetString(PyExc_TypeError,
                   "__build_class__: name is not a string");
   return NULL;
}
```

When we used __build_class__(), the first and second arguments were required, and the first had to be a function and the second a string. This section checks those requirements. Next:

```
// ... omitted ...
orig_bases = _PyTuple_FromArray(args + 2, nargs - 2);
// ... omitted ...
bases = update_bases(orig_bases, args + 2, nargs - 2);
```

Why skip the first two arguments? Because the first is the function, the second is the class name string, and starting from the third argument are the base classes (if any) for inheritance. The update_bases() function then processes these base classes, handling special cases related to inheritance—details of which we'll discuss in the next chapter. Moving on:

```
meta = _PyDict_GetItemWithError(mkw, &_Py_ID(metaclass));
```

This tries to find a "metaclass" key in the keywords dictionary and retrieves its value if present. Here, _Py_ID(metaclass) is just a string, but why write it this way? As explained before, for performance reasons, CPython pre-compiles frequently used strings and makes them available in the interpreter. "metaclass"**Error! Bookmark not defined.** is one of these. Using this mechanism allows the interpreter to use a pre-compiled string instead of creating a new one each time, improving performance. For more on other strings compiled this way, refer to Tools/build/generate_global_objects.py in the source code.

Selecting the Metaclass

Now comes the important part:

```
if (meta == NULL) {
    if (PyTuple_GET_SIZE(bases) == 0) {
        meta = (PyObject *) (&PyType_Type);
    }
    else {
        PyObject *base0 = PyTuple_GET_ITEM(bases, 0);
        meta = (PyObject *)Py_TYPE(base0);
    }
    Py_INCREF(meta);
    isclass = 1;
}
```

If no explicit `meta` is specified, the function checks if any base classes were provided. If there are none, it uses `PyType_Type` as the `meta`, which is basically the `type` class in Python. If there are base classes, Python allows multiple inheritance, so it takes the metaclass of the first base class (using `Py_TYPE(base0)` retrieves the `ob_type` member, i.e., the metaclass of `base0`). Let's continue:

```c
if (isclass) {
    winner = (PyObject *)_PyType_CalculateMetaclass((PyTypeObject *)meta,
                                                    bases);
    if (winner == NULL) {
        goto error;
    }
    if (winner != meta) {
        Py_SETREF(meta, Py_NewRef(winner));
    }
}
```

Here, the `_PyType_CalculateMetaclass()` function determines the "winner." Why do we need to determine a winner? Because with Python's multiple inheritance design, a class can have multiple base classes, potentially with different metaclasses. A resolution algorithm is therefore needed to determine which metaclass should be used. We'll discuss this resolution logic in the next chapter.

Preparing the Namespace

Moving on:

```c
if (_PyObject_LookupAttr(meta, &_Py_ID(__prepare__), &prep) < 0) {
    ns = NULL;
}
else if (prep == NULL) {
    ns = PyDict_New();
}
else {
    PyObject *pargs[2] = {name, bases};
    ns = PyObject_VectorcallDict(prep, pargs, 2, mkw);
    Py_DECREF(prep);
}
```

This code prepares the class namespace. If the metaclass (meta) defines a __prepare__ method, it uses that to prepare the namespace; otherwise, it defaults to an empty dictionary. What can you do with __prepare__ in Python? Here's an example:

```
class MetaCat(type):
    def __prepare__(name, bases):
        print(f"Hello Meta! {name} {bases}")
        return {"SPECIAL_NAME": "Hello Kitty"}

class Cat(metaclass=MetaCat):
    pass
```

With this, both the Cat class and its instances will have the .SPECIAL_NAME attribute. For more details about this feature, refer to the official documentation and PEP-3115.

- **Data model**: https://docs.python.org/3/reference/datamodel.html#preparing-the-class-namespace
- **PEP-3115**: https://peps.python.org/pep-3115/

The Birth of a Class!

Back to the original source code, the function is nearing completion:

```
cell = _PyEval_Vector(tstate, (PyFunctionObject *)func, ns, NULL, 0, NULL);
if (cell != NULL) {
    if (bases != orig_bases) {
        if (PyMapping_SetItemString(ns, "__orig_bases__", orig_bases) < 0) {
            goto error;
        }
    }
    PyObject *margs[3] = {name, bases, ns};
    cls = PyObject_VectorcallDict(meta, margs, 3, mkw);
    if (cls != NULL && PyType_Check(cls) && PyCell_Check(cell)) {
        PyObject *cell_cls = PyCell_GET(cell);
        if (cell_cls != cls) {
            if (cell_cls == NULL) {
                const char *msg =
```

CHAPTER 23   CLASSES AND WHERE THEY COME FROM

```
                    "__class__ not set defining %.200R as %.200R. "
                    "Was __classcell__ propagated to type.__new__?";
                PyErr_Format(PyExc_RuntimeError, msg, name, cls);
            } else {
                const char *msg =
                    "__class__ set to %.200R defining %.200R as %.200R";
                PyErr_Format(PyExc_TypeError, msg, cell_cls, name, cls);
            }
            Py_SETREF(cls, NULL);
            goto error;
        }
    }
}
```

We've seen `cell` in the previous chapter. If `cell` is not null, we're ready to create the class. The key step is here:

`cls = PyObject_VectorcallDict(meta, margs, 3, mkw);`

This line calls the metaclass (`meta`) to create the class object (`cls`). That's the answer to our original question:

- All classes are created by invoking their metaclass during the creation process.
- If you specify a metaclass, the specified metaclass is used to create the class.
- If you don't specify a metaclass:
  - If there are base classes, use the metaclass of the first base class.
  - If there are no base classes, use the built-in `type` as the metaclass.

In summary, every class—either user-specified or by default—has a metaclass. Because the metaclass for all built-in classes is `type`, except for those that explicitly specify a different metaclass, you can say that nearly all classes in Python are created by the `type` class.

That's why when you use `type()` to print any class, whether built-in or user-defined:

```
>>> type(object)
<class 'type'>
>>> type(int)
<class 'type'>
>>> type(str)
<class 'type'>
>>> class Dog:
...     pass
>>> type(Dog)
<class 'type'>
```

The result is always `<class 'type'>`. But if you specify your own metaclass:

```
>>> type(Cat)
<class '__main__.MetaCat'>
```

Then it reflects the metaclass you specified.

Chicken or the Egg?

If you dig deeper, you'll notice the `type` class itself also has its own metaclass specified as type:

```
>>> type(type)
<class 'type'>
```

How is that possible? How can something create itself? Let's look at the definition of PyType_Type:

```
// file: Objects/typeobject.c
PyTypeObject PyType_Type = {
    PyVarObject_HEAD_INIT(&PyType_Type, 0)
    "type",                              /* tp_name */
    sizeof(PyHeapTypeObject),            /* tp_basicsize */
    // ... omitted ...
};
```

Here you can see why the string "type" appears in the output. The macro PyVarObject_HEAD_INIT() is the key to the chicken-or-the-egg dilemma:

```
// file: Include/object.h
#define PyObject_HEAD_INIT(type)    \
    {                               \
        _PyObject_EXTRA_INIT        \
        { 1 },                      \
        (type)                      \
    },
```

This macro essentially assigns the parameter passed in (in this case, PyType_Type) to the ob_type member of the object itself. This sets the metaclass of PyType_Type to be type.

Why design it this way? If not, the story that "every class's metaclass is type" simply wouldn't hold together!

CHAPTER 24

Class Inheritance in CPython

In other programming languages, class "inheritance" might not need much explanation: it's generally about defining shared methods in a base class so that subclasses can use them directly. However, Python has an extra layer of complexity with its support for multiple inheritance, which allows a single class to inherit from multiple base classes. This makes things a bit more complicated. Well, maybe more than a bit—if you dive into the source code, it can get quite involved.

Classes and Inheritance

Creating a Class

Let's start with the basics:

```
class Animal:
    pass

class Cat(Animal):
    pass
```

Let's see what kind of bytecode is generated by these lines. Starting with the first part:

```
1           2 PUSH_NULL
            4 LOAD_BUILD_CLASS
            6 LOAD_CONST               0 (<code object Animal>)
            8 MAKE_FUNCTION            0
           10 LOAD_CONST               1 ('Animal')
           12 CALL                     2
           20 STORE_NAME               0 (Animal)
```

Most of these instructions should look familiar. Let's walk through them line by line, and this time, let's also break down the operations on the memory stack.

First, the LOAD_BUILD_CLASS instruction—which we've seen in the previous chapter—loads the __build_class__() function used for creating classes. After it's loaded, the stack looks like this:

```
+-----------------+
| __build_class__ |
+-----------------+
```

Next, the LOAD_CONST instruction loads the precompiled code object for the Animal class. At this point, the stack becomes:

```
+-----------------+
| <Code Object>   |
+-----------------+
| __build_class__ |
+-----------------+
```

The MAKE_FUNCTION 0 instruction then pops the code object off the top of the stack, uses it as a parameter, and creates a function object wrapping this code object, pushing it back onto the stack:

```
+-----------------------+
| <Animal function obj> |
+-----------------------+
| __build_class__       |
+-----------------------+
```

Next, LOAD_CONST 1 loads the string 'Animal'—this will be used as the name of the class. The stack now looks like:

```
+-----------------------+
| "Animal" string       |
+-----------------------+
| <Animal function obj> |
+-----------------------+
| __build_class__       |
+-----------------------+
```

The CALL 2 instruction pops off the top two items from the stack as arguments and calls the function that is now third from the top. So essentially, this is equivalent to __build_class__(<Animal function obj>, "Animal"). The new Animal class is then pushed back onto the stack:

```
+----------------------+
| <Animal class obj>   |
+----------------------+
```

With the class created, let's see how inheritance works.

How Does Inheritance Work?

```
  5           22 PUSH_NULL
              24 LOAD_BUILD_CLASS
              26 LOAD_CONST              2 (<code object Cat>)
              28 MAKE_FUNCTION           0
              30 LOAD_CONST              3 ('Cat')
              32 LOAD_NAME               0 (Animal)
              34 CALL                    3
              42 STORE_NAME              1 (Cat)
              44 RETURN_CONST            4 (None)
```

Most instructions are the same, but CALL 3 pops the top three elements off the stack as arguments and uses the fourth element as the function to execute. The result in this case is equivalent to:

// file: Python/pythonrun.c

__build_class__(<Cat function obj>, "Cat", <Animal class obj>)

This establishes the inheritance relationship between Cat and Animal. Let's review the implementation of the built-in __build_class__() function, which we covered in the previous chapter:

// file: Python/bltinmodule.c

static PyObject *

```c
builtin___build_class__(PyObject *self, PyObject *const *args,
Py_ssize_t nargs, PyObject *kwnames)
{
    // ... omitted ...
    orig_bases = _PyTuple_FromArray(args + 2, nargs - 2);
    // ... omitted ...
}
```

The first argument is the function object that defines the class, the second is the name of the class, and any remaining arguments are the base classes—which are packed into a tuple, allowing for any number of base classes. Well…it's not completely unlimited—technically, there's no explicit restriction, but the more base classes you specify, the more time it takes to compute the inheritance relationships, so it's not common to use an excessive number.

Method Lookup

Let's start with a simple example:

```python
class Cat:
    def hi(self):
        pass

kitty = Cat()
kitty.hi()
```

How is the `.hi()` method found when called on the `kitty` object? Let's look at the generated bytecode:

```
              4 LOAD_BUILD_CLASS
              6 LOAD_CONST               0 (<code object Cat>)
              8 MAKE_FUNCTION            0
             10 LOAD_CONST               1 ('Cat')
             12 CALL                     2
             20 STORE_NAME               0 (Cat)

  6          22 PUSH_NULL
```

CHAPTER 24   CLASS INHERITANCE IN CPYTHON

```
            24 LOAD_NAME               0 (Cat)
            26 CALL                    0
            34 STORE_NAME              1 (kitty)
7           36 LOAD_NAME               1 (kitty)
            38 LOAD_ATTR               5 (NULL|self + hi)
            58 CALL                    0
            66 POP_TOP
            68 RETURN_CONST            2 (None)
```

The first part defines the Cat class. The middle section creates the kitty instance. Once the instance is created, LOAD_NAME 1 (kitty) loads the previously created object onto the stack, and LOAD_ATTR 5 attempts to find the hi method on this object. The next CALL 0 instruction then calls the method.

Let's look at what the LOAD_ATTR 5 instruction actually does:

```
// file: Python/bytecodes.c

inst(LOAD_ATTR, (unused/9, owner -- res2 if (oparg & 1), res)) {
    // ... omitted ...
    PyObject *name = GETITEM(frame->f_code->co_names, oparg >> 1);
    if (oparg & 1) {
        PyObject* meth = NULL;
        if (_PyObject_GetMethod(owner, name, &meth)) {
            assert(meth != NULL);  // No errors on this branch
            res2 = meth;
            res = owner;  // Transfer ownership
        }
        else {
            DECREF_INPUTS();
            ERROR_IF(meth == NULL, error);
            res2 = NULL;
            res = meth;
        }
    }
    else {
```

CHAPTER 24   CLASS INHERITANCE IN CPYTHON

```
        // ... omitted ...
    }
}
```

Because the oparg for LOAD_ATTR 5 is 5, the relevant path will call the _PyObject_GetMethod(owner, name, &meth) function, which tries to find name in owner and assign it to meth. For our example, owner refers to the kitty instance, and name is "hi".

So how does Python find the specified method in an object? Let's look at the relevant source code, breaking it down into parts as it's a bit long:

```
// file: Objects/object.c

int
_PyObject_GetMethod(PyObject *obj, PyObject *name, PyObject **method)
{
    // ... omitted ...
    PyTypeObject *tp = Py_TYPE(obj);

    // ... omitted ...
    PyObject *descr = _PyType_Lookup(tp, name);

    // ... omitted ...
}
```

Omitting some of the error-checking code, the _PyType_Lookup() function's name suggests it looks for the attribute or method named name on the specified type. Diving into the function:

```
// file: Objects/typeobject.c

/* Internal API to look for a name through the MRO.
   This returns a borrowed reference, and doesn't set an exception! */
PyObject *
_PyType_Lookup(PyTypeObject *type, PyObject *name)
{
    // ... omitted ...
    res = find_name_in_mro(type, name, &error);

    // ... omitted ...
```

CHAPTER 24   CLASS INHERITANCE IN CPYTHON

```
    return res;
}
```

The comment makes it clear: this method searches through the MRO (Method Resolution Order). The function `find_name_in_mro()` is quite self-explanatory as well. The MRO is the sequence Python uses to look up methods—a somewhat complex algorithm (which we'll discuss in detail next time), but for now, just know that it controls the method lookup order.

Returning to the original `_PyObject_GetMethod()` function, let's continue:

```
descrgetfunc f = NULL;
if (descr != NULL) {
    Py_INCREF(descr);
    if (_PyType_HasFeature(Py_TYPE(descr), Py_TPFLAGS_METHOD_DESCRIPTOR)) {
        meth_found = 1;
    } else {
        f = Py_TYPE(descr)->tp_descr_get;
        if (f != NULL && PyDescr_IsData(descr)) {
            *method = f(descr, obj, (PyObject *)Py_TYPE(obj));
            Py_DECREF(descr);
            return 0;
        }
    }
}
```

Python supports a feature called "descriptors," and the `tp_descr_get` and `tp_descr_set` members correspond to the __get__ and __set__ methods of a descriptor. This code checks whether `descr` is a method descriptor.

There are two types of descriptors: data descriptors and non-data descriptors. For more details, you can refer to the official documentation. A method descriptor is a kind of non-data descriptor—it has a __get__ method, but no __set__ or __delete__ method.

CHAPTER 24   CLASS INHERITANCE IN CPYTHON

This section determines whether the object is a method descriptor and, if not, calls f(descr, obj, (PyObject *)Py_TYPE(obj)) and assigns the result to method—essentially invoking the descriptor's __get__ method in Python. Continuing further:

```
PyObject *dict;
if ((tp->tp_flags & Py_TPFLAGS_MANAGED_DICT)) {
    PyDictOrValues* dorv_ptr = _PyObject_DictOrValuesPointer(obj);
    if (_PyDictOrValues_IsValues(*dorv_ptr)) {
        PyDictValues *values = _PyDictOrValues_GetValues(*dorv_ptr);
        PyObject *attr = _PyObject_GetInstanceAttribute(obj, values, name);
        if (attr != NULL) {
            *method = attr;
            Py_XDECREF(descr);
            return 0;
        }
        dict = NULL;
    }
    else {
        dict = dorv_ptr->dict;
    }
}
else {
    PyObject **dictptr = _PyObject_ComputedDictPointer(obj);
    if (dictptr != NULL) {
        dict = *dictptr;
    }
    else {
        dict = NULL;
    }
}

if (dict != NULL) {
    Py_INCREF(dict);
    PyObject *attr = PyDict_GetItemWithError(dict, name);
    if (attr != NULL) {
        *method = Py_NewRef(attr);
```

```
        Py_DECREF(dict);
        Py_XDECREF(descr);
        return 0;
    }
    Py_DECREF(dict);

    if (PyErr_Occurred()) {
        Py_XDECREF(descr);
        return 0;
    }
}
```

This code may look a bit verbose, but its purpose is to attempt to find the specified attribute in the object's dictionary or attributes. If it's found, it stores it in method and returns from the function; if not, it continues through the other resolution logic. If nothing is found, an error will eventually be raised. Once the method is found, it is put back on the stack and executed by the next CALL 0 instruction.

In summary, LOAD_ATTR actually does quite a lot of work. When you write code like kitty.say_goodbye() in Python, this attribute access is managed by the LOAD_ATTR instruction. We've omitted many details, specifically the complex MRO (Method Resolution Order) algorithm I mentioned earlier. In multiple inheritance scenarios, this algorithm can become somewhat complicated. We'll discuss it thoroughly in the next part!

CHAPTER 25

Method Resolution Order and C3 Linearization

In this chapter, let's take a short break from reading CPython source code and focus on how Python calculates the method lookup order in multiple inheritance situations, specifically when multiple parent classes implement the same method—which one takes precedence?

The C3 Linearization Algorithm

Regarding Python's use of the C3 linearization algorithm, I'll borrow a brief description from Wikipedia:

> Python's Guido van Rossum summarizes C3 superclass linearization thus: "Basically, the idea behind C3 is that if you write down all of the ordering rules imposed by inheritance relationships in a complex class hierarchy, the algorithm will determine a monotonic ordering of the classes that satisfies all of them. If such an ordering can not be determined, the algorithm will fail."

The key here is "monotonicity," meaning that whether the inheritance relationships are simple or highly complex, the C3 linearization algorithm tries to calculate a reasonable order. If it can find such an order, the result will be the same every time.

- **C3 linearization**: https://en.wikipedia.org/wiki/C3_linearization

CHAPTER 25   METHOD RESOLUTION ORDER AND C3 LINEARIZATION

Whose Method Gets Called?

Let's start with a simple code example:

```python
class A:
    def greeting(self):
        print("Hey in A")

class B(A):
    def greeting(self):
        print("Hey in B")

class C(A):
    def greeting(self):
        print("Hey in C")

class D(B, C):
    pass

d = D()
d.greeting()
```

This is a straightforward multiple inheritance structure. Class D has two parent classes. So, when you call d.greeting(), whose method does it use? In this case, it's simple—class D's immediate parent is class B, and B defines its own greeting method, so that's the one that gets called. But why B and not C, since they are on the same level?

Let's complicate the story a bit—what if class B doesn't define the greeting() method? For example:

```python
class A:
    def greeting(self):
        print("Hey in A")

class B(A): pass

class C(A):
    def greeting(self):
        print("Hey in C")

class D(B, C): pass
```

If class B doesn't define the greeting() method, does the method lookup go up to class A, or does it move sideways to the sibling class C? Python's Method Resolution Order (MRO) determines this. You can check a class's MRO using the .mro() method:

```
>>> D.mro()
[<class '__main__.D'>, <class '__main__.B'>, <class '__main__.C'>, <class '__main__.A'>, <class 'object'>]
```

The order is D -> B -> C -> A and finally Python's base class object. So when you call d.greeting() and class B does not define the method, the next in order is class C, and its greeting method will be called.

Python's MRO uses the C3 Linearization Algorithm, which has been adopted since Python 2.3. The purpose of this algorithm is to find a reasonable inheritance order so that every class' methods are resolved predictably.

What about before Python 2.3? Before that, Python used depth-first search (DFS) to determine the MRO. For the example above, DFS would yield D -> B -> A -> C as the order, which could cause problems in certain situations, such as the notorious diamond inheritance problem.

MRO Calculation

Single Inheritance

Let's start with a simple case—single inheritance. To keep things straightforward, let's just use pass in each class:

```
class A: pass
class B(A): pass
```

CHAPTER 25   METHOD RESOLUTION ORDER AND C3 LINEARIZATION

The inheritance hierarchy looks like this:

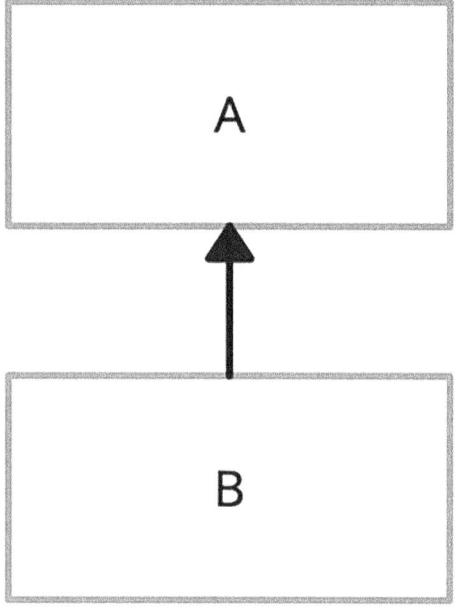

Single inheritance

Before calculating the MRO for A, it's important to note that although class A doesn't explicitly inherit another class, in Python 3, it will implicitly inherit from object. So, the hierarchy actually looks like this:

CHAPTER 25   METHOD RESOLUTION ORDER AND C3 LINEARIZATION

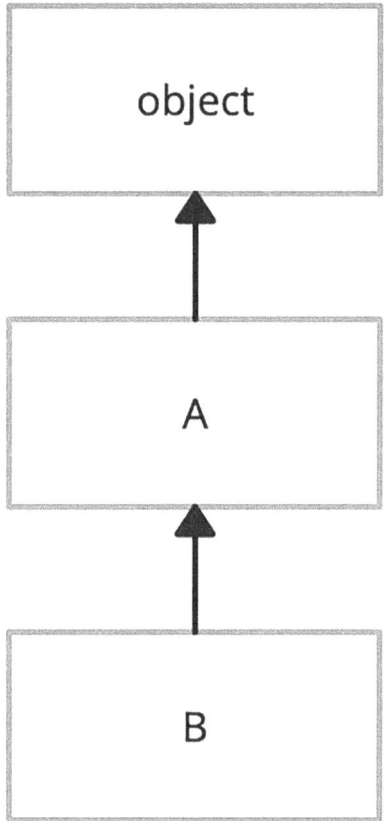

Single inheritance full

Let's start from the top with the object class. We'll use L<Class> to denote the linearization order (i.e., the MRO):

L<object> = [object]

Since object is at the top, its MRO is just [object]. Now for class A:

L<A> = [A] + merge(L<object>, [object])

At first glance, this formula may look complicated, but it's actually just the current class plus the merged, unique sequence of its parent linearizations and parent lists.

247

CHAPTER 25   METHOD RESOLUTION ORDER AND C3 LINEARIZATION

The merging process selects the first "good head" from the heads of the lists. A "good head" must not appear further down any other list or, if so, must only appear as the head of those lists. This is akin to untangling threads and finding a proper loose end to pull.

Let's step through the calculation. First, expand L<object>:

```
L<A> = [A] + merge([object], [object])
```

Since there's only a single object, it becomes our good head. Remove it from the lists and prepend to the result:

```
L<A> = [A, object]
```

This case is simple, but let's look at B:

```
L<B> = [B] + merge(L<A>, [A])
```

Expand L<A>:

```
L<B> = [B] + merge([A, object], [A])
```

Now, for the merging procedure (simplifying the rules):

1. If the head of a list (e.g., A) is not present (or is the head) in all other lists, it's a good head. Take it, then repeat.

2. If not, try the next list in order.

3. Keep repeating until all elements are added in order.

Here, A appears as the head in both lists, so it's a good head. Remove it from all lists:

```
L<B> = [B, A] + merge([object])
```

The remaining is straightforward:

```
L<B> = [B, A, object]
```

Let's check with .mro():

```
>>> A.mro()
[<class '__main__.A'>, <class 'object'>]
>>> B.mro()
[<class '__main__.B'>, <class '__main__.A'>, <class 'object'>]
```

Looks correct. Now let's move on to multiple inheritance, which is more complex.

Multiple Inheritance

Let's look at a simple example of multiple inheritance:

```
class A: pass
class B(A): pass
class C(A): pass
class D(B, C): pass
```

The inheritance diagram looks like this:

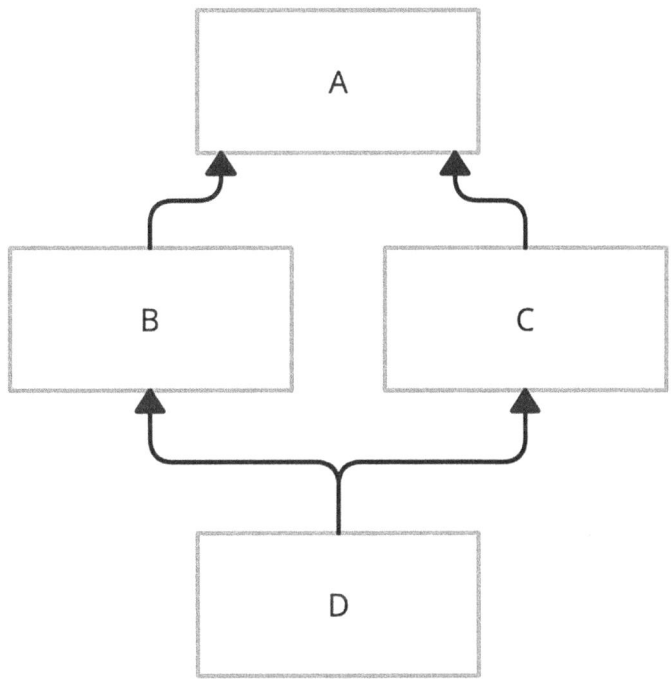

Multiple inheritance simple

Both L<A>, L<B>, and L<C> are as before:

```
L<B> = [B, A, object]
L<C> = [C, A, object]
```

Let's focus on L<D>:

L<D> = [D] + merge(L<B>, L<C>, [B, C])

Expand L<B> and L<C>:

L<D> = [D] + merge([B, A, object], [C, A, object], [B, C])

Start by looking for a good head. The head B exists as the head in the last list, so it's a good head. Remove B:

L<D> = [D, B] + merge([A, object], [C, A, object], [C])

Next, try A, but in the [C, A, object] list, A isn't the head. So we check C, which is a good head—remove C:

L<D> = [D, B, C] + merge([A, object], [A, object], [A, object])

Now A is the head in all lists, so take it:

L<D> = [D, B, C, A] + merge([object], [object], [object])

Finally, remove object:

L<D> = [D, B, C, A, object]

Let's verify:

```
>>> D.mro()
[<class '__main__.D'>, <class '__main__.B'>, <class '__main__.C'>, <class '__main__.A'>, <class 'object'>]
```

Matches our calculation.

In general, the order seems to be: move up first, then across sibling classes, then up again, until reaching `object`. But let's see a more complicated scenario.

A More Complex Inheritance Example

Here's the code:

```
class A: pass
class B: pass
class C(A, B): pass
```

CHAPTER 25   METHOD RESOLUTION ORDER AND C3 LINEARIZATION

```
class D(B): pass
class E(C): pass
class F(D, C): pass
class G(F, E): pass
```

That's a bit more complex:

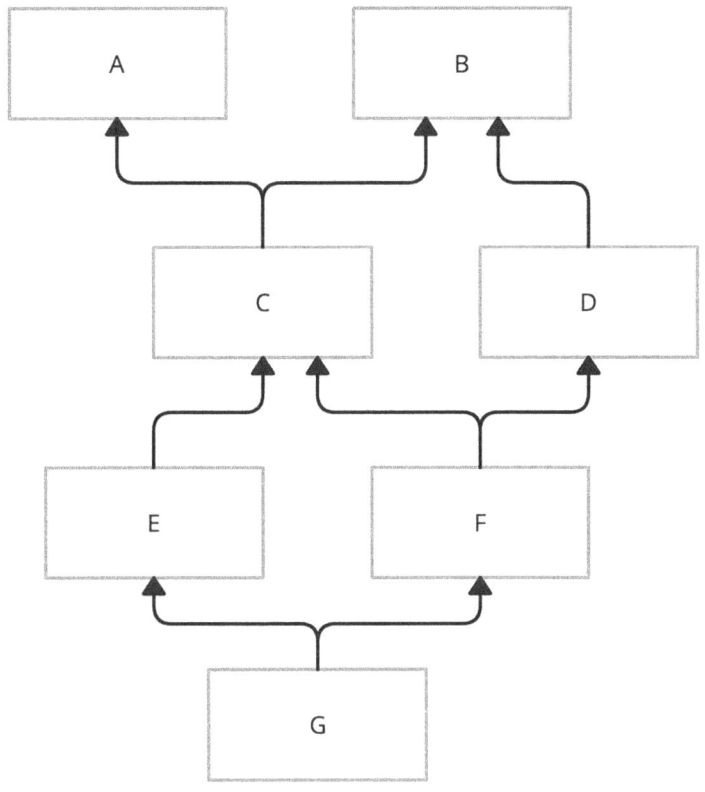

Multiple inheritance complex

Let's start step by step:

```
L<A> = [A, object]
L<B> = [B, object]
L<C> = [C, A, B, object]
```

Class D is still single inheritance:

```
L<D> = [D, B, object]
```

251

CHAPTER 25   METHOD RESOLUTION ORDER AND C3 LINEARIZATION

Now for L<E>:

L<E> = [E] + merge(L<C>, [C])

Expand L<C>:

L<E> = [E] + merge([C, A, B, object], [C])

C is a good head; remove it:

L<E> = [E, C] + merge([A, B, object])

Only one list remains:

L<E> = [E, C, A, B, object]

Now, L<F>:

L<F> = [F] + merge(L<D>, L<C>, [D, C])

Expand L<D> and L<C>:

L<F> = [F] + merge([D, B, object], [C, A, B, object], [D, C])

D is a good head; remove it:

L<F> = [F, D] + merge([B, object], [C, A, B, object], [C])

B can't be selected yet since in [C, A, B, object] it's not the head. Try C, which is a good head; remove it:

L<F> = [F, D, C] + merge([B, object], [A, B, object])

Still, B isn't a good head yet, but A is, so remove it:

L<F> = [F, D, C, A] + merge([B, object], [B, object])

Now, both lists start with B, so finalize:

L<F> = [F, D, C, A, B, object]

Lastly, for L<G>:

L<G> = [G] + merge(L<F>, L<E>, [F, E])

252

Expand L<F> and L<E>:

L<G> = [G] + merge([F, D, C, A, B, object], [E, C, A, B, object], [F, E])

Let's fast-forward a bit for brevity:

L<G> = [G, F] + merge([D, C, A, B, object], [E, C, A, B, object], [E])
L<G> = [G, F, D] + merge([C, A, B, object], [E, C, A, B, object], [E])
L<G> = [G, F, D, E] + merge([C, A, B, object], [C, A, B, object])
L<G> = [G, F, D, E, C, A, B, object]

Again, the process is upward then across, repeating as needed. Let's check F and G with .mro():

```
>>> F.mro()
[<class '__main__.F'>, <class '__main__.D'>, <class '__main__.C'>, <class '__main__.A'>, <class '__main__.B'>, <class 'object'>]
>>> G.mro()
[<class '__main__.G'>, <class '__main__.F'>, <class '__main__.D'>, <class '__main__.E'>, <class '__main__.C'>, <class '__main__.A'>, <class '__main__.B'>, <class 'object'>]
```

Everything checks out.

While the steps may seem complicated, the overall procedure is consistent. Thanks to the C3 linearization algorithm, Python ensures a unique, deterministic, and orderly inheritance sequence, even in complex multiple inheritance scenarios.

What If It Can't Be Calculated?

Here's another example:

```
class A: pass
class B(A): pass
class C(A): pass
class D(B, C): pass
class E(C, D): pass
```

CHAPTER 25   METHOD RESOLUTION ORDER AND C3 LINEARIZATION

The inheritance structure is:

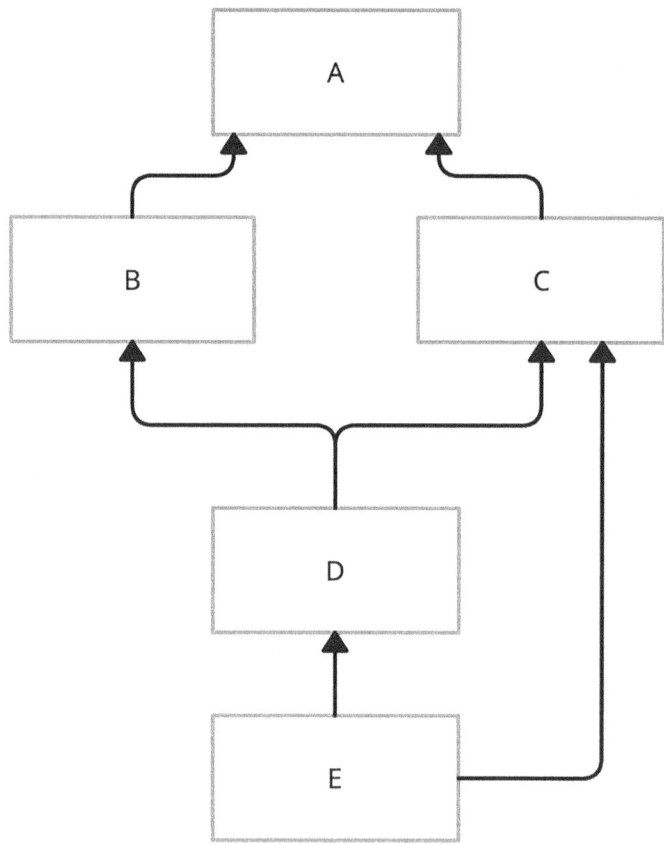

Multiple inheritance does not work

```
L<A> = [A, object]
L<B> = [B, A, object]
L<C> = [C, A, object]
```

Now for L<D>:

```
L<D> = [D] + merge(L<B>, L<C>, [B, C])
```

Expand L<B> and L<C>:

```
L<D> = [D] + merge([B, A, object], [C, A, object], [B, C])
```

Proceeding quickly:

```
L<D> = [D, B] + merge([A, object], [C, A, object], [C])
L<D> = [D, B, C] + merge([A, object], [A, object])
L<D> = [D, B, C, A, object]
```

Now for L<E>:

```
L<E> = [E] + merge(L<C>, L<D>, [C, D])
```

Expand L<C> and L<D>:

```
L<E> = [E] + merge([C, A, object], [D, B, C, A, object], [C, D])
```

Try to merge: C is not a good head; try D next, also not a good head; try the following C, still no luck. In short, there's no possible good head, so the inheritance hierarchy cannot satisfy the C3 linearization and merging rules. In this situation, Python will raise a TypeError:

```
TypeError: Cannot create a consistent method resolution
order (MRO) for bases C, D
```

"Not every romance ends with fond memories 🎵🎵."

Not all multiple inheritance hierarchies can produce a valid MRO. If you encounter this, consider if such complexity is truly necessary, or solve it by adjusting the inheritance order.

In the next chapter, we'll take a look at how the C3 algorithm is implemented inside CPython.

CHAPTER 26

The Role of super() in Multiple Inheritance

In the previous chapter, we gave a brief introduction to the C3 linearization algorithm. You can calculate it manually or use the built-in .mro() method on a class to inspect its Method Resolution Order (MRO). In this chapter, we'll follow the trail of the .mro() method and see how this algorithm is implemented in CPython.

Algorithm Implementation

Preparation Before Merging

Since every class has a .mro() method, we can trace the implementation via the type_methods member of PyType_Type:

```
// file: Objects/typeobject.c
static PyObject *
type_mro_impl(PyTypeObject *self)
{
    PyObject *seq;
    seq = mro_implementation(self);
    if (seq != NULL && !PyList_Check(seq)) {
        Py_SETREF(seq, PySequence_List(seq));
    }
    return seq;
}
```

CHAPTER 26   THE ROLE OF SUPER() IN MULTIPLE INHERITANCE

It looks like mro_implementation() returns a sequence, which is likely what we're looking for:

// file: Objects/typeobject.c

```
static PyObject *
mro_implementation(PyTypeObject *type)
{
    // ... omitted ...
    PyObject *bases = lookup_tp_bases(type);
    Py_ssize_t n = PyTuple_GET_SIZE(bases);
    for (Py_ssize_t i = 0; i < n; i++) {
        PyTypeObject *base = _PyType_CAST(PyTuple_GET_ITEM(bases, i));
        if (lookup_tp_mro(base) == NULL) {
            // ... error handling ...
        }
        assert(PyTuple_Check(lookup_tp_mro(base)));
    }
    // ... omitted ...
}
```

First, it retrieves the direct bases of the current class. For example:

```
class A: pass
class B: pass
class C(A, B): pass
```

For class C, its direct base classes are A and B. If you follow the implementation of lookup_tp_bases(), you'll see that the subsequent for loop uses the lookup_tp_mro() function to check whether each base class has an MRO. If not, an error is raised.

Let's look at how lookup_tp_bases() and lookup_tp_mro() are implemented:

// file: Objects/typeobject.c

```
static inline PyObject *
lookup_tp_bases(PyTypeObject *self)
{
    return self->tp_bases;
}
```

258

CHAPTER 26   THE ROLE OF SUPER() IN MULTIPLE INHERITANCE

```c
static inline PyObject *
lookup_tp_mro(PyTypeObject *self)
{
    return self->tp_mro;
}
```

Pretty straightforward: they simply access the tp_bases and tp_mro members. Moving further down:

```c
// file: Objects/typeobject.c

// ... omitted ...
if (n == 1) {
    PyTypeObject *base = _PyType_CAST(PyTuple_GET_ITEM(bases, 0));
    PyObject *base_mro = lookup_tp_mro(base);
    Py_ssize_t k = PyTuple_GET_SIZE(base_mro);
    PyObject *result = PyTuple_New(k + 1);
    if (result == NULL) {
        return NULL;
    }

    PyTuple_SET_ITEM(result, 0, Py_NewRef(type));
    for (Py_ssize_t i = 0; i < k; i++) {
        PyObject *cls = PyTuple_GET_ITEM(base_mro, i);
        PyTuple_SET_ITEM(result, i + 1, Py_NewRef(cls));
    }
    return result;
}
// ... omitted ...
```

When n == 1, meaning there is only one base class, the function follows a simpler flow: it creates an empty tuple, puts the current class at the first position, then iterates over the parent's MRO, appending each entry:

```c
// file: Objects/typeobject.c

// ... omitted ...
    PyObject **to_merge = PyMem_New(PyObject *, n + 1);
    // ... error handling ...
```

CHAPTER 26   THE ROLE OF SUPER() IN MULTIPLE INHERITANCE

```
    for (Py_ssize_t i = 0; i < n; i++) {
        PyTypeObject *base = _PyType_CAST(PyTuple_GET_ITEM(bases, i));
        to_merge[i] = lookup_tp_mro(base);
    }
    to_merge[n] = bases;

    PyObject *result = PyList_New(1);
    // ... error handling ...

    PyList_SET_ITEM(result, 0, Py_NewRef(type));
    if (pmerge(result, to_merge, n + 1) < 0) {
        Py_CLEAR(result);
    }
    PyMem_Free(to_merge);

    return result;
// ... omitted ...
```

Here, the for loop aggregates the MROs of all base classes into the to_merge array and adds the current class itself, preparing for the merging process.

Merging

The actual merging occurs in the pmerge() function:

```
// file: Objects/typeobject.c
static int
pmerge(PyObject *acc, PyObject **to_merge, Py_ssize_t to_merge_size)
{
    int res = 0;
    Py_ssize_t i, j, empty_cnt;
    int *remain;

    remain = PyMem_New(int, to_merge_size);

    // ... error handling ...
    for (i = 0; i < to_merge_size; i++)
        remain[i] = 0;
```

260

CHAPTER 26   THE ROLE OF SUPER() IN MULTIPLE INHERITANCE

```
again:
  empty_cnt = 0;
  for (i = 0; i < to_merge_size; i++) {
      PyObject *candidate;

      PyObject *cur_tuple = to_merge[i];

      if (remain[i] >= PyTuple_GET_SIZE(cur_tuple)) {
          empty_cnt++;
          continue;
      }

      candidate = PyTuple_GET_ITEM(cur_tuple, remain[i]);
      for (j = 0; j < to_merge_size; j++) {
          PyObject *j_lst = to_merge[j];
          if (tail_contains(j_lst, remain[j], candidate))
              goto skip;
      }
      res = PyList_Append(acc, candidate);
      if (res < 0)
          goto out;

      for (j = 0; j < to_merge_size; j++) {
          PyObject *j_lst = to_merge[j];
          if (remain[j] < PyTuple_GET_SIZE(j_lst) &&
              PyTuple_GET_ITEM(j_lst, remain[j]) == candidate) {
              remain[j]++;
          }
      }
      goto again;
   skip: ;
  }

  if (empty_cnt != to_merge_size) {
      set_mro_error(to_merge, to_merge_size, remain);
      res = -1;
  }
```

261

```
    out:
      PyMem_Free(remain);
      return res;
}
```

The implementation here isn't very hard to follow. It starts by allocating memory for an array called `remain` and initializing it all to 0. This array will contain the current index for each list that is being merged. The algorithm then selects the next best candidate and uses the `tail_contains()` function to check if this candidate appears later in any of the other lists. If so, it skips this candidate with `goto skip` and tries the next one. If a "good head" (a suitable candidate) is found, it is added to the result, and all pointers that point to this entry are advanced by one. This process repeats until all elements are placed or an error occurs.

If there are still elements left to process but no suitable candidate is found, an error is returned. This essentially reproduces the manual calculation we explored in the previous chapter. Next, let's discuss the `super()` function, which is also closely related to MRO.

Family Feuds

Let's start with a simple code example:

```python
class Animal:
    def sleep(self):
        print("Zzzzz")

class Cat(Animal):
    def sleep(self):
        super().sleep()

kitty = Cat()
kitty.sleep()
```

If you have experience in other object-oriented languages, you can probably guess that `super().sleep()` is calling the superclass's `.sleep()` method. Running the code indeed prints "Zzzzz". However, Python's `super()` function is not entirely the same as what you might have learned in other languages. Did you notice that it's `super()`, not just `super`? We'll revisit this point shortly. For now, let's look at how `super()` is implemented.

Super!

Let's check the bytecode instructions:

```
8            4 LOAD_GLOBAL             0 (super)
            14 LOAD_DEREF              1 (__class__)
            16 LOAD_FAST               0 (self)
            18 LOAD_SUPER_ATTR         5 (NULL|self + sleep)
            22 CALL                    0
            30 POP_TOP
            32 RETURN_CONST            0 (None)
```

Here we encounter a LOAD_SUPER_ATTR 5 instruction we haven't seen before. Tracing into this instruction, you'll see it invokes the global super() function via PyObject_Vectorcall(), creating an instance. In fact, super in Python is a global function, but, more accurately, it is itself a class:

```
>>> super
<class 'super'>
```

Just like int or str, it's a built-in class. Using what we've learned before, you can guess there's a type named PySuper_Type. We can follow the tp_init member of PySuper_Type to see what happens when an instance is created:

```
// file: Objects/typeobject.c
static int
super_init(PyObject *self, PyObject *args, PyObject *kwds)
{
    // ... omitted ...
    if (super_init_impl(self, type, obj) < 0) {
        return -1;
    }
    return 0;
}
```

CHAPTER 26   THE ROLE OF SUPER() IN MULTIPLE INHERITANCE

Let's go deeper into the actual implementation: super_init_impl():

```c
// file: Objects/typeobject.c

static inline int
super_init_impl(PyObject *self, PyTypeObject *type, PyObject *obj) {
    superobject *su = (superobject *)self;
    PyTypeObject *obj_type = NULL;
    if (type == NULL) {
        PyThreadState *tstate = _PyThreadState_GET();
        _PyInterpreterFrame *frame = _PyThreadState_GetFrame(tstate);
        if (frame == NULL) {
            PyErr_SetString(PyExc_RuntimeError,
                            "super(): no current frame");
            return -1;
        }
        int res = super_init_without_args(frame, frame->f_code,
        &type, &obj);

        if (res < 0) {
            return -1;
        }
    }

    // ... omitted ...
    Py_XSETREF(su->type, (PyTypeObject*)Py_NewRef(type));
    Py_XSETREF(su->obj, obj);
    Py_XSETREF(su->obj_type, obj_type);
    return 0;
}
```

If super() is called without arguments, control goes into the super_init_without_args() function and passes the current Frame and Code Object:

```c
// file: Objects/typeobject.c

static int
super_init_without_args(_PyInterpreterFrame *cframe, PyCodeObject *co,
                        PyTypeObject **type_p, PyObject **obj_p)
```

```
{
    // ... omitted ...
    PyTypeObject *type = NULL;
    int i = PyCode_GetFirstFree(co);
    for (; i < co->co_nlocalsplus; i++) {
        PyObject *name = PyTuple_GET_ITEM(co->co_localsplusnames, i);
        if (_PyUnicode_Equal(name, &_Py_ID(__class__))) {
            PyObject *cell = _PyFrame_GetLocalsArray(cframe)[i];
            // ... error handling ...
            type = (PyTypeObject *) PyCell_GET(cell);
            // ... error handling ...
            break;
        }
    }
    // ... omitted ...
    *type_p = type;
    *obj_p = firstarg;
    return 0;
}
```

This function retrieves the `__class__` variable from the Code Object, which points to the current class. So, in Python, when you call `super()` without arguments, it can still determine the current class and object from the current frame.

Whose Child Is It?

So in the previous example, inside the `Cat` class, does `super()` produce an instance of `Cat` or `Animal`? While from a result perspective it might seem like a superclass instance, in reality, it's neither. The `super()` function creates an instance of the `PySuper_Type` class, which acts as a proxy object with references to the current class and object. If you inspect the object created by `super()`, you'll see something like:

`<super: <class 'Cat'>, <Cat object>>`

CHAPTER 26   THE ROLE OF SUPER() IN MULTIPLE INHERITANCE

It's neither Cat nor Animal; it's the proxy object created by the super class. When you call a method on this proxy, such as super().sleep(), it triggers the tp_getattro member for PySuper_Type:

// file: Objects/typeobject.c

```
static PyObject *
super_getattro(PyObject *self, PyObject *name)
{
    superobject *su = (superobject *)self;

    if (PyUnicode_Check(name) &&
        PyUnicode_GET_LENGTH(name) == 9 &&
        _PyUnicode_Equal(name, &_Py_ID(__class__)))
        return PyObject_GenericGetAttr(self, name);

    return do_super_lookup(su, su->type, su->obj, su->obj_type, name, NULL);
}
```

Here, su is our proxy object. The function checks if we are accessing the __class__ attribute, for example, with super().__class__. If so, the generic PyObject_GenericGetAttr() function returns <class 'super'>. The length check for 9 is a small performance trick: since the length of '__class__' is 9, checking length is faster than comparing full strings.

If another attribute (like sleep) is being accessed, the function goes into do_super_lookup(). Before exploring this function, let me clarify the state of the su proxy object and its members:

- su is the proxy object itself.
- su->type is the class where super() was constructed. Since no parameter was given, Python infers this from the current frame, in this case, Cat.
- su->obj is the current instance, i.e., self.
- su->obj_type is the actual type of the current object, also Cat here.

CHAPTER 26   THE ROLE OF SUPER() IN MULTIPLE INHERITANCE

At this point, type and obj_type happen to be the same, but they can differ. See what happens if we add another level of inheritance:

```python
class Animal:
    def sleep(self):
        print("Zzzzz")

class Cat(Animal):
    def sleep(self):
        super().sleep()

class Kitty(Cat):
    pass

k = Kitty()
k.sleep()
```

When k.sleep() is called, the proxy object created by super() has the following state:

- su->type is the class where super() was called: Cat.
- su->obj is k, the instance.
- su->obj_type is the actual type of k, which is Kitty.

While here they seem the same, they may differ depending on the context. Now let's look at the do_super_lookup() function:

```c
// file: Objects/typeobject.c

static PyObject *
do_super_lookup(superobject *su, PyTypeObject *su_type, PyObject *su_obj,
                PyTypeObject *su_obj_type, PyObject *name, int *method)
{
    // ... omitted ...
    res = _super_lookup_descr(su_type, su_obj_type, name);
    // ... omitted ...
}
```

CHAPTER 26   THE ROLE OF SUPER() IN MULTIPLE INHERITANCE

This function makes use of the provided type and object information to resolve the method. If you pursue _super_lookup_descr():

```c
// file: Objects/typeobject.c
static PyObject *
_super_lookup_descr(PyTypeObject *su_type, PyTypeObject *su_obj_type,
PyObject *name)
{
    // ... omitted ...
    mro = lookup_tp_mro(su_obj_type);
    // ... omitted ...

    i++;

    // ... omitted ...
    do {
        PyObject *obj = PyTuple_GET_ITEM(mro, i);
        PyObject *dict = lookup_tp_dict(_PyType_CAST(obj));
        // ... omitted ...
        res = PyDict_GetItemWithError(dict, name);
        // ... omitted ...
        i++;
    } while (i < n);
}
```

It starts looking in the MRO of su->obj_type (in the previous example, Kitty), not from the class where super() was called (Cat). The important line is i++, meaning the search starts from the second element in the MRO, thus avoiding recursively retrieving the same method and causing an infinite loop.

For those who have used other programming languages, it may seem counterintuitive that the search starts from the type of the object itself rather than directly from the superclass. But why did Python design it this way?

CHAPTER 26   THE ROLE OF SUPER() IN MULTIPLE INHERITANCE

Solving Family Feuds

Multiple inheritance can cause the Diamond Problem. For example:

```
class Animal:
    def sleep(self):
        print("Zzzzz")

class Bird(Animal):
    def sleep(self):
        print("I can sleep standing up.")
        super().sleep()

class Fish(Animal):
    def sleep(self):
        print("I can sleep without closing my eyes.")
        super().sleep()

class Cat(Bird, Fish):
    def sleep(self):
        print("Purr purr~")
        super().sleep()

kitty = Cat()
kitty.sleep() # What gets printed?
```

What do you think this prints? The tricky part is figuring out who `super().sleep()` refers to in the `Bird` class. If you're thinking in terms of other languages, you might expect it to refer to `Animal.sleep()`.

Let's consider the state of `super()` inside the `Bird` class:

- `su` is the proxy object.
- `su->type` is contextually inferred as the `Bird` class.
- `su->obj` is the current instance, in this case, `kitty`.
- `su->obj_type` is the actual class of the object, which is `Cat`.

From the source code, we see that Python begins searching the MRO of su->obj_type (i.e., Cat), not the MRO of Bird. The MRO of Cat is Cat -> Bird -> Fish -> Animal. Python will find the Bird class, then proceed to the next in line, which is Fish. As a result, the output will be:

```
Purr purr~
I can sleep standing up.
I can sleep without closing my eyes.
Zzzzz
```

If you want a concise explanation of Python's super(): it finds the current class's MRO and starts searching from the class after the current one in the MRO.

If the search simply moved from Bird directly to the superclass Animal, then Fish.sleep() would be skipped, deviating from the intended inheritance order specified by the MRO. Python uses the C3 linearization algorithm to get the correct MRO and, with the design of super(), resolves the complications of multiple inheritance.

- **Diamond problem**: http://en.wikipedia.org/wiki/Diamond_problem

Specifying the Superclass

In the above examples, super() was always called without arguments, but in fact, super() can take parameters:

```python
class Animal:
    def sleep(self):
        print("Zzzzz")

class Cat(Animal):
    def sleep(self):
        super(Cat, self).sleep()
```

This explicitly sets su->type to Cat and su->obj to self, so Python doesn't need to infer from the current frame. However, in most cases, the parameterless super() is sufficient and more concise.

Quick Quiz: Who Am I?

Here's a simple question for you. What does this code print?

```python
class Person:
    name = "Walter White"
    def say_my_name(self):
        print(self.name)

class Heisenberg(Person):
    name = "Heisenberg"
    def say_my_name(self):
        super().say_my_name()

heisenberg = Heisenberg()
heisenberg.say_my_name()  # What will be printed?
```

You might expect `"Walter White"` from the `Person` class to be printed, but the result is `"Heisenberg"`.

Why? Think about who `self` points to inside the proxy object created by `super()`, and the answer will be clear. :)

CHAPTER 27

The Generator Object and the Yield Statement

Generators are a fascinating feature in Python. They allow you to produce values one at a time, rather than generating all values at once. This trait makes generators particularly useful when handling large datasets or infinite data collections. There are several ways to create a generator in Python, and one common approach is to use the `yield` keyword to define a generator function. For example:

```
def three_numbers():
    yield 520
    yield 1450
    yield 9527

nums = three_numbers()
```

When you inspect `nums`, you'll find it is a generator object:

```
>>> type(nums)
<class 'generator'>
```

You can then use the built-in `next()` function to retrieve the next value, until there are no more values to yield. In this chapter, we'll take a look at how generators are implemented in Python.

CHAPTER 27   THE GENERATOR OBJECT AND THE YIELD STATEMENT

The Generator Class

Let's first examine the bytecode of the above code, starting with the upper section:

```
0            0 RESUME                   0

1            2 LOAD_CONST               0 (<code object three_numbers>)
             4 MAKE_FUNCTION            0
             6 STORE_NAME               0 (three_numbers)

7            8 PUSH_NULL
            10 LOAD_NAME                0 (three_numbers)
            12 CALL                     0
            20 STORE_NAME               1 (nums)
            22 RETURN_CONST             1 (None)
```

We have previously seen these instructions—they are quite similar to defining a regular function. However, the lower portion differs:

```
1            0 RETURN_GENERATOR
             2 POP_TOP
             4 RESUME                   0

2            6 LOAD_CONST               1 (520)
             8 YIELD_VALUE              1
            10 RESUME                   1
            12 POP_TOP

3           14 LOAD_CONST               2 (1450)
            16 YIELD_VALUE              1
            18 RESUME                   1
            20 POP_TOP

4           22 LOAD_CONST               3 (9527)
            24 YIELD_VALUE              1
            26 RESUME                   1
            28 POP_TOP
            30 RETURN_CONST             0 (None)
```

```
    >>   32 CALL_INTRINSIC_1        3 (INTRINSIC_STOPITERATION_ERROR)
         34 RERAISE                 1
ExceptionTable:
  4 to 30 -> 32 [0] lasti
```

Wow! There are several unfamiliar instructions, and the execution seems to jump around. To keep things concise, let's summarize first:

- The instruction RETURN_GENERATOR is fairly self-explanatory—it creates a generator object.

- YIELD_VALUE sends the current value from the generator back to the caller and suspends the function's execution. For example, in the above example, `yield 1` yields the value 1 to the caller, and the function pauses at that point.

- RESUME resumes the suspended generator and continues execution from the point where the YIELD_VALUE instruction paused, usually triggered by calling the built-in next() function or the generator's .send() method.

Let's take a look at the RETURN_GENERATOR instruction first:

```c
// file: Python/bytecodes.c

inst(RETURN_GENERATOR, (--)) {
    // ... omitted ...
    PyFunctionObject *func = (PyFunctionObject *)frame->f_funcobj;
    PyGenObject *gen = (PyGenObject *)_Py_MakeCoro(func);
    // ... omitted ...
}
```

This instruction fetches the function object from the stack, then uses the _Py_MakeCoro() function to build a generator object (where Coro is short for Coroutine). Inside _Py_MakeCoro(), the make_gen() function is called to actually create the generator object:

```c
// file: Objects/genobject.c

static PyObject *
make_gen(PyTypeObject *type, PyFunctionObject *func)
```

CHAPTER 27   THE GENERATOR OBJECT AND THE YIELD STATEMENT

```
{
    PyCodeObject *code = (PyCodeObject *)func->func_code;
    int slots = _PyFrame_NumSlotsForCodeObject(code);
    PyGenObject *gen = PyObject_GC_NewVar(PyGenObject, type, slots);
    if (gen == NULL) {
        return NULL;
    }
    gen->gi_frame_state = FRAME_CLEARED;
    gen->gi_weakreflist = NULL;
    gen->gi_exc_state.exc_value = NULL;
    gen->gi_exc_state.previous_item = NULL;
    assert(func->func_name != NULL);
    gen->gi_name = Py_NewRef(func->func_name);
    assert(func->func_qualname != NULL);
    gen->gi_qualname = Py_NewRef(func->func_qualname);
    _PyObject_GC_TRACK(gen);
    return (PyObject *)gen;
}
```

To put it simply, this process converts a function object into a generator. However, this would be too much of an oversimplification. Here, the function first calculates how much space the object requires and then uses PyObject_GC_NewVar() to allocate a generator object. The generator can have several states:

// file: Include/internal/pycore_frame.h

```
typedef enum _framestate {
    FRAME_CREATED = -2,
    FRAME_SUSPENDED = -1,
    FRAME_EXECUTING = 0,
    FRAME_COMPLETED = 1,
    FRAME_CLEARED = 4
} PyFrameState;
```

A newly created generator has the state FRAME_CLEARED, meaning it hasn't been executed yet.

CHAPTER 27   THE GENERATOR OBJECT AND THE YIELD STATEMENT

That said, you may have heard that generators are supposed to use less memory. While this is generally true, you may notice here that generators do need memory, and sometimes more, since they must store various states. The main benefit of generators is their "lazy evaluation" property—they only generate the next value when it's needed, rather than all values at once. For large or even infinite containers, this can indeed save memory since it avoids expanding all items at once, but for small collections, generators might actually use more memory than a standard list or tuple due to the overhead of maintaining state.

Let's see what the `PyGenObject` structure looks like:

```
// file: Include/cpython/genobject.h
```

```
typedef struct {
    _PyGenObject_HEAD(gi)
} PyGenObject;
```

After macro expansion, it becomes:

```
typedef struct {
    PyObject ob_base;
    PyObject *gi_weakreflist;
    PyObject *gi_name;
    PyObject *gi_qualname;

    _PyErr_StackItem gi_exc_state;
    PyObject *gi_origin_or_finalizer;

    char gi_hooks_inited;
    char gi_closed;
    char gi_running_async;

    int8_t gi_frame_state;

    PyObject *gi_iframe[1];
} PyGenObject;
```

Here, `gi_name` and `gi_qualname` are the generator's name fields, `gi_frame_state` indicates the current execution state, and `gi_exc_state` is for exception handling (which we'll clarify with examples soon). The `gi_iframe[1]` at the end—this flexible array member—is a pattern we've encountered before.

CHAPTER 27   THE GENERATOR OBJECT AND THE YIELD STATEMENT

yield, Please!

In the bytecode listing above, notice the instruction YIELD_VALUE 1. As the name implies, this corresponds to the yield keyword. Let's see what it does:

// file: Python/bytecodes.c

```
inst(YIELD_VALUE, (retval -- unused)) {
    assert(frame != &entry_frame);
    PyGenObject *gen = _PyFrame_GetGenerator(frame);
    gen->gi_frame_state = FRAME_SUSPENDED;
    _PyFrame_SetStackPointer(frame, stack_pointer - 1);
    tstate->exc_info = gen->gi_exc_state.previous_item;
    gen->gi_exc_state.previous_item = NULL;
    _Py_LeaveRecursiveCallPy(tstate);
    _PyInterpreterFrame *gen_frame = frame;
    frame = cframe.current_frame = frame->previous;
    gen_frame->previous = NULL;
    _PyFrame_StackPush(frame, retval);
    goto resume_frame;
}
```

What happens here is that the generator object associated with the current Frame is retrieved. Its state is set to suspended (FRAME_SUSPENDED), because yield returns a value, so the stack pointer needs adjusting. In between, some exception-handling takes place (to be discussed in detail soon). Lastly, _PyFrame_StackPush(frame, retval) places the return value on the previous Frame, i.e., the Frame of the caller. As described earlier, the YIELD_VALUE instruction yields the value back to the caller and suspends the function's execution.

Let's revisit these two lines, which handle exceptions:

```
tstate->exc_info = gen->gi_exc_state.previous_item;
gen->gi_exc_state.previous_item = NULL;
```

These lines transfer the exception state to ensure exceptions are appropriately handled. What does this mean? Here's an example:

CHAPTER 27 THE GENERATOR OBJECT AND THE YIELD STATEMENT

```python
def simple_generator():
    try:
        yield 100
        raise ValueError("Hey Hey Hey")
    except:
        yield "Hey"
gen = simple_generator()
print(next(gen))   # Prints 100
print(next(gen))   # What does this print?
```

The first call to next() prints 100 as expected. Despite expectations that the generator is now exhausted, a second call to next() actually prints "Hey", which arises from the yield inside the except block. What's going on?

On the first next(), the generator starts, encounters yield 100, suspends execution, and returns 100. At this moment, the generator is paused (FRAME_SUSPENDED) and hasn't yet reached the raise statement. When next() is called a second time, execution resumes where it left off. The raise ValueError("Hey Hey Hey") triggers an exception, which is caught by the generator's except block. Inside this block, another yield outputs "Hey", and execution suspends again.

The generator stores the exception state in previous_item, allowing correct exception handling when the generator resumes.

Next, Please!

To obtain the next value from a generator, you can use Python's built-in next() function—but how is this actually implemented?

```c
// file: Python/bltinmodule.c

static PyObject *
builtin_next_impl(PyObject *module, PyObject *iterator,
                  PyObject *default_value)
{
    PyObject *res;

    // ... error handling ...
```

279

```
    res = (*Py_TYPE(iterator)->tp_iternext)(iterator);
    if (res != NULL) {
        return res;
    } else if (default_value != NULL) {
        if (PyErr_Occurred()) {
            if(!PyErr_ExceptionMatches(PyExc_StopIteration))
                return NULL;
            PyErr_Clear();
        }
        return Py_NewRef(default_value);
    } else if (PyErr_Occurred()) {
        return NULL;
    } else {
        PyErr_SetNone(PyExc_StopIteration);
        return NULL;
    }
}
```

This function looks up the `tp_iternext` slot. Let's follow it to the definition for PyGen_Type:

// file: Objects/genobject.c

```
static PyObject *
gen_iternext(PyGenObject *gen)
{
    PyObject *result;
    assert(PyGen_CheckExact(gen) || PyCoro_CheckExact(gen));
    if (gen_send_ex2(gen, NULL, &result, 0, 0) == PYGEN_RETURN) {
        if (result != Py_None) {
            _PyGen_SetStopIterationValue(result);
        }
        Py_CLEAR(result);
    }
    return result;
}
```

The real focus here is on the gen_send_ex2() function, but before going further, let's look at this check:

```
if (result != Py_None) {
    _PyGen_SetStopIterationValue(result);
}
```

This may seem counterintuitive: Why is _PyGen_SetStopIterationValue() called when result is not Py_None? Consider the outer if condition:

```
if (gen_send_ex2(gen, NULL, &result, 0, 0) == PYGEN_RETURN) {
    // ... omitted ...
}
```

The gen_send_ex2 function executes the generator's Frame. If execution completes, it returns PYGEN_RETURN, and result contains the returned value.

Normally, you wouldn't explicitly write a return in a generator—it just raises StopIteration internally when exhausted. But if you do write an explicit return statement inside a generator, such as:

```
def simple_gen():
    yield 100
    return 9999
```

During the call to gen_send_ex2(), result is set to 9999. If you try this in the REPL:

```
>>> s = simple_gen()
>>> next(s)
100
```

The first call prints 100 as expected. Now, the generator should be exhausted, and another call to next(s) raises an exception, but notice the result:

```
>>> next(s)
Traceback (most recent call last):
  File "<stdin>", line 1, in <module>
StopIteration: 9999
```

The StopIteration exception includes the value 9999. That's exactly what _PyGen_SetStopIterationValue(result) accomplishes.

So, what is gen_send_ex2() mainly responsible for?

- It handles the generator's behavior based on its current state—such as FRAME_CREATED, FRAME_EXECUTING, or FRAME_COMPLETED.
- When execution begins, it sets the state to FRAME_EXECUTING and uses _PyEval_EvalFrame() to execute the generator's Frame.

It must be said—using generators is quite straightforward, but the implementation under the hood is rather complex. It can be quite dizzying to follow…orz.

CHAPTER 28

How Iterators Work Internally

Iterators are widely used in Python. They let us traverse various "containers" without having to use a conventional for loop, as is common in other programming languages. These so-called containers are not limited to lists—dictionaries, strings, and ranges can all be iterated over in a similar way. In this chapter, we'll explore how iterators are implemented.

The Iterator Protocol

Python features three related concepts: iteration, iterable, and iterator. Let's do a quick recap:

- **Iteration**: A noun referring to the process of looping through all the elements inside an object.
- **Iterable**: An adjective describing an object that can be iterated over; in this chapter, "iterable object" refers to this.
- **Iterator**: A noun representing a container-like object that lets us traverse its elements using specific methods.

According to Python's definition, any object that implements the "iterator protocol" qualifies as an iterator. The iterator protocol is straightforward: as long as an object implements the __iter__() and __next__() magic methods, it is considered an iterator. This is the Python-level definition; next, we'll look at how it is implemented in CPython.

To create an iterator in Python, you can use the built-in function iter():

```
iter([9, 5, 2, 7])
```

CHAPTER 28 HOW ITERATORS WORK INTERNALLY

Let's start by looking at the implementation of this function in the source code:

// file: Python/clinic/bltinmodule.c.h

```c
static PyObject *
builtin_iter(PyObject *module, PyObject *const *args, Py_ssize_t nargs)
{
    PyObject *return_value = NULL;
    PyObject *object;
    PyObject *sentinel = NULL;

    if (!_PyArg_CheckPositional("iter", nargs, 1, 2)) {
        goto exit;
    }
    object = args[0];
    if (nargs < 2) {
        goto skip_optional;
    }
    sentinel = args[1];
skip_optional:
    return_value = builtin_iter_impl(module, object, sentinel);

exit:
    return return_value;
}
```

It appears that the actual implementation resides in the builtin_iter_impl() function:

// file: Python/bltinmodule.c

```c
static PyObject *
builtin_iter_impl(PyObject *module, PyObject *object, PyObject *sentinel)
{
    if (sentinel == NULL)
        return PyObject_GetIter(object);
    if (!PyCallable_Check(object)) {
        PyErr_SetString(PyExc_TypeError,
                        "iter(object, sentinel): object must be callable");
```

```
        return NULL;
    }
    return PyCallIter_New(object, sentinel);
}
```

This is fairly straightforward: if a "sentinel" is not provided, it directly calls PyObject_GetIter(); otherwise, it calls PyCallIter_New(). But what exactly does the sentinel mean here?

Halt! Password, Please!

The sentinel means that if the iterator returns a value equal to the sentinel, iteration should stop. Let's look at an example:

```python
from random import randint

numbers = iter(lambda: randint(1, 10), 7)

for num in numbers:
    print(num)
```

Since I've passed 7 as the second argument to iter(), the above code will continually generate random numbers between 1 and 10 until the number 7 is produced. If no sentinel is provided, the iteration would continue indefinitely.

Let's start by looking at the simpler PyCallIter_New() function:

```c
// file: Objects/iterobject.c

PyObject *
PyCallIter_New(PyObject *callable, PyObject *sentinel)
{
    calliterobject *it;
    it = PyObject_GC_New(calliterobject, &PyCallIter_Type);
    if (it == NULL)
        return NULL;
    it->it_callable = Py_NewRef(callable);
    it->it_sentinel = Py_NewRef(sentinel);
    _PyObject_GC_TRACK(it);
    return (PyObject *)it;
}
```

Here, an object of structure type `calliterobject` is created to store the iterator's information:

```
// file: Objects/iterobject.c
typedef struct {
    PyObject_HEAD
    PyObject *it_callable;
    PyObject *it_sentinel;
} calliterobject;
```

This structure is fairly simple. Let's also look at the structure of PyCallIter_Type:

```
// file: Objects/iterobject.c
PyTypeObject PyCallIter_Type = {
    PyVarObject_HEAD_INIT(&PyType_Type, 0)
    "callable_iterator",                    /* tp_name */
    sizeof(calliterobject),                 /* tp_basicsize */
    0,                                      /* tp_itemsize */
    // ... omitted ...
    0,                                      /* tp_richcompare */
    0,                                      /* tp_weaklistoffset */
    PyObject_SelfIter,                      /* tp_iter */
    (iternextfunc)calliter_iternext,        /* tp_iternext */
    calliter_methods,                       /* tp_methods */
};
```

The key points here are `tp_iter` and `tp_iternext`. The `tp_iter` member returns the iterator object itself, and `tp_iternext` is responsible for returning the next element. These directly correspond to the __iter__ and __next__ methods mentioned earlier in the iterator protocol.

```
// file: Objects/object.c
PyObject *
PyObject_SelfIter(PyObject *obj)
{
    return Py_NewRef(obj);
}
```

CHAPTER 28   HOW ITERATORS WORK INTERNALLY

This simply returns the iterator object itself. Now let's look at the calliter_iternext() function:

```
// file: Objects/iterobject.c

static PyObject *
calliter_iternext(calliterobject *it)
{
    PyObject *result;
    // ... error handling ...

    result = _PyObject_CallNoArgs(it->it_callable);
    if (result != NULL && it->it_sentinel != NULL){
        int ok;

        ok = PyObject_RichCompareBool(it->it_sentinel, result, Py_EQ);
        if (ok == 0) {
            return result;
        }

        if (ok > 0) {
            Py_CLEAR(it->it_callable);
            Py_CLEAR(it->it_sentinel);
        }
    }
    else if (PyErr_ExceptionMatches(PyExc_StopIteration)) {
        PyErr_Clear();
        Py_CLEAR(it->it_callable);
        Py_CLEAR(it->it_sentinel);
    }
    Py_XDECREF(result);
    return NULL;
}
```

In the middle, it uses the PyObject_RichCompareBool() function to check if the returned value equals the sentinel. If it does, iteration stops and both it_callable and it_sentinel are cleared. Otherwise, it returns the element.

287

CHAPTER 28 HOW ITERATORS WORK INTERNALLY

Another noteworthy detail: if the iterator raises StopIteration, PyErr_Clear() is called to clear the error status, and iteration stops. This is why, when we fetch the next item using next() and there is nothing left, StopIteration is thrown. But within a for loop or list comprehension, this error is internally handled and does not propagate.

This process is fairly easy to understand. Next, let's examine another function: PyObject_GetIter(), which is a bit more complex:

```c
// file: Objects/abstract.c

PyObject *
PyObject_GetIter(PyObject *o)
{
    PyTypeObject *t = Py_TYPE(o);
    getiterfunc f;

    f = t->tp_iter;
    if (f == NULL) {
        if (PySequence_Check(o))
            return PySeqIter_New(o);
        return type_error("'%.200s' object is not iterable", o);
    }
    else {
        PyObject *res = (*f)(o);
        if (res != NULL && !PyIter_Check(res)) {
            PyErr_Format(PyExc_TypeError,
                         "iter() returned non-iterator "
                         "of type '%.100s'",
                         Py_TYPE(res)->tp_name);
            Py_SETREF(res, NULL);
        }
        return res;
    }
}
```

It first checks whether the tp_iter member is implemented. If so, it calls it directly:

```c
PyObject *res = (*f)(o);
```

CHAPTER 28   HOW ITERATORS WORK INTERNALLY

This line does exactly that. There are some interesting details here, but let's come back to them.

If the `tp_iter` member is not implemented, it checks whether the object is a sequence. If it is, it creates a general-purpose sequence iterator using PySeqIter_New(). Let's look at its implementation:

```
// file: Objects/iterobject.c

PyObject *
PySeqIter_New(PyObject *seq)
{
    seqiterobject *it;

    if (!PySequence_Check(seq)) {
        PyErr_BadInternalCall();
        return NULL;
    }
    it = PyObject_GC_New(seqiterobject, &PySeqIter_Type);
    if (it == NULL)
        return NULL;
    it->it_index = 0;
    it->it_seq = Py_NewRef(seq);
    _PyObject_GC_TRACK(it);
    return (PyObject *)it;
}
```

This function creates a `seqiterobject` structure, defined as follows:

```
// file: Objects/iterobject.c

typedef struct {
    PyObject_HEAD
    Py_ssize_t it_index;
    PyObject *it_seq;
} seqiterobject;
```

CHAPTER 28   HOW ITERATORS WORK INTERNALLY

it_index keeps track of the current position during iteration, while it_seq points to the sequence object being iterated. Let's also check the structure for PySeqIter_Type:

```
// file: Objects/iterobject.c

PyTypeObject PySeqIter_Type = {
    PyVarObject_HEAD_INIT(&PyType_Type, 0)
    "iterator",                             /* tp_name */
    sizeof(seqiterobject),                  /* tp_basicsize */
    // ... omitted ...
    0,                                      /* tp_richcompare */
    0,                                      /* tp_weaklistoffset */
    PyObject_SelfIter,                      /* tp_iter */
    iter_iternext,                          /* tp_iternext */
    seqiter_methods,                        /* tp_methods */
    0,                                      /* tp_members */
};
```

Here, the tp_iter member also just returns itself. Let's look at the implementation for tp_iternext:

```
// file: Objects/iterobject.c

static PyObject *
iter_iternext(PyObject *iterator)
{
    seqiterobject *it;
    PyObject *seq;
    PyObject *result;

    assert(PySeqIter_Check(iterator));
    it = (seqiterobject *)iterator;
    seq = it->it_seq;
    // ... error handling ...

    result = PySequence_GetItem(seq, it->it_index);
    if (result != NULL) {
        it->it_index++;
        return result;
    }
```

```
    if (PyErr_ExceptionMatches(PyExc_IndexError) ||
        PyErr_ExceptionMatches(PyExc_StopIteration))
    {
        PyErr_Clear();
        it->it_seq = NULL;
        Py_DECREF(seq);
    }
    return NULL;
}
```

The PySequence_GetItem() function retrieves the element at the index specified by it_index. If it is successful, the result is returned and the index is incremented. If an IndexError or StopIteration occurs, PyErr_Clear() is called and iteration stops, without raising an exception.

Different Types of Iterators?

When you pass different iterable objects to the iter() function, you'll receive different types of iterator objects. Let's take a look at the various iterator objects that can be produced:

```
>>> iter([])
<list_iterator object>

>>> iter(range(0))
<range_iterator object>

>>> iter({})
<dict_keyiterator object>

>>> iter('hello')
<str_ascii_iterator object>

>>> iter('Dragon Ball')
<str_iterator object>
```

CHAPTER 28   HOW ITERATORS WORK INTERNALLY

Why are there so many types? This is because different types of iterable objects have their own iterator implementations. In the PyObject_GetIter() function, this line:

```
PyObject *res = (*f)(o);
```

calls the implementation of the tp_iter member and passes the current iterable object to it. Different data types may have different implementations of tp_iter. For example, here is the implementation for lists:

```
// file: Objects/listobject.c
static PyObject *
list_iter(PyObject *seq)
{
    _PyListIterObject *it;

    // ... error handling ...
    it = PyObject_GC_New(_PyListIterObject, &PyListIter_Type);
    if (it == NULL)
        return NULL;
    it->it_index = 0;
    it->it_seq = (PyListObject *)Py_NewRef(seq);
    _PyObject_GC_TRACK(it);
    return (PyObject *)it;
}
```

This function creates an iterator object of type PyListIter_Type, whose tp_iternext is implemented as follows:

```
// file: Objects/listobject.c
static PyObject *
listiter_next(_PyListIterObject *it)
{
    PyListObject *seq;
    PyObject *item;

    // ... error handling ...
```

```
    if (it->it_index < PyList_GET_SIZE(seq)) {
        item = PyList_GET_ITEM(seq, it->it_index);
        ++it->it_index;
        return Py_NewRef(item);
    }

    it->it_seq = NULL;
    Py_DECREF(seq);
    return NULL;
}
```

The implementation of tp_iternext for lists is relatively simple. If the input is a string, the iterator created depends on whether the string contains only ASCII characters or uses other encodings. Dictionaries and ranges have their unique mechanisms as well. Therefore, different iterator objects are seen as above.

If you're interested, you can follow the same logic to trace the tp_iternext implementations of iterator objects produced by ranges, strings, and dictionaries. This will help you understand how different iterator objects work.

Both generators covered in the previous chapter and the iterators described here can be used with the next() function, but the implementation of iterators is much simpler. :)

CHAPTER 29

Understanding Descriptors in Python

Descriptors are a fascinating and important feature in Python. Many seemingly straightforward syntax elements are actually built upon descriptors, even though you might not realize that you are already using them. Descriptors allow us to perform additional actions behind the scenes when we read, set, or invoke attributes and methods on objects. Furthermore, they form the foundation for many functionalities that we now take for granted.

Descriptors are categorized into two types: data descriptors and non-data descriptors. The difference lies in which specific methods they implement. In this chapter, we'll explore how descriptors are implemented in CPython.

When Calling Methods

In CPython, when you want to retrieve an attribute from an object, the type's `tp_getattro` member determines how the attribute is fetched. In most cases, `tp_getattro` points to the `PyObject_GenericGetAttr()` function. Judging from its name, you can probably guess that this is a generic attribute accessor.

Let me give you an example:

```python
class Cat:
    race = "Feline"

    def __init__(self, name, age):
        self.name = name
        self.age = age

kitty = Cat("Kitty", 18)
print(kitty.name)
```

CHAPTER 29   UNDERSTANDING DESCRIPTORS IN PYTHON

What happens when the last line tries to print `kitty.name`? Or, to phrase it differently: How is this `.name` attribute actually found? Let's examine the bytecode:

```
              4 LOAD_BUILD_CLASS
              6 LOAD_CONST              0 (<code object Cat>)
              8 MAKE_FUNCTION           0
             10 LOAD_CONST              1 ('Cat')
             12 CALL                    2
             20 STORE_NAME              0 (Cat)

    9        22 PUSH_NULL
             24 LOAD_NAME               0 (Cat)
             26 LOAD_CONST              2 ('凯蒂')
             28 LOAD_CONST              3 (18)
             30 CALL                    2
             38 STORE_NAME              1 (kitty)

   10        40 PUSH_NULL
             42 LOAD_NAME               2 (print)
             44 LOAD_NAME               1 (kitty)
             46 LOAD_ATTR               6 (name)
             66 CALL                    1
             74 POP_TOP
             76 RETURN_CONST            4 (None)
```

Most of these instructions we've covered previously, so nothing unusual there. What stands out is that when reading the `.name` attribute, the LOAD_ATTR instruction is used. This instruction is responsible for fetching the `name` attribute from the `kitty` object. As discussed in earlier chapters, if we trace what this instruction does, it eventually leads to the _PyObject_GetMethod() function. This function spans several lines and contains a sequence of logic checks. Let's go through it step by step.

Attribute Lookup Process

```
// file: Objects/object.c

// ... omitted ...
PyTypeObject *tp = Py_TYPE(obj);
```

```
// ... omitted ...
PyObject *descr = _PyType_Lookup(tp, name);
descrgetfunc f = NULL;
if (descr != NULL) {
    Py_INCREF(descr);
    if (_PyType_HasFeature(Py_TYPE(descr), Py_TPFLAGS_METHOD_DESCRIPTOR)) {
        meth_found = 1;
    } else {
        f = Py_TYPE(descr)->tp_descr_get;
        if (f != NULL && PyDescr_IsData(descr)) {
            *method = f(descr, obj, (PyObject *)Py_TYPE(obj));
            Py_DECREF(descr);
            return 0;
        }
    }
}
// ... omitted ...
```

Py_TPFLAGS_METHOD_DESCRIPTOR is a flag used to mark whether an object has the "method descriptor" property. If it does, it's noted, and the lookup continues. We'll discuss method descriptors in more detail later.

Next, we focus on the line f = Py_TYPE(descr)->tp_descr_get. If the descriptor implements the tp_descr_get member and is a data descriptor, its function is called and its result returned—no further lookups are done. The function used to determine whether the descriptor is a data descriptor, PyDescr_IsData(), is straightforward:

```
// file: Objects/descrobject.c
int
PyDescr_IsData(PyObject *ob)
{
    return Py_TYPE(ob)->tp_descr_set != NULL;
}
```

CHAPTER 29   UNDERSTANDING DESCRIPTORS IN PYTHON

It simply checks if tp_descr_set has been implemented. If so, it is a data descriptor; if not, it's a non-data descriptor. This matches our conceptual understanding of data and non-data descriptors. The following section is a bit longer:

```c
// file: Objects/object.c
// ... omitted ...
PyObject *dict;

if ((tp->tp_flags & Py_TPFLAGS_MANAGED_DICT)) {
    PyDictOrValues* dorv_ptr = _PyObject_DictOrValuesPointer(obj);
    if (_PyDictOrValues_IsValues(*dorv_ptr)) {
        PyDictValues *values = _PyDictOrValues_GetValues(*dorv_ptr);
        PyObject *attr = _PyObject_GetInstanceAttribute(obj, values, name);
        if (attr != NULL) {
            *method = attr;
            Py_XDECREF(descr);
            return 0;
        }
        dict = NULL;
    }
    else {
        dict = dorv_ptr->dict;
    }
}
else {
    PyObject **dictptr = _PyObject_ComputedDictPointer(obj);
    if (dictptr != NULL) {
        dict = *dictptr;
    }
    else {
        dict = NULL;
    }
}
if (dict != NULL) {
    Py_INCREF(dict);
    PyObject *attr = PyDict_GetItemWithError(dict, name);
```

CHAPTER 29 UNDERSTANDING DESCRIPTORS IN PYTHON

```c
    if (attr != NULL) {
        *method = Py_NewRef(attr);
        Py_DECREF(dict);
        Py_XDECREF(descr);
        return 0;
    }
    Py_DECREF(dict);

    if (PyErr_Occurred()) {
        Py_XDECREF(descr);
        return 0;
    }
}
// ... omitted ...
```

Although this snippet looks complex, it's essentially doing one thing: it tries to find the `name` attribute in the instance's dictionary. If found, it returns it; if not, it continues the search. Moving on:

```c
// file: Objects/object.c

// ... omitted ...
if (meth_found) {
    *method = descr;
    return 1;
}
// ... omitted ...
```

Recall the earlier check for method descriptors? If found, the method descriptor is set to the `method` variable, and the search stops. Otherwise, lookup proceeds:

```c
// file: Objects/object.c

// ... omitted ...
if (f != NULL) {
    *method = f(descr, obj, (PyObject *)Py_TYPE(obj));
    Py_DECREF(descr);
    return 0;
}
// ... omitted ...
```

By this point, f represents a non-method, non-data descriptor—it is, in fact, a non-data descriptor. At this step, the __get__() method of the descriptor is called and its result returned. If the object is not even a descriptor:

```
// file: Objects/object.c
if (descr != NULL) {
    *method = descr;
    return 0;
}
// ... omitted ...
```

Here, descr is most likely the class attribute found by _PyType_Lookup(tp, name). In our earlier example, this would be the race attribute of the Cat class.

If nothing is found during the above process, the final step is straightforward:

```
// ... omitted ...
PyErr_Format(PyExc_AttributeError,
            "'%.100s' object has no attribute '%U'",
            tp->tp_name, name);

set_attribute_error_context(obj, name);
return 0;
// ... omitted ...
```

An AttributeError is raised—end of process!

Process Summary

Let me summarize the entire attribute lookup process and clarify some terminology:

- Descriptor (D)
- Data descriptor (DD)
- Non-data descriptor (NDD)
- Method descriptor (MD)

Process:

1. Check if the attribute is a D:
   - 1A. If it is, and it is a DD, then its __get__() method is called and its result returned.
   - 1B. If it is just an MD, note its presence and continue searching.
2. Search the object's __dict__ for the attribute:
   - 2A. If found, return it.
   - 2B. If not, proceed to step 4.
3. If step 1B found an MD, set it to the method variable and stop the search.
4. For a NDD found in step 1A, call its __get__() method and return the result.
5. If none of the above, assume it is a normal class attribute (not a D) and return it directly.
6. If still not found, raise AttributeError.

Method Descriptors

In Python, method descriptors are a class of descriptors that implement part of the descriptor protocol; in particular, they only implement the __get__() method. Therefore, they can also be considered a type of non-data descriptor.

How is a method descriptor defined in Python? It's actually quite simple, and you probably already know how. Here's an example:

```
class Cat:
  def meow(self):
    print("Meow Meow")
kitty = Cat()
```

CHAPTER 29 UNDERSTANDING DESCRIPTORS IN PYTHON

That's it. Wait, isn't that just a regular instance method? Yes, but it is a method descriptor. Let me demonstrate in the REPL:

```
>>> type(Cat.meow)
<class 'function'>
>>> hasattr(Cat.meow, '__get__')
True

>>> kitty = Cat()
>>> type(kitty.meow)
<class 'method'>
>>> hasattr(kitty.meow, '__get__')
True
```

See? Both functions and methods have a __get__() method—this is the defining feature of a method descriptor.

When a class function is accessed, its __get__() method is called, returning a bound method. This bound method automatically includes the instance (self) or class (cls) as the first argument. So writing the following two ways is equivalent:

```
>>> kitty.meow()
Meow Meow
>>> Cat.meow.__get__(kitty, Cat)()
Meow Meow
// file: Objects/funcobject.c
PyTypeObject PyFunction_Type = {
    PyVarObject_HEAD_INIT(&PyType_Type, 0)
    "function",
    sizeof(PyFunctionObject),
    // ... omitted ...
    0,                                          /* tp_dict */
    func_descr_get,                             /* tp_descr_get */
    0,                                          /* tp_descr_set */
    offsetof(PyFunctionObject, func_dict),      /* tp_dictoffset */
```

CHAPTER 29 UNDERSTANDING DESCRIPTORS IN PYTHON

```
    0,                            /* tp_init */
    0,                            /* tp_alloc */
    func_new,                     /* tp_new */
};
```

The implementation of its `tp_descr_get` member is as follows:

```
static PyObject *
func_descr_get(PyObject *func, PyObject *obj, PyObject *type)
{
    if (obj == Py_None || obj == NULL) {
        return Py_NewRef(func);
    }
    return PyMethod_New(func, obj);
}
```

If an instance is passed in, a bound method is returned; otherwise, the original function is returned. Whether the instance is our adorable `kitty` or the `Cat` class itself depends on how the method is called.

Reflecting on step 3 of our process summary: if the attribute is a method descriptor, it is set directly to the `method` variable, and the lookup stops. This is why, when accessing the `kitty.meow` attribute, if there is a `meow` method defined via `def`, it will correctly find the method.

In conclusion, descriptors are truly everywhere in Python. You are already using them, even if you aren't consciously aware of their presence.

CHAPTER 30

Exception Handling Internals in CPython

Computer programs might not make mistakes, but humans do—and often. Some are intentional, some accidental, and some entirely unforeseen. Regardless of the situation, we need a mechanism to handle these issues, and that's where exception handling comes in.

Most programming languages have similar constructs. In Python, exceptions are handled using the `try...except...` keywords. In this chapter, we'll look at the reality behind exception handling—specifically, how it's implemented in CPython.

Exception Handling

Let's start with a simple example:

```python
try:
    1 / 0  # This line will cause an error
    print("Hello World")
except Exception as e:
    print(f"Something went wrong! {e}")
```

When you run the code above, the division by zero (1/0) triggers a `ZeroDivisionError` exception, which is caught and handled in the `except` block. But how does this work? Let's inspect the bytecode generated for this code. Since it's a bit lengthy, we'll break it down in parts:

```
2             4 LOAD_CONST               0 (1)
              6 LOAD_CONST               1 (0)
              8 BINARY_OP               11 (/)
             12 POP_TOP
```

```
3           14 PUSH_NULL
            16 LOAD_NAME              0 (print)
            18 LOAD_CONST             2 ('Hello World')
            20 CALL                   1
            28 POP_TOP
            30 RETURN_CONST           4 (None)
      >>    32 PUSH_EXC_INFO
// ... omitted ...
```

This appears fairly straightforward, except for the PUSH_EXC_INFO instruction at the end—there's nothing else particularly new. The two lines in the try block correspond directly to bytecode instructions. Although we know that the BINARY_OP instruction for division will cause a runtime error, this is only determined during execution, not during compilation. Unless there is a syntax error, bytecode compilation simply generates instructions; whether an error occurs or not will only be known when the Python VM executes the bytecode.

Stacking Up

So, what does the PUSH_EXC_INFO instruction do? The name suggests it pushes exception information onto a stack. Let's check the source code:

// file: Python/bytecodes.c

```c
inst(PUSH_EXC_INFO, (new_exc -- prev_exc, new_exc)) {
    _PyErr_StackItem *exc_info = tstate->exc_info;
    if (exc_info->exc_value != NULL) {
        prev_exc = exc_info->exc_value;
    }
    else {
        prev_exc = Py_None;
    }
    assert(PyExceptionInstance_Check(new_exc));
    exc_info->exc_value = Py_NewRef(new_exc);
}
```

This instruction saves the new exception new_exc into the current thread's exception stack (exc_info->exc_value). If there was already an existing unhandled exception, it is taken out and stored in prev_exc for subsequent use.

Why do we need an exception stack? Because exception handling does not always resolve all issues: if an error occurs within an except block, it can propagate to another exception handler, and this process may repeat. Thus, having a stack is sensible. So, what is _PyErr_StackItem? Let's look at this structure:

```
// file: Include/cpython/pystate.h
typedef struct _err_stackitem {
    PyObject *exc_value;
    struct _err_stackitem *previous_item;
} _PyErr_StackItem;
```

Aside from the exc_value member we just saw, it also has a previous_item member pointing to the previous stack item. This allows for exception chaining, so exceptions can be processed layer by layer during handling.

Exception Table

Normally, we would continue examining the flow, but let's scroll to the bottom of the bytecode to see something new—the ExceptionTable:

```
ExceptionTable:
  4 to 28 -> 32 [0]
  32 to 40 -> 84 [1] lasti
  42 to 62 -> 74 [1] lasti
  74 to 82 -> 84 [1] lasti
```

We may not have seen this before, but its meaning is fairly easy to understand. For instance, 4 to 28 -> 32 [0] means that if any instruction from bytecode 4 to 28 throws an exception, execution will jump to instruction 32. Similarly, the other lines represent exception handling for other ranges. The indexes like 32 [0], 74 [1], and so on likely refer to different exception handlers. In the same try block, there may be multiple except blocks, so this points to which handler will process a given exception.

Entry Portals

Looking at the bytecode, instructions at positions 32 (PUSH_EXC_INFO), 74 (LOAD_CONST), and 84 (COPY) are preceded by a >> marker. Instruction 82 (RERAISE) also has this, but we'll return to that later. The >> marker designates an "entry portal"—for our example, it's the start of an exception handling block. This is not unique to try...except...; even if...else... can contain the >> marker. For example:

```
a = 100
if a > 0:
    print("Positive")
else:
    print("Negative")
```

The compiled bytecode looks like this:

```
// ... omitted ...
  2           6 LOAD_NAME                0 (a)
              8 LOAD_CONST               1 (0)
             10 COMPARE_OP              68 (>)
             14 POP_JUMP_IF_FALSE        9 (to 34)
// ... omitted ...
  5     >>   34 PUSH_NULL
             36 LOAD_NAME                1 (print)
             38 LOAD_CONST               3 ('Negative')
             40 CALL                     1
// ... omitted ...
```

Depending on the result of the test, execution "jumps" to different instructions. Our focus, however, is exception handling.

Exception Type Matching

Now, we know the BINARY_OP instruction can cause an exception at runtime. According to the ExceptionTable, execution will jump to instruction 32, push the exception onto the stack, and continue:

```
4           34 LOAD_NAME                1 (Exception)
            36 CHECK_EXC_MATCH
            38 POP_JUMP_IF_FALSE       21 (to 82)
            40 STORE_NAME               2 (e)
```

Entering the except block, let's focus on the CHECK_EXC_MATCH instruction:

```c
// file: Python/bytecodes.c
inst(CHECK_EXC_MATCH, (left, right -- left, b)) {
    assert(PyExceptionInstance_Check(left));
    if (check_except_type_valid(tstate, right) < 0) {
        DECREF_INPUTS();
        ERROR_IF(true, error);
    }

    int res = PyErr_GivenExceptionMatches(left, right);
    DECREF_INPUTS();
    b = res ? Py_True : Py_False;
}
```

Here, left is the caught exception instance—in our example, it would be a ZeroDivisionError object. right is the exception type you're trying to match—in our case, it's Exception. This instruction checks whether left is a subclass of (or matches) right. If yes, it returns Py_True; otherwise, it returns Py_False, corresponding to Python's True and False. Also, left remains on the stack for the next instruction.

Most textbooks (including my own) stress that you should catch specific exception types—i.e., prefer except ZeroDivisionError as e: instead of catching the generic Exception. I took a shortcut in this example and simply caught all exceptions, so here, left is the current exception value (ZeroDivisionError) and right is Exception. Matching these, b will be Py_True (Python's True).

But what do we do with this Boolean value? The next instruction, POP_JUMP_IF_FALSE 21, is self-explanatory:

```c
// file: Python/bytecodes.c
inst(POP_JUMP_IF_FALSE, (cond -- )) {
    if (Py_IsFalse(cond)) {
        JUMPBY(oparg);
    }
}
```

CHAPTER 30 EXCEPTION HANDLING INTERNALS IN CPYTHON

```
        else if (!Py_IsTrue(cond)) {
            int err = PyObject_IsTrue(cond);
            DECREF_INPUTS();
            if (err == 0) {
                JUMPBY(oparg);
            }
            else {
                ERROR_IF(err < 0, error);
            }
        }
    }
}
```

Since our computed value is False, we'd jump to the instruction indicated, which in this case is RERAISE 0. This re-raises the exception so that the next handler can attempt to handle it. However, since we actually get True, we proceed to the next instruction, which stores the exception instance (left) into the variable e.

Handling the Exception

Continuing:

```
  5          42 PUSH_NULL
             44 LOAD_NAME               0 (print)
             46 LOAD_CONST              3 ('Something went wrong! ')
             48 LOAD_NAME               2 (e)
             50 FORMAT_VALUE            0
             52 BUILD_STRING            2
             54 CALL                    1
             62 POP_TOP
             64 POP_EXCEPT
             66 LOAD_CONST              4 (None)
             68 STORE_NAME              2 (e)
             70 DELETE_NAME             2 (e)
             72 RETURN_CONST            4 (None)
    >>       74 LOAD_CONST              4 (None)
```

The upper part assembles the error message string. There's a new instruction here: POP_EXCEPT:

// file: Python/bytecodes.c

```
inst(POP_EXCEPT, (exc_value -- )) {
    _PyErr_StackItem *exc_info = tstate->exc_info;
    Py_XSETREF(exc_info->exc_value, exc_value);
}
```

This implementation is straightforward: it retrieves the current thread's exception stack and sets its `exc_value` to the processed exception. The `Py_XSETREF` macro assigns the new value and releases the old one. The net result is that the topmost exception is removed from the stack, making way for the next possible exception handler (if any).

That's about the entire flow for a `try...except...` block in Python. Not too complex—right? :)

Finally!

Now, let's add a `finally` block to the original example:

```python
try:
    1 / 0  # This line will cause an error
    print("Hello World")
except Exception as e:
    print(f"Something went wrong! {e}")
finally:
    print("Finally Finish! Python is Awesome!")
```

In Python, the `finally` block always executes, regardless of whether an exception occurred. Let's see how the bytecode changes. To keep it concise, I'll just show the parts that differ significantly:

```
  2           4 LOAD_CONST               0 (1)
              6 LOAD_CONST               1 (0)
              8 BINARY_OP               11 (/)
             12 POP_TOP

  3          14 PUSH_NULL
             16 LOAD_NAME                0 (print)
             18 LOAD_CONST               2 ('Hello World')
```

CHAPTER 30   EXCEPTION HANDLING INTERNALS IN CPYTHON

```
              20 CALL                    1
              28 POP_TOP

  7    >>    30 PUSH_NULL
              32 LOAD_NAME               0 (print)
              34 LOAD_CONST              5 ('Finally Finish! Python is
                                            Awesome!')
              36 CALL                    1
              44 POP_TOP
              46 RETURN_CONST            4 (None)
       >>    48 PUSH_EXC_INFO
```

The instructions are mostly the same, and the `finally` block appears in this sequence as well. However, there is now a >> marker preceding bytecode 30. This position is not referenced in the ExceptionTable, since the `finally` block always executes and does not require a jump based on exceptions.

Continuing:

```
  5           58 PUSH_NULL
              60 LOAD_NAME               0 (print)
              62 LOAD_CONST              3 ('Something went wrong! ')
              64 LOAD_NAME               2 (e)
              66 FORMAT_VALUE            0
              68 BUILD_STRING            2
              70 CALL                    1
              78 POP_TOP
              80 POP_EXCEPT
              82 LOAD_CONST              4 (None)
              84 STORE_NAME              2 (e)
              86 DELETE_NAME             2 (e)
              88 JUMP_BACKWARD          30 (to 30)
       >>    90 LOAD_CONST              4 (None)
```

The only new instruction here is `JUMP_BACKWARD`, which jumps back to a specific bytecode position—in this case, to instruction 30, which is the start of the `finally` block. This ensures that, regardless of whether an exception occurs, the `finally` block is always executed.

Index

A

Abstract Syntax Tree (AST), 26, 27, 118
Animal.sleep(), 269
.append()method, 141
AST, *see* Abstract Syntax Tree (AST)
AttributeError, 300, 301

B

b.cpython-312.pyc, 27
BINARY_OP instruction, 306, 308
BINARY_SUBSCR instruction, 39
breakpoint set--name main, 112
__build_class__()function, 225, 226
builtin___build_class__()function, 29
BuiltinImporter, 70, 71
builtin_iter_impl()function, 284
BUILTINS(), 210
__builtins__variable, 224
Built-in type
    build and run, 54–55
    create new type, 49
    define methods, 50–51
    parameterized initialization, 56–58
    PyKitty_Type, 49, 51–53, 57
Bytecode, 27, 29, 73, 75, 91, 121–131

C

calliter_iternext()function, 287
calliterobject, 286
__call__method, 30, 196

Cat class, 25, 30, 237, 265, 266, 269, 270
Cell object, 215
    cell_contents attribute, 222
    co_cellvars, 220
    hey()function, 216
    hi()function, 216
    localsplus array, 217
    PyCell_New()function, 216
    PyCellObject, 215, 217
    structure, cell, 215
ChatGPT, 4
CHECK_EXC_MATCHinstruction, 309
Classes, 223
    BUILDINS(), 224, 225
    Cat class, 225
    class statement, 223
    create instances, 223
    inheritance, 233, 235, 236
        Animal class, 235
        __build_class__()function, 235
        create class, 234–236
        .hi()method, 236
    LOAD_BUILD_CLASS, 224, 225
    metaclass, 227–232
    namespace, 229
    as objects, 223
    PyClassObject, 223
    PyType_Type, 228, 231, 232
    update_bases()function, 227
    use type(), 231
__class__variable, 265, 266
.clear()method, 139, 168

INDEX

C3 linearization algorithm, 243, 245, 253, 255
Closures
    __closure__attribute, 222
    func_closuremember, 219
    hey()function, 218
    LOAD_CLOSURE, 2, 217, 218
    MAKE_FUNCTION, 218
    oparg, 218
co_* attributes, 220, 221
co_consts, 74, 75
Code object, 185, 191, 220
    __code__, 190
    func_code member, 184
    future module, 185
    init_code()function, 189
    LOAD_CONST instruction, 184
    makecode()function, 187
    optimize_and_assemble()function, 186
    _PyAssemble_MakeCodeObject()
        function, 187
    _PyAST_Compile()function, 184
    _PyCode_New(), 188
    PyCodeObject, 185
_code_to_hash_pyc(), 127
_code_to_timestamp_pyc(), 127
./configure command, 7
COPY_FREE_VARS 1, 219
co_varnames attribute, 220
C programming skills, 1
CPython, 1
    in C, 4
    development tools, 3
    floating point numbers (see Floating
        point numbers)
    in Parser/tokenizer.c, 26
    project structure, 5–13
    "small integers", 76
cpython-292, 27

CPython project
    ./configure command, 7
    directories, 6, 7
        Doc, 6
        Grammar, 6
        Include, 6
        Lib, 6
        Mac, 6
        Misc, 6
        modules, 6
        objects, 6
        Parser, 6
        PC, 6
        PCbuild, 6
        --prefix option, 7
        Programs, 7
        Python, 7
        python.exe, 8
        structure, 5
        Tools, 7
    REPL, 8–11, 13
CPython source code, 1, 2
    #ifdef conditional compilation
        directives, 3
    original code, 2
    3.12.6 version, 2
    VS Code, 3

D

Debuggers, 111
#define, 17
def keyword, 181
__delete__method, 239
Depth-first search (DFS), 245
Descriptors, 295
    AttributeError, 300, 301
    data descriptors, 295, 297

__get__() method, 300
LOAD_ATTR instruction, 296
method descriptor, 297, 299, 301–303
method variable, 299
.name attribute, 296
non-data descriptors, 295
PyDescr_IsData(), 297
PyObject_GenericGetAttr(), 295
Py_TPFLAGS_METHOD_DESCRIPTOR, 297
tp_getattromember, 295
DFS, *see* Depth-first search (DFS)
d.greeting(), 244, 245
__dict__, 34
Dictionaries (dict) object, 145
    add element, 149–153
    dict_new, 148
    allocation, 166–167
    DKIX_EMPTY, 149
    handle hash collisions, 154–157
    insertdict(), 159, 161
    insertion_resize(), 161
        insert_to_emptydict()function, 159
    internal structure, 145
    load factor, 163
    lookup process, 157–158
    mapping, 146
    memory, 167–168
    PyDictKeysObject, 147, 149
    PyDictObject structure, 146, 147, 162, 163
    PyDict_Type, 147
    Py_EMPTY_KEYS, 148, 149
dk_indices array, 153, 157
DK_IS_UNICODE(), 160
dk_log2_index_bytes, 163
dk_usable, 162, 164, 165, 167
do_super_lookup() function, 266, 267

E

Empty tuples, 172, 259
Enclosing variables, 206–208, 211–213
Exception handling, 305
    BINARY_OP instruction, 306, 308
    CHECK_EXC_MATCH instruction, 309
    entry portal, 308
    exception stack, 307
    ExceptionTable, 307, 308, 312
    except ZeroDivisionError, 309
    JUMP_BACKWARD, 312
    PUSH_EXC_INFO instruction, 306
    _PyErr_StackItem, 307
    Py_XSETREF macro, 311
    ZeroDivisionError exception, 305
ExceptionTable, 307, 308, 312
exit(), 11, 13
exit_unwind label, 204

F

_find_and_load() function, 65
_find_and_load_unlocked() function, 66, 67, 70
find_name_in_mro() function, 239
find_spec() class method, 70
Flexible Array Member, 170, 200
float_as_number, 85
Floating point numbers, 81
    arithmetic operations, 85
    bias, 84
    comparisons, 88
    C's double, 84
    IEEE 754 double precision format, 83, 84
    infinity, 86, 88

Floating point numbers (*cont.*)
    NaN, 87, 88
    PyFloat_FromDouble(), 82, 89
    PyFloat_MAXFREELIST, 89
    PyFloatObject, 82
    PyObject_Malloc(), 83
    structure, 81, 82
for loop, 283, 288
Frame object, 199
    dying, 204
    entry_frame, 202
    _f_frame_data, 200
    f_frame member, 200
    f_funcobj, 200
    f_locals, 201
    localsplus, 201
    _PyEval_EvalFrameDefault
        function, 201
    _PyEvalFrameClearAndPop()
        function, 204
    PyFrameObject, 201
    _PyInterpreterFrame, 200, 201, 204
    PyThreadState, 202
Free variable, 219
FrozenImporter, 70, 71
func_code member, 184
func_get_code function, 194
func_set_code function, 195
Function object
    access attributes, 194–195
    __code__ attribute, 192, 194, 195
    as code object, 192
    definition, 191
    func_code, 192
    MAKE_FUNCTION instruction,
        192, 193
    oparg, 193
    PyFunctionObject, 193, 195

PyFunction_Type, 195
Vectorcall, 196–198

G

generate_cases.py, 203
Generator object, 273
    gi_name and gi_qualname, 277
    "lazy evaluation" property, 277
    make_gen(), 275
    next() function, 273, 275, 279
    _PyFrame_StackPush (frame,
        retval), 278
    PyGenObject, 277
    _PyGen_SetStopIterationValue(), 281
    PyGen_Type, 280
    _Py_MakeCoro(), 275
    PyObject_GC_NewVar(), 276
    RETURN_GENERATOR, 275
    YIELD_VALUE, 275, 278
gen_send_ex2() function, 281, 282
__get__() method, 300–302
__get__ method, 239, 240
GETITEM(), 208
GETLOCAL macro, 206, 207
get_small_int() function, 79
GLOBALS(), 210, 211
Global variables, 205
greeting() method, 244, 245
greeting.c file, 11, 12
greeting.h file, 11–13

H

handle_system_exit() function, 13
header (.h) file, 11, 49
"Hello CPython", 10, 11
hello() function, 205

hello.py file, 116, 117, 122, 128–130
hey()function, 216–219, 222
hi()function, 216
.hi()method, 236

I, J

import_find_and_load(), 65, 69
import_from()function, 66, 67
__import__function, 63
import_get_module()function, 65
importlib._bootstrap._find_and_load(), 65
importlib's import_module()function, 65
import_name()function, 62, 64
Include/dictobject.hfile, 145
Include/internal/pycore_runtime_init_generated.h file, 108
Include/internal/pycore_unicodeobject_generated.h file, 108
Include/object.h file, 34
Include/pytypedefs.h file, 15
Inheritance hierarchies, 246, 255
__init__()function, 25, 31
__init__method, 56
insertdict()function, 159, 161, 164
.insert()method, 142
insertion_resize()function, 160, 161, 166
insert_to_emptydict()function, 152, 159, 164
inspect.currentframe(), 222
Integers, 73, 78
    astronomical numbers, 77–78
    bytecode process, 73
    co_consts, 74
    LOAD_CONST instruction, 73, 75
    PyLong_FromLong(), 73, 75, 79
    PyLongObject, 74, 75
    "small integer", 79–80

STORE_NAME instruction, 73
isnan(), 87
IS_SMALL_INT macro, 79
Iterable object, 283, 292
Iteration, 283, 285, 287, 288, 290
Iterator object, 286, 291–293
    calliter_iternext()function, 287
    iter() function, 291
    PyErr_Clear(), 288, 291
    PyListIter_Type, 292
    PyObject_GetIter() function, 292
    PyObject_RichCompareBool() function, 287
    tp_iternext, 293
    types, 292
Iterator protocol, 283, 286
Iterators, 283
iter() function, 283, 285, 291

K

kitty = Cat(), 30
kitty_backflip function, 51, 52
kitty_dealloc function, 51
kitty_greeting function, 51, 52, 57
KittyObject, 50, 56
kittyobject.c, 49
kittyobject.h, 49
kitty_repr function, 51, 52
k.sleep(), 267

L

len() function, 44, 45
list_append function, 42, 141
LIST_APPEND_METHODDEF, 42
list_ass_slice(), 144
list_concat() function, 43

list_extend(), 44
list_inplace_concat(), 43
list_insert function, 142
list_length(), 45
listobject.c, 51, 52
List objects
    .append()method, 141
    .insert() method, 142
    .remove() method, 143
    create and initialize, 134–137
    list_ass_slice(), 144
    list_resize() function, 137
    new_allocated, 140
    newsize, 139
    over-allocation, 137, 140–141
    PyListObject, 134
    PyObject_VAR_HEAD, 134
    PyVarObject, 134
    reallocation, 138–139
    structure, 133
list_remove function, 143
list_resize() function, 137, 139, 140, 142, 143
list_richcompare() function, 46
LOAD_ATTR instruction, 237, 238, 241
LOAD_BUILD_CLASS instruction, 234
LOAD_BUILD_CLASS operation, 28
LOAD_CONST instruction, 191, 234
LOAD_FAST instruction, 206–208, 213
LOAD_GLOBAL instruction, 206, 208, 210, 213
Local, enclosing, global, built-in (LEGB), 205, 213
localsplus, 206, 207
Local variables, 206, 207, 213
lv_tag, 76, 77

M

Macros, 17
"Magic number", 125–127
main function, 113
main.py, 69
MAKE_FUNCTION instruction, 184, 191–193, 234
make_gen() function, 275
make install command, 8
marshal.loads(), 129
maybe_freelist_push() function, 175, 176
maybe_pyc_file() function, 122, 123
memcpy() function, 103, 104
Metaclass, 227–232
Method resolution order (MRO), 239, 241
    and C3 linearization algorithm, 245
    DFS, 245
    inheritance structure, 254
    lookup_tp_bases() function, 258
    lookup_tp_mro() function, 258
    merge, 260–262
    mro_implementation(), 258
    .mro() method, 245, 257
    multiple inheritance, 249
        complex, 250–253
        does not work, 255
        simple, 249, 250
    single inheritance, 246–248
    to_mergearray, 260
Module import mechanism, 61
    BuiltinImporter, 70
    "Crazy side-effects!" comment, 67–69
    FrozenImporter, 70
    import_find_and_load(), 69
    IMPORT_FORM instruction, 66, 67
    IMPORT_FROM instruction, 62
    IMPORT_NAME instruction, 62
    PathFinder, 70

STORE_NAME instruction, 61
Monotonicity, 243
mp_ass_subscript, 99
mp_length function, 45
mp_subscript, 40
MRO, *see* Method resolution order (MRO)
.mro() method, 245, 248, 253, 257
mro_implementation(), 258
Multiple inheritance, 269, 270

N

Namespace, 208, 210, 211
NaN, *see* Not a Number (NaN)
__new__() function, 25, 31
new_keys_object()
       function, 152, 156, 163
next() function, 273, 275, 279, 288, 293
Non-empty tuples, 173–174
Not a Number (NaN), 87, 88

O

ob_digit array, 76, 77
ob_fval, 82, 83
ob_item array, 169–171, 174, 179
Objects
    PyObject (*see* PyObject)
ob_refcnt, 17–21
ob_size, 24
ob_type, 17, 22, 90
oparg, 193
Opcodes, 129–131
Over-allocation, 137, 140, 141

P, Q

Parser/tokenizer.c, 26
PathFinder, 70, 71

Person class, 271
pmerge() function, 260
__prepare__ method, 229
printf(), 9, 51
PUSH_EXC_INFO instruction, 306
PyArg_ParseTupleAndKeywords()
       function, 57
PyASCIIObject, 93, 95–97, 107, 151
_PyAST_Compile(), 27, 119
_PyBuiltin_Init() function, 53
Py_BytesMain() function, 113, 123
__pycache__ directory, 27, 122
PyCallIter_New() function, 285
PyCallIter_Type, 286
PyCell_New()function, 216
PyCellObject, 212, 213
.pyc file, 27, 121, 124
    for app.py, 122
    hello.cpython-312.pyc, 122
    for hello.py, 122
    hello.pyc file, 129
    maybe_pyc_file()
       function, 122, 123
    opcode.h, 130
    py_compile.compile(), 128
    pyrun_file(), 123
    python app.py, 122
PyCodeObject function, 185, 186, 189
PyCode_Type, 220
_Py_COMMON_FIELDS(func_), 183
PyCompactUnicodeObject, 93, 95, 96
py_compile module, 122, 127
py_compile.compile(), 128
_Py_Dealloc(), 21
PyDescr_IsData(), 297
PyDict_Clear() function, 168
_PyDict_GetItemWithError(), 224
PyDictKeyEntry, 155

INDEX

PyDictKeysObject, 146, 147, 149, 152, 153, 156
PyDictKeysObject structure, 162, 163
PyDictObject, 145, 146
PyDict_SetItem(), 150, 208
_PyDict_SetItem_Take2(), 150
PyDict_Type, 147, 149
PyDictUnicodeEntry, 155
PyDictValues, 146, 147
Py_EMPTY_KEYS, 148, 149, 152
PyEval_EvalCode() function, 119
_PyEval_EvalFrameDefault function, 201
_PyEvalFrameClearAndPop() function, 204
_Py_FdIsInteractive() function, 116
.py files, 122
PyFloat_FromDouble() function, 82, 89, 90
PyFloat_MAXFREELIST, 89
PyFloatObject, 82, 86, 90
PyFloat_Type, 84
PyFunctionObject, 182, 183, 193, 195
PyFunction_Type, 194, 195
PyGenObject, 277
PyGen_Type, 280
_Py_ID(metaclass), 227
_Py_IMMORTAL_REFCNT, 21
PyImport_GetMagicNumber(), 125
PyImport_GetModule(), 67
PyImport_ImportModuleLevelObject() function, 64
Py_INCREF() function, 57
_PyInterpreterFrame, 200, 201, 204
_Py_IsImmortal() function, 21
PyKittyObject, 50
PyKitty_Type, 49, 51–53, 57
_PyList_AppendTakeRefListResize(), 142
PyList_AsTuple(), 174

PyListIter_Type, 292
PyListObject, 50
PyList_Type, 23, 37, 46, 49, 52, 134, 137, 141
PyLong_FromLong() function, 73, 75, 79
PyLongObject, 74, 75, 82
_PyLongValue, 75–77
pymain_main() function, 113
pymain_run_file() function, 114
pymain_run_file_obj() function, 115
pymain_run_python() function, 114
_Py_MakeCoro() function, 275
PyMapping_Size(), 45
PyMem_Free(), 118
_Py_NewReference(), 19
PyObject
    #ifdef, 16
    Include/object.h, 16
    Include/pytypedefs.h file, 15
    macros, 17
    ob_refcnt, 18–20
    PyObject_HEAD, 134
    _PyObject_HEAD_EXTRA, 17, 18
    _PyObject_Init(), 137
    _PyObject_InitVar(), 137
    PyObject_Malloc(), 137
    PyObject_VAR_HEAD, 134
    _PyObject_VAR_SIZE(), 136
    PyTypeObject, 22
    PyVarObject, 24, 134
PyObject_GC_NewVar(), 276
PyObject_GenericGetAttr() function, 295
PyObject_GetItem(), 211, 224
PyObject_GetIter() function, 285, 288, 292
_PyObject_GetMethod() function, 238, 239, 296
PyObject_Hash() function, 151
PyObject_HEAD, 50, 95, 197, 200, 215

_PyObject_HEAD_EXTRA, 17, 18
_PyObject_Init(), 19, 83
PyObject_Malloc(), 83
_PyObject_New() function, 19
PyObject_RichCompareBool()
    function, 287
PyObject_SetItem(), 208
PyObject_Size(), 44
PyObject_VAR_HEAD, 24
PyObject_Vectorcall(), 263
_PyParser_ASTFromFile() function, 118
_PyRun_AnyFileObject(), 115
pyrun_file() function, 117
_PyRun_InteractiveLoopObject()
    function, 8, 9
_PyRun_SimpleFileObject() function, 116
PySeqIter_New(), 289
PySequenceMethods, 45
PySequence_Tuple(), 173
_Py_SINGLETON() macro, 172
_Py_SIZE_ROUND_UP(), 136
PySlice_AdjustIndices() function, 106
PySlice_Type, 105
_Py_Specialize_LoadGlobal() function, 209, 210
_Py_Specialize_UnpackSequence(), 178
Py_ssize_t, 18
PySuper_Type class, 263, 265, 266
Python, 1, 4, 111
    code, 121, 126
    descriptors (*see* Descriptors)
    floating point numbers (*see* Floating
        point numbers)
    function object, 191
    functions, 181
    generators, 293
        (*see also* Generator object)
    integers (*see* Integers)

Python 2.3, 245
python app.py command, 122
Python/compile.c file, 185, 186
python.exe, 8, 112
python hello.py, 111, 114
Python/pythonrun.c, 8
Python Virtual Machine (PVM), 27, 181
_PyTokenizer_Get(), 26
Py_TPFLAGS_HAVE_VECTORCALL
    flag, 196
Py_TPFLAGS_METHOD_
    DESCRIPTOR, 297
_PyTuple_FromArray(), 174
PyTuple_GET_ITEM() macro, 171
PyTuple_MAXFREELIST, 176
PyTuple_NFREELISTS, 176
PyTupleObject, 169
PyTuple_Type, 170, 174, 177
Py_TYPE(), 90
_PyType_AllocNoTrack() function,
    135, 148
_PyType_CalculateMetaclass()
    function, 228
PyType_GenericAlloc() function, 135
PyType_GenericNew() function, 134
_PyType_Lookup() function, 238
_PyType_Lookup(tp, name), 300
PyTypeObject, 22, 33, 146
    definition, 33, 34
    list type, 36
        list addition, 42–44
        list comparison, 46–48
        list methods, 41–42
        number of elements, 44–45
        print list, 37–39
        use bracket operator, 39–40
    tp_alloc, 34
    tp_as_mapping, 35

INDEX

PyTypeObject (*cont.*)
    tp_as_number, 35
    tp_as_sequence, 35
    tp_base, 34
    tp_basicsize, tp_itemsize, 34
    tp_call, 35
    tp_dealloc, 34
    tp_descr_getand tp_descr_set, 35
    tp_dict, 34
    tp_doc, 35
    tp_flags, 35
    tp_getset, 35
    tp_init, 34
    tp_members, 35
    tp_methods, 35
    tp_name, 34
    tp_new, 34
    tp_richcompare, 35
    tp_strand tp_repr, 35
_PyType_PreHeaderSize(), 137
PyType_Type, 29, 49, 104, 228, 231, 232, 257
_PyUnicode_FastCopyCharacters, 102
PyUnicode_KIND, 103
PyUnicode_New() function, 92, 97
PyUnicodeObject, 93, 95–97
PyUnicode_Type, 96
PyUnicodeWriter(), 39
PyVarObject, 24, 134
PyVarObject_HEAD_INIT(), 232
PyVectorcall_Call() function, 196, 197
Py_XSETREF() function, 57

R

Read-Eval-Print Loop (REPL), 8–11, 13
REPL, *see* Read-Eval-Print Loop (REPL)
.remove() method, 143

RETURN_GENERATOR instruction, 275
run_eval_code_obj() function, 119, 123
run_mod() function, 118

S

say_something() function, 9, 11–13
Scopes, variables, 205, 206
__set__ method, 239
SIZEOF_VOID_P, 136
"Small integer", 76, 79–80
small_ints array, 80
.SPECIAL_NAME attribute, 229
sq_concat, 43
sq_inplace_concat, 43
sq_item, 40
sq_length method, 45
SSTATE_INTERNED_IMMORTAL, 108
SSTATE_INTERNED_IMMORTAL_STATIC, 108
SSTATE_INTERNED_MORTAL, 108
SSTATE_NOT_INTERNED, 108
StopIteration, 288, 291
STORE_FAST instruction, 207, 213
STORE_NAME instruction, 208
String, 91, 101
    copy operations, 102–105
    create, 91
    encoding conversion, 96–98
    "immortal" objects, 108
    immutable, 98–99
    interning, 107–109
    LOAD_CONSTinstruction, 91
    objects, 92–95
    slice operation, 104–106
    state struct, 95
        ascii, 96
        compact, 96

interned, 95
kind, 96
statically_allocated, 96
structure, 95–96
hash, 95
length, 95
PyObject_HEAD, 95
super() function, 262–270
super_init_impl(), 264
super_init_without_args() function, 264
super().sleep(), 262, 266, 269
sys.meta_path, 70, 71
sys.modules dictionary, 65–67, 69

T

tail_contains() function, 262
.to_bytes() method, 126
Tokenization, 25
tok_get() function, 26
tp_alloc, 34
tp_as_mapping, 35, 39, 40, 45
tp_as_mapping structure, 98
tp_as_number, 35
tp_as_sequence, 35, 39, 40, 42, 45
tp_base, 34
tp_basicsize, 34, 136
tp_call, 35
tp_call member, 195, 196
tp_call() member method, 30
tp_dealloc, 23, 34
tp_descr_get, 35
tp_descr_get member, 297, 303
tp_descr_set, 35
tp_dict, 34
tp_doc, 35
tp_flags, 35
tp_getset, 35

tp_init, 34
tp_itemsize, 34, 136, 137
tp_iter member, 286, 288–290, 292
tp_iternext member, 286, 290, 292, 293
tp_members, 35
tp_methods, 35, 52
tp_name, 23, 34
tp_new, 34
tp_repr, 35
tp_repr member, 51, 52
tp_richcompare, 35, 46
tp_str, 35
tuple() class, 173
tuple_as_mapping member, 177
tupledealloc(), 174
tuple_get_empty(), 172
tuple_new() function, 170
tuple_new_impl() function, 171, 172
Tuples, 169
create, 170
deallocation mechanism, 174–177
empty tuple, 172
non-empty, 173–174
**ob_items, 170
modification function, 177
PyTupleObject structure, 169
unpack, 178–180
tuplesubscript(), 177
type_call() function, 30, 31
TypeError, 255
type->tp_new() function, 31
_typeobject, 22, 24

U

unicode_get_hash(), 151
unicode_getitem(), 99, 105
unicode_subscript() function, 106

INDEX

UNPACK_SEQUENCE, 178
UNPACK_SEQUENCE_TUPLE, 179
UNPACK_SEQUENCE_TWO_TUPLE, 179
update_bases()function, 227

V, W, X

Variable scope, 205, 206
Vector, 196
Vectorcall, 196
    Py_TPFLAGS_HAVE_VECTORCALL
        flag, 196
    PyVectorcall_Call() function, 196

tp_vectorcall_offset, 197
Vim, 3
Visual Studio Code (VS Code), 3, 4
VS Code, *see* Visual Studio Code
       (VS Code)

Y

YIELD_VALUE instruction, 275, 278

Z

Zed, 4
ZeroDivisionError object, 309

GPSR Compliance

The European Union's (EU) General Product Safety Regulation (GPSR) is a set of rules that requires consumer products to be safe and our obligations to ensure this.

If you have any concerns about our products, you can contact us on

ProductSafety@springernature.com

In case Publisher is established outside the EU, the EU authorized representative is:

Springer Nature Customer Service Center GmbH
Europaplatz 3
69115 Heidelberg, Germany